Handbook of English Fundamentals

CORRECTION CHART

4 ⁹⁵

[Concluded overleaf]

CORRECTION CHART

HANDBOOK OF ENGLISH FUNDAMENTALS

Donald W. Emery
Professor Emeritus, University of Washington

John M. Kierzek
Late of Oregon State University

Peter Lindblom
Miami-Dade Community College

Macmillan Publishing Co., Inc.
New York

Collier Macmillan Publishers
London

Macmillan Publishing Co., Inc.
866 Third Avenue, New York, New York 10022

Collier Macmillan Canada, Ltd.

Library of Congress Cataloging in Publication Data

Emery, Donald William, (date)
    Handbook of English fundamentals.

    "A portion of this material has been reprinted from
English fundamentals . . . and . . . of English fundamentals,
Form C."
    Includes index.
    1. English language—Rhetoric.   2. English
language—Grammar—1950–   I. Kierzek, John M.,
(date)   joint author. II. Lindblom, Peter D.,
(date)   joint author. III. Title.
PE1408.E474   808'.042   77-4957
ISBN 0-02-332940-8

Printing: 1 2 3 4 5 6 7 8   Year: 8 9 0 1 2 3 4

PREFACE

Handbook of English Fundamentals springs from an old and illustrious line, *English Fundamentals,* first published in 1933 and now popular in its sixth edition. *English Fundamentals* is designed for students of writing who wish to work through a review of standard English usage and the first principles of writing short papers; *Handbook* is intended for those who wish to have a convenient, brief reference book to guide them in the application of those principles to their own writing. *English Fundamentals* has been refined and sharpened in the process of going through five revisions; it has been modified and improved in response to comments from teachers, out of respect for the language, and from a wish to serve the needs of student writers more effectively. *Handbook* has benefited from the same accumulated efforts at improvement, for much of its instruction and explanation has been adapted from *English Fundamentals.*

Handbook organizations vary. At one end of the range stands the strict progression from simple principle to complex; at the other is the alphabetical reference catalogue. The first extreme seems too pedagogical for a book that may prove most useful when it is not read cover to cover in the order of its content. The last variation, although predictable and convenient, confounds the inquirer who knows everything about the inquiry but its name. In determining our table of contents, we have tried to learn from all the systems practiced and to arrange material in ascending order from mechanical detail to theoretical principle and taste. *Handbook* is arranged so that the user will come first to the guidance most commonly sought in the process of writing revision: punctuation, mechanics, capitalization, and spelling. Each element is presented in an easily remembered statement or direction, and that statement is then amplified and explained through clear examples so that users can not only refresh their memory of the rule itself but reinforce past instruction and experience by reflecting on the discussion of the principle and the examples.

Next in the order of presentation are discussions of sentence structure and usage. The principles are set out in concise statements designed for easy, rapid reference and application; they are discussed and illustrated so that users can acquire a working knowledge and a clear understanding.

Part IV offers a treatment of the grammar and structure of the sentence. This section provides a quick review of any part of sentence construction and analysis that may have slipped the user's mind. A review of basic sentence patterns and variations on those basic patterns encourages development of varied sentence structures and leads directly and logically to a review of the principles of coordination and subordination so necessary for the production of writing that is logically consistent and stylistically pleasing.

The final section of the book consists of an overview of the basic steps in the process of composing and writing various assignments that may face a student. A guide to taking essay tests provides directions and guidelines for organizing thinking and writing for essay examinations. Steps for reviewing notes as well as directions for the actual composition process take the student from study sessions to the final written version of the examination. A clear, cogent, brief discussion of the principles of the paragraph and the essay builds on the instructions for essay writing and guides the student in the development of brief essays and papers. Finally, a thorough discussion of a practical process for research and term paper writing leads the writer from the development of a working bibliography to the final, properly documented draft. Numerous models for footnote and bibliography forms demonstrate correct documentation.

The final section comprises two appendixes. The first is a basic discussion of style offering examples of what passes as good style and directions for avoiding the traps of what is condemned as poor or weak. The second appendix, a glossary of grammatical terms, permits a quick reference to principles and elements by name and reinforces the student's knowledge of terms without clouding the issues with obscure or overtechnical definitions.

In every part of *Handbook of English Fundamentals* we have tried to explain each item briefly and clearly. Our attitude is essentially prescriptive and conservative, not because we deny language the right to change but because we believe a writer should first choose expression according to what *is* considered correct rather than what *will* be. What is standard is the handbook's domain; what will be is in the hands of tomorrow's authors.

Among the many debts of gratitude we owe to persons who have helped in the creation of *Handbook of English Fundamentals,* that to the memory of John M. Kierzek and to his part in former editions of *English Fundamentals* is paramount. His daughter, Marian Leyrer, who allowed us to use his name and his work, deserves no small thanks. We also express our appreciation to Anthony English of Macmillan, who contributed much to the preparation of the appendix "Reminders About Style," and whose editorial guidance through the entire production of the book has been invaluable. Finally, to all the students who used and instructors who taught *English Fundamentals* a most sincere thanks. Their loyalty to that book has done much to shape this one.

D. W. E.

P. L.

CONTENTS

PART V
Essay Tests, Paragraphs, Essays, and Research Papers

Part I
Principles of Form

PUNCTUATION

I. COMMAS

Commas are used to separate certain parts of the sentence so that written communication will be clear and direct. Commas are also used to set off words, phrases, or clauses that break into the normal word order of a sentence. Notice that these interrupters are *set off* by commas. This means that, although interrupters that begin or end a sentence will have only one comma, any such unit that comes in the interior of the sentence will have *two* commas, one before it and one after it.

P 1. Use a comma before the coordinating conjunctions *and, but, for, or, nor, yet* when they join the clauses of a compound sentence.

A compound sentence contains two or more independent clauses. (See also P 15–1 and P 16 for other punctuation problems with compound units.)

> I placed the typed sheet on his desk, and he picked it up and read it slowly. His face turned red, but he did not say a word. I knew he was angry, for he rose and stamped out of the room.

P 2. Use commas to separate the items of a series.

A series is composed of three or more words, phrases, or clauses of equal grammatical rank. A series usually takes the form of *a, b, and c;* sometimes it may be *a, b, or c.* In journalistic writing the comma is omitted before *and* or *or;* in more formal writing it is generally not omitted. The beginning writer will do well to follow formal practice.

1

The old house was empty, cold, dark, and uninviting. [Four adjectives.]

The jury was made up of two preachers, six housewives, three laborers, and a farmer. [Four nouns.]

She rushed into the house, up the stairs, and into her room. [Phrases.]

I told him which way to go, what to carry, and how to dress. [Phrases.]

P 3. Use commas to separate coordinate adjectives preceding a noun.

A comma separating two adjectives signifies that the two adjectives are equal in their modifying force. A comma is not used when the modifier closer to the noun has more importance as an identifier of the noun. Thus we use a comma with "a difficult, unfair examination" but not with "a difficult final examination." Another explanation is that in the first example "difficult" and "unfair" modify "examination" with equal force, whereas in the second example "difficult" really modifies the unit "final examination."

The problem here is to determine when adjectives are coordinate, that is, equal in modifying value. Two tests may prove helpful, although each of them rests upon a kind of intuitive ability to recognize normal and natural English:

1. If the insertion of *and* between the modifiers results in an acceptable reading, the adjectives are equal and a comma should be used. "A difficult *and* unfair examination" would sound correct to most native speakers of English, but "a difficult *and* final examination" would not.

2. If the adjectives sound natural in reversed position, they are equal and should be separated by a comma. Thus we could say "an unfair, difficult examination" but normally not "a final difficult examination" without meaning something quite different from a difficult final examination.

When you use a noun preceded by more than two adjectives, you should test the adjectives by pairs, the first with the second, the second with the third, and so on. It may help you to know that we usually do not use commas before adjectives denoting size or age. And you must remember that we never use a comma between the last adjective and the noun.

Observe how the use of the above-mentioned tests results in punctuation like the following:

a tall, dark, and handsome gentleman	a tall, dark, handsome gentleman
the dark, cold, drafty classroom	a neat, courteous little boy
a heavy, soiled leather ball	her funny little upturned
a mean old local gossip	nose

P 4. Use commas after most introductory modifiers, especially if the modifier is long and not closely restrictive.

Modern usage varies considerably; you must depend on your own good sense and judgment. The following explanations will provide a general guide:

1. Put commas after introductory adverbial clauses except those that are short or in no need of special emphasis. No hard-and-fast rule governs this situation. The inexperienced writer would probably do well to use commas after all introductory adverbial clauses except very short time clauses.

> Although none of us really enjoyed the performance, we applauded politely.
> If what you say is true, quick action is required.
> Before an undergraduate can participate in these sports, he must take a physical examination.
> Whenever I see him I remember his youthful awkwardness.
> When George sleeps the rest of us must be quiet.

2. Put commas after introductory verbal phrase modifiers.

> Having climbed the steep trail up Cougar Mountain, Bob decided to take some pictures. To get the best view of the valley, he walked to the edge of the cliff. After opening his rucksack, he searched for his new telephoto lens.

3. Put commas after introductory absolute elements, such as phrases, sentence adverbs, mild exclamations, and after *yes* and *no*.

> In fact, there was no way to keep the front door closed. Well, what are we to do now? No, we are not in danger. Certainly, I'll put a chair against it.

4. Ordinarily, do not put commas after introductory prepositional phrases unless they need special emphasis or happen to be very long. But long introductory prepositional phrases are not common in modern writing.

After a heavy dinner we usually went for a walk in the meadow. Beyond the meadow was a grove of birches. In early summer many birds nested there.

P 5. Use a comma between any two words that might be mistakenly read together.

Before, he had been industrious and sober.
Once inside, the dog scampered all over the furniture.
While we were eating, the table collapsed.
After we had washed, Mother prepared breakfast.
Ever since, he has been afraid of deep water.
Shortly after ten, thirty new recruits appeared.
Whatever is, is right.

P 6. Use commas to set off nonrestrictive clauses and phrases.

Adjective clauses and phrases are either restrictive or nonrestrictive.

> The restrictive modifier, the kind that is not set off by commas, *is essential to the identification of the word being modified.*

The grade *that I received on my report* pleased me.
The girl *sitting next to me* chewed gum noisily.

Commas would not be used in these sentences. You can see that without the modifiers ("The grade pleased me"; "The girl chewed gum noisily"), the subjects are not identified. What grade, what girl are we talking about? But when we add the modifiers we identify the *particular* grade and the *particular* girl. In other words, this kind of modifier restricts the meaning of a general noun to one specific member of its class.

The other type, the nonrestrictive modifier, requires commas to set it off.

> The nonrestrictive modifier supplies additional or incidental information about the word being modified, *but the information is not needed for identifying purposes.*

(However, don't get into the habit of thinking that a nonrestrictive modifier is necessarily unimportant; if it has no importance to the meaning of the sentence, it has no right to be in the sentence.) If the noun being modified does not require identification, the modifier following it will be nonrestrictive and will require commas. It follows, then, that nonrestrictive modifiers will be found following proper nouns (*Mount Everest, Philadelphia, Mrs. Frank Lockwood*); nouns already identified (the oldest *boy* in his class, his only *grandchild*); and one-of-a-kind nouns (Alice's *mother,* the *provost* of the college, the *writer* of the editorial).

Examine these additional examples contrasting restrictive and nonrestrictive modifiers. Notice in the last pair of sentences how the writer, by using or not using commas, can sometimes give important information to the reader.

> The man *whose car had been wrecked* asked us for a ride. [Restrictive.]
> Mr. Ash, *whose car had been wrecked,* asked us for a ride. [Nonrestrictive.]
> Anyone *wishing more detailed information* should write to the secretary.
> My father, *wishing more detailed information,* wrote to the secretary.
> I visited an old and close friend *who plans to become a minister.*
> I visited my oldest and closest friend, *who plans to become a minister.*
> A woman *at the far end of the head table* summoned a waiter.
> Professor Angela Cheney, *at the far end of the head table,* summoned a waiter.
> My brother-in-law *who lives in Akron* is a chemist. [The writer has more than one brother-in-law. The restrictive clause is needed to distinguish this brother-in-law from other brothers-in-law.]
> My brother-in-law, *who lives in Akron,* is a chemist. [Since identification is not required, the writer is telling us that he has only one brother-in-law.]

P 7. Use commas to set off most appositives. (See also P 15-5.)

An appositive is a noun unit that immediately follows a noun or pronoun and stands for the same thing.

> The new boy, *the one with red hair,* likes me.
> The colonel, *a friend of many years,* advised me to stay.
> Mr. McClure, *our science teacher,* told me about it.

P 8. Use commas to set off absolute phrases.

An absolute phrase, which consists of a noun or a pronoun plus a verbal, usually modifies the sentence as a whole, not any special part of it. (See pages 128–129.)

> *The cat being away,* the mice will play.

My work having been finished, I went to see Alice.
He sat there in silence, *his left cheek twitching as usual.*
He stood in the doorway, *his wet cloak dripping water on the rug,* and
waited for some sign of recognition.

P 9. Use commas to set off parenthetical expressions.

Parenthetical expressions are words, phrases, or clauses that break
into the sentence to explain, to emphasize, to qualify, or to point
the direction of the thought.

The text, *moreover,* had not been carefully proofread.
You will find, *for example,* that the format is not attractive.
His appearance, *I must say,* was not prepossessing.

P 10. Use commas to set off words used in direct address.

And now, *ladies and gentlemen,* let us adjourn.
I tell you, *Carol,* that we were all proud of you.
"You were justified, *Miss Faire,*" she said, "in refusing the gift."
"*Henry,* your theme must be rewritten," said his teacher.

P 11. Use commas to set off expressions designating the speaker in direct quotations.

"With your permission," *he replied,* "there's nothing I'd rather do."
"That must do," *he said,* "until we think of something better."

Other marks may be used instead of the comma if the sentence
justifies their use.

"How shall I tell him?" asked Mary timidly. [Question mark after
question.]
"Silence!" he shouted. "Get to work at once!" [Exclamation
point.]
"Two of the buildings are firetraps," replied the comptroller;
"moreover, the library needs a new roof." [See P 16 for the use
of the semicolon.]

P 12. Use commas to set off degrees, titles, and the like when they follow names.

Henry Lyle, *Ph.D.,* gave the opening address.
The new ambassador is Peter Jones, *Esq.*
Harold Titus, *Jr., chairman of the board,* has resigned.

P 13. Use commas to set off negative insertions used for emphasis, units out of their position, and short interrogative clauses combined with statements.

Our plane was a DC-3, *not the jet we had expected.*
Tired and footsore, the hikers finally reached camp.
The hikers finally reached camp, *tired and footsore.*
[*But*] The tired and footsore hikers finally reached camp.
You had a good time, *didn't you?*
You recall, *don't you,* our first meeting?

P 14. Use commas to set off items in dates and addresses.

On July 14, *1904,* in a little cottage at 316 High Street, *Mayville, Illinois,* the wedding took place.

(Journalistic practice usually omits the comma *after* the year and the state.)

P 15. Do not use unnecessary commas.

Normally, commas are *not* used in the following positions (the superfluous commas are circled):

1. Before a coordinating conjunction joining two verbs, complements, phrases, or subordinate clauses.

I had studied hard ⊙ but failed the test.
If I can finish studying ⊙ and you can find four dollars, we'll go out for a pizza.

2. Between a subject and its verb or between a verb and its complement.

The man at the far end of the head table ⊙ is my uncle.
None of us will ever understand ⊙ how you got such a good grade.

3. Between adjectives that are not coordinate (see P 3) or between the final adjective and the noun being modified. (Usually commas are not used before adjectives denoting age or size.)

a serviceable ⊙ iron frying pan
a likable, outgoing ⊙ sort of person
this delightful ⊙ little ⊙ old man

4. To set off restrictive clauses and phrases. (See P 6.)

My first-round opponent was a fellow ⊙ who had captained his college golf team.
You may use the raincoat ⊙ hanging on the hook next to mine.

5. To set off restrictive appositives. Appositives like those shown in P 7 are called loose or nonrestrictive appositives and are set off by commas. But an appositive may sometimes function the same way that a restrictive adjective clause functions, that is, it may identify a preceding noun that, without the appositive, could refer to any one member of a class. An appositive of this sort is not set off.

> my brother ⊙ Jack; the poet ⊙ Keats; the apostle ⊙ Paul; the preposition ⊙ *to*

6. To set off the year following the month rather than the day of the month or before the zip-code number.

> After July ⊙ 1978 ⊙ his mail should be sent to 1675 East Union Street, Seattle, Washington ⊙ 98122.

II. SEMICOLONS

The semicolon, a separator with more weight than the comma, is used only between sentence units that are grammatically equal. Side-by-side independent clauses without coordinating conjunctions often present the writer with a choice between a semicolon, making one sentence with two related ideas, or a period, making two sentences with the ideas more conspicuously separated.

P 16. Use a semicolon between independent clauses not joined by a coordinating conjunction.

In compound sentences that do not use a coordinating conjunction there may be no connective between the clauses, the second clause may begin with an adverbial modifier, or the second clause may begin with a **conjunctive adverb** such as *however, therefore, moreover, consequently,* and the like.

> These are only a few of the urgent problems concerning our ecology; many more exist. [No connective.]
> You must first fill out the application form; later you will be interviewed. [Adverb with second clause.]
> The public must live with these decisions; therefore the public should have a voice in the debates. [Conjunctive adverb with second clause.]

The misuse of a comma between independent clauses in compound sentences without coordinating conjunctions results in an error called the **comma fault** or the **comma splice.** At this point it might be helpful to remind you of three related sentence types involving the compounding of sentence units:

1. A simple sentence with two verbs joined by a coordinating conjunction. Normal punctuation: none. (See P 15–1.)

> We worked all day on the car but could not find the trouble.

2. A compound sentence with the two independent clauses joined by a coordinating conjunction. Normal punctuation: a comma before the conjunction. (See P 1.)

> We worked all day on the car, and now it runs well.

3. A compound sentence without one of the coordinating conjunctions joining the independent clauses. (The second clause often begins with an adverbial unit or a conjunctive adverb.) Normal punctuation: a semicolon.

> We worked all day on the car; it now runs well.
> We worked all day on the car; now it runs well.
> We worked all day on the car; consequently, it now runs well.

P 17. Use a semicolon before the coordinating conjunction in a compound sentence if an emphatic balance is desired or if other punctuation is used at several points.

> The trustees refused to release any of the funds; nor did they show any sympathy for my dire needs.
> Mr. Berry's disposition, we all admit, is very pleasant; but office routine is too often upset by his tardiness, his addiction to practical jokes, and his rather juvenile frivolity.

P 18. Use semicolons to separate most clauses arranged in the form of a series.

Three or more *short* independent clauses in a series may be separated by commas.

> Larry fetched the water, Mort built the fire, and I opened the cans of soup.

But long clauses—independent clauses especially, but sometimes dependent clauses also—are better separated by semicolons, particularly if there is other punctuation within the clauses.

> The first week of the tour called for long hops and little free time; the second week, with longer rest periods in Amsterdam and Antwerp, was less exhausting; but the third week, which took us

to four countries in seven days, left us numb and bewildered. [Three lengthy independent clauses in series, with internal punctuation.]

These dark days will be worth all they have cost if they show us that happiness is not a matter of money; if they force upon us the joy of achievement, the thrill of creative effort; if they teach us that our true destiny is to serve, to the best of our ability, our fellow man. [Three lengthy adverbial clauses in series, with internal punctuation.]

P 19. Do _not_ use a semicolon to separate a subordinate clause or phrase from the independent clause.

Although prospects for increased profits for the third quarter seem hopeful, [not ;] the dividend rate will remain the same.

The dissident group withdrew their proposal, [not ;] the results of the first vote having shown the futility of attempts at reform.

III. Apostrophes, Colons, Dashes

P 20. Use an apostrophe to form the possessive (genitive case) of nouns.

Any noun, whether singular or plural, that does not end in _s_ forms its possessive by adding an apostrophe and _s_.

a boy's hat, the horse's tail, Carol's car, men's shoes, children's toys

All plural nouns that end in _s_ form the possessive by adding an apostrophe after the _s_.

boys' hats, horses' tails, the Smiths' home, ladies' dresses

With singular nouns ending in _s_ no hard-and-fast rule can be made. With short words especially, an apostrophe and _s_ are added. But if the added _s_ syllable makes the word awkward to pronounce, only an apostrophe is added. With some words usage allows either of the forms.

this class's behavior, Mr. Jones' (or Jones's) house, Keats' (or Keats's) poetry, Archimedes' law

P 21. Use an apostrophe to form the possessive case of indefinite pronouns (but not of other pronouns).

anybody's game, someone's gloves, somebody else's sweater, each other's rights

(But note the possessive forms of these pronouns: his, hers, its, ours, yours, theirs, whose.)

P 22. Use an apostrophe to stand for the omitted material in contractions.

> We've decided that you're the logical candidate.
> They're members of the class of '79, aren't they?
> It's eleven o'clock, and Henry's still in bed.

You must learn to distinguish carefully between the following pairs of contractions and possessives:

it's [it is]	its	who's [who is]	whose
there's [there is]	theirs	you're [you are]	your
they're [they are]	their		

P 23. Use an apostrophe to form the plural of letters, numbers, symbols, and words used as words.

> Your *T*'s and *7*'s look alike. So do your *3*'s and *8*'s. Your *n*'s, *m*'s, and *u*'s all look like a wavy line. Don't use so many *and*'s in your writing, and never use *&*'s as substitutes for them.

P 24. Do *not* use an apostrophe to form the plural of either a common or a proper noun.

> **WRONG:** Our neighbor's, the Allen's and the Murray's, recently bought new Honda's.
> **RIGHT:** Our neighbors, the Allens and the Murrays, recently bought new Hondas.

P 25. Use a colon (:) at the end of a complete clause introducing a series, a statement, a quotation, and so forth.

> The apostrophe has three uses: to form possessives, to indicate contractions, and to form certain plurals.
> A few nervous giggles greeted the speaker's opening remark: "Ladies, gentlemen, and others."
> Our organization has one purpose: to combat industrial pollution. [A comma normally sets off an appositive. A colon sets off an appositive emphatically, but it should be used only when the appositive is introduced by a complete independent clause.]
> All hikers must bring the following: a flashlight, a small ax, and a waterproof tarpaulin.

P 26. Use a colon to separate the clauses of a compound sentence if the second clause is a logical explanation, restatement, or development of the first.

This book is unlike most anthologies: it contains only selections approved by students.

The ode is a special type of lyric: its theme is exalted and its style elevated.

P 27. Follow conventional practice in using colons in formal salutations, time notations, and in Biblical and bibliographic citations.

Dear Ms. Collins:
To whom it may concern:
9:40 A.M.
Luke 4:7
New York: Macmillan Publishing Co., Inc.

P 28. Do *not* use a colon before a series when the introductory material is not a complete clause.

In other words, do not use a colon to separate a verb from its complement or a preposition from its object.

FAULTY: All hikers must bring: a flashlight, a small ax, and a waterproof tarpaulin.

FAULTY: The things a hiker must bring are: a flashlight, a small ax, and a waterproof tarpaulin.

FAULTY: The hiker's equipment should consist of: a flashlight, a small ax, and a waterproof tarpaulin.

P 29. Use a dash (—) to show an abrupt change in thought in the sentence.

NOTE: The dash in script must be longer than a hyphen. On a typewriter the dash is formed from two hyphens (—) with no space between it and the letters preceding and following it.

"I suggest that we now—but perhaps we should first hear a reading of the minutes of the last meeting," said the chairperson.

P 30. Use dashes to set off a parenthetical insertion that abruptly breaks the continuity of a sentence. (See also P 48.)

Superior students—notice that I said superior—need not take the test.

For example, Archilochus, the almost legendary "inventor" of the iambic measure—he flourished in the seventh century B.C.—was thought to have wielded more than natural powers in his invectives against his enemies.

—ROBERT C. ELLIOTT
"The Satirist and Society"

P 31. Use dashes to set off an appositive series, to avoid a piling up of commas.

> The division of the book into genres—poems, short stories, novellas, dramas—has advantages and disadvantages.

P 32. Use a dash before a summarizing statement following a listing of items.

> Fraternity rushing, hazing, all-night bull sessions, contempt for scholarship—all these were *de rigueur* in my college days.

P 33. Use a dash only when you can justify its use; it is not a substitute for other marks.

> FAULTY: Her oldest friend—Olga Trent—visited her after the funeral.
> FAULTY: We had hunted in these fields before—but this time the farmer refused our request.

IV. QUOTATION MARKS

P 34. Use double quotation marks (" ") to enclose the exact words of a quoted speech.

Quotation marks always come in pairs. The marks show the beginning and the end of a speech, whether it is part of a sentence, one sentence, or several sentences. If a speech is interrupted by material showing who said it, quotation marks set off the quoted material from the explanatory material. If you are quoting a speech of more than one sentence, you do not need to put quotation marks around each separate sentence. Use them where the directly quoted material begins and where it ends or is interrupted. In recording dialogue, a change of speaker requires a new paragraph.

> On the main road a motorist stopped him and asked, "What's that over there? A house on fire?"
> "It was," said Miles. "It's almost out now."

"Looks like a big place. Only Government property, I suppose?"
"That's all," said Miles.

—EVELYN WAUGH
Tactical Exercise

P 35. Do *not* use quotation marks to set off an indirect quotation, which is a statement giving the substance but not the direct words of a speech.

DIRECT: Peggy answered, "I worked hard on this. I checked all my data."

INDIRECT: Peggy answered that she had worked hard and checked all her data.

P 36. Use quotation marks to set off words referred to as words and slang used in a formal context. (See also M 2.)

It was very neatly written, and, except that "friend" was written "freind" and one of the "S's" was the wrong way round, the spelling was correct all the way through.

—GEORGE ORWELL
Animal Farm

The witness told the jury that he had recently been released from the "slammer."

P 37. Use single quotation marks (' ') to enclose a speech within a speech or a quoted word within a speech.

"I wonder what he meant," said Betty, "when he said, 'There are wheels within wheels.'"
"Did you know," he asked, "that 'boondoggle,' now applied to 'make-work' projects, had an earlier very different meaning?"

P 38. Use quotation marks to set off subdivisions of books, names of songs, and titles of units of less than book length, such as short stories, short poems, essays, and articles. (For quotation marks and italics, see M 1.)

The second chapter of *Moby-Dick* is entitled "The Carpet-Bag."
Nanki-Poo sings "A Wandering Minstrel I" early in Act I of *The Mikado.*
Our anthology includes "Threes," a poem from Sandburg's *Smoke and Steel.*
The first article I read for my research paper was John Lear's "How Hurricanes Are Born" in the *Saturday Review.*

P 39. Use other marks with terminal quotation marks as follows:

1. The period and the comma always come inside the quotation marks.

> "Come in," said my uncle, "and take off your coat."

2. The semicolon and the colon always come outside the quotation marks.

> Mr. Lowe said, "I heartily endorse this candidate"; unfortunately, most of the audience thought he said "hardly" instead of "heartily."
>
> The speaker closed with these words from Arnold's "Dover Beach": "Ah, love, let us be true to one another."

3. The question mark and the exclamation mark come within the quotation marks if the quoted material is a question or an exclamation; otherwise they come outside.

Your problem here will be with the question mark; an exclamation mark outside the quotation marks is possible in only a most contrived kind of sentence.

> "Good Heavens!" he exclaimed. "Is that the best you can do?"
> Mother asked, "Where were you this morning?"
> Did she say, "I came home early"? [The question mark belongs to the whole sentence, not to the quoted part.]
> Did Mother ask, "Where were you this morning?" [Note that only one question mark is used after a double question like this.]
> "Do you have trouble," Mary asked, "spelling words like 'exceed' and 'supersede'?" [The question mark applies to the entire question, not to the single quoted word.]

P 40. Follow standard printing practice when you reproduce extended quoted material, as you may sometimes do in a research paper.

If the quoted excerpt extends through two or more paragraphs, use quotation marks at the beginning of each paragraph but at the end of only the final paragraph. If you are typing your paper, you may follow the usual printing practice of indenting five extra spaces from both sides (ten spaces to indicate paragraphs) and single-spacing the extended quotation. If you use this system, no quotation marks are needed.

V. END MARKS

P 41. Use a period after a declarative or imperative sentence.

This study hall is too noisy. Please stop your whispering.

P 42. Use a period after acceptable abbreviations.

A few abbreviations are proper in the ordinary sort of writing, such as *Mr., Mrs., Ms., Messrs., Dr.,* before names; *Jr., Sr., Esq., D.D., Ph.D.,* and so forth, after names. No period is used with *Miss;* and *Ms.,* used instead of *Miss* or *Mrs.* when marital state is not indicated, is usually considered an abbreviation and uses a period, although some modern dictionaries have entries for it either with or without a period.

The following, correct in footnotes, bibliographies, and tabulations, should be written out in ordinary writing: *e.g.* (*for example*), *etc.* (*and so forth*), *i.e.* (*that is*), *p., pp.* (*page, pages*), *vol.* (*volume*), *viz.* (*namely*).

B.C., A.D., A.M., and *P.M.,* used with numerals, are to be used only when necessary for clarity. The following are correct in addresses but must be spelled out in ordinary writing: *Ave.* (*Avenue*), *St.* (*Street*), *Blvd.* (*Boulevard*), *Co.* (*Company*).

In modern usage, the "alphabet" forms of various governmental or intergovernmental agencies; social, business, or professional organizations; and phrases used in scientific contexts are usually not followed by periods: *TVA, SEC, NASA, CIA, UNESCO, NATO, CARE, USO, CBS, PTA, ICBM, GNP, mph, rpm.* When in doubt, consult your dictionary.

P 43. Avoid abbreviating common words in your writing.

> **POOR:** Last Mon. P.M. I met my two older bros., who live in N.Y. Chas. works for a mfg. co. there. Thos. attends NYU. He's coming home for Xmas.
>
> **RIGHT:** Last Monday afternoon I met my two older brothers, who live in New York. Charles works for a manufacturing company there. Thomas attends New York University. He's coming home for Christmas.

P 44. Use a question mark (?) after a direct question, which is an utterance that calls for an answer. (For the use of question marks with quotation marks, see P 39.)

But use a period, not a question mark, after an indirect question, which is a *statement* giving the substance of a question but not the exact words that would be used in a direct question.

> **DIRECT:** Who goes there? Is that you? When do we eat? How much do I owe you?
>
> "Who goes there?" he demanded. [In dialogue.]
> Did he ask, "Where does this road lead to?" [Note single question mark.]
>
> **INDIRECT:** She asked me how old I was. I wondered why she would ask such a question. [Note that periods are used. These are statements, not direct questions.]

P 45. Use a question mark, usually within parentheses, to show doubt about the accuracy of a date or number.

> Attila, King of the Huns, born in 406(?), became known as "the Scourge of God."
> Attila the Hun (406?–453) became notorious for his vandalism and cruelty.

P 46. Use an exclamation point (!) after statements of strong feeling.

The exclamation mark is used sparingly in modern writing and should be reserved for special situations that call for strong emphasis. The mild exclamations, such as *oh, goodness, well, yes, no,* are followed by commas, not exclamation points. Be sure to place the exclamation mark after the exclamation itself.

> "Help! I'm slipping!" he shouted. [Note period after *shouted.*]
> "Stop that!" she screamed. [Do not put the exclamation point after *screamed.*]
> Well, it was exciting, wasn't it? Oh, I had a pleasant time.

P 47. Avoid the use of question marks and exclamation points to show humor or sarcasm.

> **POOR:** The first speaker's humorous (?) speech was much too long.
>
> **POOR:** Joe's budget allows twelve (!) dollars a day for expenses in New York.

VI. PARENTHESES AND BRACKETS

P 48. Use parentheses ( ) to set off a parenthetical or illustrative insertion in a sentence.

In Oregon (and Massachusetts, and Texas, for that matter) they will tell you that Oregon is a lot more.

—PHILIP WYLIE
Generation of Vipers

Commas and dashes are also used to set off parenthetical material. (See P 9 and P 30.) Of these marks, the commas show the weakest separation and are usually adequate when the writer wishes to show that the inserted material is closely related to the rest of the sentence.

CORRECT: Pete's decision, most of us agree, was a wise one.

Dashes and parentheses show a more distinct separation between the supplementary material and the main idea of the sentence. They often may be used interchangeably.

CORRECT: If there were aspects of the new world that were not perfect—child labor, for example—progress would take care of them.

CORRECT: If there were aspects of the new world that were not perfect (child labor, for example), progress would take care of them.

P 49. Other marks of punctuation may be used after the end parenthesis but not at the beginning.

If the parenthetical material stands as a complete sentence beginning with a capital letter, the end mark comes within the parentheses.

It consisted of a brass medal (they were really some old horsebrasses which had been found in the harness-room), to be worn on Sundays and holidays.

—GEORGE ORWELL
Animal Farm

Frost's local reputation grew slowly (his first poems, remember, were published in England).

Frost's local reputation grew slowly. (His first poems, remember, were published in England.)

P 50. Use parentheses to enclose numbers in a listing and inserted bits of incidental information, such as dates, titles, and so forth.

The verb forms shown in these columns are (1) the infinitive, (2) the past tense, (3) the past participle, and (4) the third person singular of the present tense.

Do not be deceived by your opponent's diminished but still substantial (15-point) lead in the polls.

Representative of this school of criticism are Ransom's *The New Criticism* (1941) and Brooks' *The Well Wrought Urn* (1947).

Senator Church (D., Idaho) spoke against the amendment.

P 51. Use square brackets [   ] within quoted excerpts to enclose explanatory material inserted by the one doing the quoting.

In his *London Journal* Boswell writes, "He [Samuel Johnson] is a very big man, is troubled with sore eyes, the palsy, and the King's evil."

P 52. Use square brackets to enclose *sic* (meaning *thus*) following a misspelling, a misused word, or some other type of error to show that the misuse actually occurs in the quoted material.

One indignant taxpayer wrote, "Why aren't our young people being taught grammer [*sic*] and spelling?"

MECHANICS

I. Italics

In handwritten or typewritten papers, underlining (`type-script like this`) is the equivalent of italics in printed material (*type like this*). The average writer needs to know only a few of the conventions regarding the use of italics and should be aware that in a few situations usage between italics and quotation marks is divided.

M 1. Italicize (underline) titles of book-length publications (books, magazines, plays); newspapers; movies; works of art and music; and names of ships, aircraft, and spacecraft. (See P 38 for the use of quotation marks with subdivisions of books.)

Lord of the Flies [book]
Saturday Review [magazine]
A Streetcar Named Desire [play]
Wall Street Journal [newspaper]

Gone With the Wind [movie]
Duchamp's *Nude Descending a Staircase* [painting]
Mozart's *Requiem* [music]
Lusitania [ship]
Lindbergh's *Spirit of St. Louis* [aircraft]
Soyuz 23 [spacecraft]

M 2. Italicize (underline) words, letters, and numerals referred to as words, letters, and numerals. (See P 36 for a similar use of quotation marks.)

I misread the *q* for a *g.*
A simile uses a connective—*like, as,* or *than*—to compare two things from different classes.
The *ie/ei* digraph has several pronunciations: *niece, weight, friend, heir, height, foreign,* and *view.*

M 3. Italicize (underline) most foreign words.

Your dictionary will give you help in determining which foreign words should be underlined and which have become so thoroughly accepted in our language that they should be treated like regular English words.

> If a satirist presents, say, a clergyman as a fool or hypocrite, he is, *qua* satirist, attacking neither a man nor a church.
>
> —NORTHROP FRYE
> *Anatomy of Criticism*

Don't let this become an *idée fixe* with you.
Honi soit qui mal y pense is the motto of the Order of the Garter.
One ex officio member of the committee criticized our agenda.
    [No underlining needed. "Ex officio" and "agenda," although clearly foreign in origin, have become naturalized.]

II. NUMERALS

M 4. In general, spell out numbers that can be expressed in one or two words; use numerals for other numbers.

eighteen workmen	276 workmen
nine dollars	1,620 dollars
over two million votes	2,375,069 votes
one and a half	$1\frac{3}{16}$

M 5. Use numerals for dates using day and year, street numbers, hours of the day when followed by A.M. or P.M., page and chapter numbers of a book, percentages and decimals, and sums of money after the dollar sign ($).

on June 7, 1926   on 7 June 1926
at 107 South 104 Street [*but*] at 725 Fourth Avenue
at 9:00 A.M. [*but*] at nine in the morning
on page 83 of chapter 4
a service charge of 2 percent
The .0375 dividend rate yielded $1,640.72.

M 6. Except in technical writing, do not begin a sentence with a numeral.

If the number is too cumbersome to spell out, recast the sentence.

WRONG: 150 people applied for the job.
RIGHT: One hundred fifty people applied for the job.
WRONG: 1,257 degrees were awarded last June.
RIGHT: Last June 1,257 degrees were awarded.

III. HYPHENS

The use of a hyphen to form a single word from two or more words poses a problem for writers and lexicographers; few matters of written English are so subject to change and to divided usage. The writer's recourse is an up-to-date dictionary, and he or she would be wise not to search for reasons behind what may appear to be arbitrary decisions. (Why, for instance, are these three sequential entries written as they are in *Webster's Third New International Dictionary:* the noun *fire stop* as two words, the verb *fire-stop* hyphenated, and the noun *firestopping* as one word?)

Certain principles and conventions, however, are quite generally followed:

M 7. Use a hyphen to divide a word that must be broken at the end of a line.

1. Divide a word only between syllables. Do not divide a word before a single vowel even when it is a syllable by itself. (Consult your dictionary for problems of syllabic division.)

inte-/grate [*not*] integ-/rate
defi-/nite [*not*] def-/inite

2. With words having a prefix or a suffix, divide the word after the prefix syllable and before the suffix syllable.

inter-/collegiate [*not*] intercol-/legiate
govern-/ess [*not*] gov-/erness

3. Do not divide a word so that a single letter ends or begins a line.

enough [*not*] e-/nough
many [*not*] man-/y

M 8. When two or more words combine to form an adjectival modifier, use hyphens if the unit precedes the noun; do not use hyphens if the modifier follows the noun or if its first word is an adverb ending in *ly*.

I deplore his devil-may-care attitude.
I admire your well-kept lawn.
Your lawn is always well kept. [No hyphen.]
I admire your neatly trimmed beard. [No hyphen.]

Note that this use of the hyphen can sometimes determine an exact meaning:

a stack of twenty-dollar bills; a stack of twenty dollar bills.
all-American boys; all American boys.
a bad-check writer; a bad check writer.

M 9. Use hyphens with compound numbers from twenty-one through ninety-nine and with fractions used before a noun.

Twenty-two others claimed the one-third share of the reward money, but they received only one eighth.

M 10. Use hyphens, particularly with prefixes and suffixes, to avoid awkward combinations of letters or to distinguish between two meanings of a word.

anti-intellectualism
pre-Aztec
her doll-like face
his annoying busy-ness
re-cover the couch [recover the money]

IV. Elliptical Periods

Sometimes a writer wishes to use quoted material but wants to shorten it while still keeping exact words of the original. Three or four spaced periods (elliptical periods or dots) are used in the quoted excerpt to show where material in the original has been omitted.

M 11. **Use three elliptical periods (. . .) to show an omission within a quoted sentence; use four dots (. . . .) to show the omission of two or more complete sentences or the omission of words at the end of a sentence.**

ORIGINAL: With bitterness the British soldiers who felt proud of their fighting at Mons found themselves caught up in continued retreat. Such was their Commander's anxiety to remove them from the danger of von Kluck's enveloping arm that he gave them no rest. Under a blazing sun the soldiers, without proper food or sleep, shuffled along, hardly awake, and when halted fell asleep instantly, standing up. Smith-Dorrien's Corps fought constant rearguard actions as the retreat from Mons began, and although Kluck's pursuit kept them under heavy artillery fire, the Germans were unable to hold the British to a standstill.

—BARBARA W. TUCHMAN
The Guns of August

SHORTENED QUOTATION: With bitterness the British soldiers . . . found themselves caught up in continued retreat. . . . Smith-Dorrien's Corps fought constant rearguard actions as the retreat from Mons began. . . .

CAPITALIZATION

C 1. **Capitalize the first word of every sentence, every quoted sentence or fragment, every transitional fragment, and every line of poetry.**

The building needs repairs. How much will it cost? Please answer me. Mr. James said, "We'll expect your answer soon." She replied, "Of course." And now to conclude.

Whenas in silks my Julia goes,
Then, then (methinks) how sweetly flows
That liquefaction of her clothes.
Next, when I cast mine eyes and see
That brave vibration each way free;
O how that glittering taketh me!

—ROBERT HERRICK, "Upon Julia's Clothes"

NOTE: Follow the practice of the author when quoting poetry that intentionally omits conventional capitalization.

C 2. Capitalize proper nouns and adjectives derived from them.

A proper noun designates by name an individual person, place, or thing that is a member of a group or class. Do not capitalize common nouns, which are words naming a group or class.

Doris Powers, woman; France, country; Tuesday, day; January, month; Christmas Eve, holiday; Shorewood High School, high school; Carleton College, college; *Mauretania,* ship; Fifth Avenue, boulevard; White House, residence

Elizabethan drama, Restoration poetry, Chinese peasants, Indian reservation, Red Cross assistance

C 3. Do not capitalize nouns and derived forms that, although originally proper nouns, have acquired special meanings.

When in doubt, consult your dictionary.

a set of china; a bohemian existence; plaster of paris; pasteurized milk; a mecca for golfers; set in roman type, not italics

C 4. Capitalize names of religions, references to deities, and most words having religious significance.

Bible, Biblical, Old Testament, Holy Writ, Jewish, Catholic, Sermon on the Mount, Koran, Talmud

C 5. Capitalize titles of persons when used with the person's name.

When the title is used alone, capitalize it only when it stands for a specific person of high rank.

I spoke briefly to Professor Jones. He is a professor of history.
We visited the late President Johnson's ranch in Texas.
Jerry is president of our art club.
Tonight the President will appear on national television.
The secretary of our local lawyers' association wrote to the Attorney General.

C 6. Capitalize names denoting family relationship but not when they are preceded by a possessive.

This rule is equivalent to saying that you capitalize when the word serves as a proper noun.

At that moment Mother, Father, and Aunt Lucy entered the room.
My mother, father, and aunt are very strict about some things.

C 7. Capitalize points of the compass when they refer to actual regions but not when they refer to directions.

Before we moved to the West, we lived in the South for a time.
You drive three miles east and then turn north on the Pacific Highway.

C 8. Capitalize names of academic subjects as they would appear in college catalogue listings, but in ordinary writing capitalize only names of languages.

I intend to register for History 322 and Sociology 188.
Last year I took courses in history, sociology, German, and Latin.

C 9. Do not capitalize names of the seasons.

summer, fall, autumn, winter, spring

C 10. In titles of books, short stories, plays, essays, and poems, capitalize the first word and all other words except the articles (*a, an, the*) and short prepositions and conjunctions.

Last semester I wrote reports on the following: Shaw's *The Intelligent Woman's Guide to Socialism and Capitalism,* Joyce's *A Portrait of the Artist as a Young Man,* Pirandello's *Six Characters in Search of an Author,* Poe's "The Fall of the House of Usher," Yeats' "An Irish Airman Foresees His Death," and Frost's "Stopping by Woods on a Snowy Evening."

SPELLING

Very likely many of you agree with Mr. Tulliver of *The Mill on the Floss,* who "found the relation between spoken and written language, briefly known as spelling, one of the most puzzling things in this puzzling world." But you should gain some comfort from two facts: Spelling is, in varying degree, a problem that troubles everyone, even an English teacher; and anyone can improve his or her spelling.

Regular reference to your dictionary and careful proofreading of your writing are practices that, if they become habitual with you, will greatly reduce the number of your spelling errors.

The material given in this spelling section will help you master common words that you use in everyday writing. The spelling rules and the reminders about the formation of plural nouns should not only fix in your mind the spelling of some of our most troublesome words but also show you some phonetic principles that determine the spelling of hundreds of words in our language. The list of words similar in sound includes the most troublesome homophones. (Homophones are words like *right/write, see/sea* that sound alike but have different meanings and spellings.) If the sentences showing the uses of the words similar in sound do not clear up for you the points of confusion, refer to a dictionary for more detailed information.

I. SPELLING RULES

Sp 1. In words ending in silent *e,* drop the *e* before a suffix beginning with a vowel and retain the *e* before a suffix beginning with a consonant.

After *c* or *g,* if the suffix begins with *a* or *o,* the *e* is retained to preserve the soft sound of the *c* or *g.*

DROP e BEFORE A VOWEL

bride	+ al	—bridal	mobile	+ ity	—mobility
cure	+ ing	—curing	noise	+ y	—noisy
fame	+ ous	—famous	remove	+ able	—removable
force	+ ible	—forcible	white	+ ish	—whitish
imagine	+ ary	—imaginary	write	+ er	—writer

RETAIN e BEFORE A CONSONANT

excite	+ ment	—excitement	life	+ like	—lifelike

hate	+ ful	—hateful	lone	+ some	—lonesome
hope	+ less	—hopeless	pale	+ ness	—paleness

RETAIN e AFTER c OR g, IF THE SUFFIX
BEGINS WITH a OR o

advantage + ous	—advantageous	service + able	—serviceable
notice + able	—noticeable	outrage + ous	—outrageous

EXCEPTIONS: acreage, awful, dyeing ("changing the color of"), ninth, singeing ("burning slightly"), wholly, wisdom.

(See also "Variant Spellings," page 32.)

Sp 2. In words with *ie* or *ei* when the sound is long *e*, use *i* before *e* except after *c*.

USE i BEFORE e

apiece	frontier	priest
belief	grieve	reprieve
fiend	niece	shriek
fierce	pierce	thievery

EXCEPT AFTER c

ceiling	conceive	perceive
conceited	deceit	receipt

EXCEPTIONS: You can remember the common exceptions to this rule by memorizing this nonsense sentence: *Neither financier seized either species of weird leisure.*

Sp 3. In words of one syllable and words accented on the last syllable, ending in a single consonant preceded by a single vowel, double the final consonant before a suffix beginning with a vowel.

WORDS OF ONE SYLLABLE—SUFFIX BEGINS
WITH A VOWEL

ban	—banned	hit	—hitting	rid	—riddance
bid	—biddable	hop	—hopping	Scot	—Scottish
dig	—digger	quit	—quitter	stop	—stoppage
drag	—dragged	[*qu*	= consonant]	wet	—wettest

ACCENTED ON LAST SYLLABLE—SUFFIX BEGINS
WITH A VOWEL

abet	—abetting	equip	—equipping	regret	—regrettable
allot	—allotted	occur	—occurrence	repel	—repellent

NOT ACCENTED ON LAST SYLLABLE—SUFFIX BEGINS
WITH A VOWEL

differ	—different	hasten	—hastened	prefer	—preferable
happen	—happening	open	—opener	sharpen	—sharpened

SUFFIX BEGINS WITH A CONSONANT

allot	—allotment	color	—colorless	sad	—sadness
big	—bigness	king	—kingdom	sin	—sinful

An apparent exception to this rule affects a few words formed by the addition of *ing, ed,* or *y* to a word ending in *c.* To preserve the hard sound of the *c,* a *k* is added before the vowel of the suffix, resulting in such spellings as *frolicking, mimicked, panicked, panicky, picnicked,* and *trafficking.*

Another irregularity applies to such spellings as *quitting* and *equipped.* One might think that the consonant should not be doubled, reasoning that the final consonant is preceded by two vowels, not by a single vowel. But because *qu* is phonetically the equivalent of *kw,* the *u* is a consonant when it follows *q.* Therefore, since the final consonant is actually preceded by a single vowel, the consonant is doubled before the suffix. (See also "Variant Spellings," pages 32–33.)

Sp 4. With words ending in *y* preceded by a consonant, change *y* to *i* when adding a suffix. Retain the *y* if it is preceded by a vowel.

ENDING IN y PRECEDED BY A CONSONANT

ally	—allies	easy	—easiest	pity	—pitiable
busy	—busily	icy	—icier	study	—studies
cloudy	—cloudiness	mercy	—merciless	try	—tried

ENDING IN y PRECEDED BY A VOWEL

boy	—boyish	coy	—coyness	enjoy	—enjoying
buy	—buys	donkey	—donkeys	stay	—staying

EXCEPTIONS: The *y* is retained in words like the following: *babyish, carrying, ladylike, studying.*

Note also that with spellings like *soliloquy/soliloquies* and *colloquy/colloquies* the plural spelling is not exceptional; the final *y* is preceded by *u,* a consonant when used with *q.* (See Sp 3.)

Sp 5. Do not confuse words that are similar in sound but different in spelling.

1. **accept:** I should like to accept your first offer.
   except: He took everything except the rugs.

2. **advice:** Free advice is usually not worth much.
   advise: Mr. Hull said he would advise me this term.

3. **affect:** His forced jokes affect me unfavorably.
   effect: His humor has a bad effect. Let us try to effect a lasting peace.

4. **all ready:** They were all ready to go home.
   already: They had already left when we telephoned the house.

5. **all together:** Now that we are all together, let us talk it over.
   altogether: They were not altogether pleased with the results.

6. **altar:** In this temple was an altar to the Unknown God.
   alter: One should not try to alter or escape history.

7. **canvas:** We used a piece of canvas to shelter us from the wind.
   canvass: The candidate wanted to canvass every person in his precinct.

8. **capital:** capital letter; capital gains; capital punishment; capital crime.
   Capitol: Workmen are painting the dome of the Capitol.

9. **cite:** He cited three good examples.
   site: The site of the new school has not been decided upon.
   sight: They were awed by the sight of so much splendor.

10. **coarse:** The coarse sand blew in my face.
    course: We discussed the course to take. Of course he may come with us.

11. **complement:** Find the complement in this sentence.
    compliment: It is easier to pay a compliment than a bill.

12. **consul:** Be sure to look up the American consul in Rome.
    council: He was appointed to the executive council.
    counsel: I sought counsel from my friends. They counseled moderation. He employed counsel to defend him.

13. **desert:** Out in the lonely desert he tried to desert from his regiment.
    dessert: We had apple pie for dessert.

14. **dining:** We eat dinner in our dining room. Dining at home is pleasant.
    dinning: Stop dinning that song into my ears!

15. **formerly:** He was formerly a student at Beloit College.
    formally: You must address the presiding judge formally and
        respectfully.

16. **instance:** For instance, he was always late to class.
    instants: As the car turned, those brief instants seemed like
        hours.

17. **its:** Your plan has much in its favor. [Possessive of *it*.]
    it's: It's too late now for excuses. [Contraction of *it is*.]

18. **later:** It is later than you think.
    latter: Of the two novels, I prefer the latter.

19. **lose:** You must not lose your purse.
    loose: He has a loose tongue. The dog is loose again.

20. **past:** It is futile to try to relive the past.
    passed: She smiled as she passed me. She passed the test.

21. **peace:** He was picked up for disturbing the peace.
    piece: I'd like another piece of pie.

22. **personal:** Write him a personal letter.
    personnel: The personnel here is a select group.

23. **presence:** We are honored by your presence.
    presents: The child demanded expensive presents.

24. **principal:** The principal of a school; the principal [chief]
        industry; the principal and the interest.
    principle: He is a man of high principles.

25. **quiet:** You must keep quiet.
    quite: You have been quite good all day.

26. **shone:** The cat's eyes shone in the dark.
    shown: He hasn't shown us his best work.

27. **stationary:** The stationary benches could not be moved.
    stationery: He wrote a letter on hotel stationery.

28. **statue:** It was a statue of a pioneer.
    stature: Athos was a man of gigantic stature.
    statute: The law may be found in the 1917 book of statutes.

29. **than:** She sings better than I.
    then: She screamed; then she fainted.

30. **their:** It wasn't their fault. [Possessive pronoun.]
    there: You won't find any gold there. [Adverb of place.]
    they're: They're sure to be disappointed. [Contraction of *they
        are*.]

31. **to:** Be sure to speak to him. [Preposition.]
    too: He is far too old for you. [Adverb.]
    two: The membership fee is only two dollars. [Adjective.]

32. **whose:** Whose book is this? [Possessive pronoun.]
    who's: I wonder who's with her now. [Contraction of *who is*.]

Sp 6. Follow these general principles in the spelling of plural nouns:

1. Plurals of most nouns are regularly formed by the addition of *s*. But if the singular noun ends in an *s* sound (*s, sh, ch, x, z*), *es* is added in order to form a new syllable in pronunciation.

crab, crabs	foe, foes	kiss, kisses	tax, taxes
lamp, lamps	box, boxes	church, churches	lass, lasses

2. Nouns ending in *y* form their plurals according to the spelling rule. (See Sp 4.)

toy, toys	army, armies	fly, flies	attorney, attorneys
key, keys	lady, ladies	sky, skies	monkey, monkeys

3. Some words ending in *o* (including all musical terms and all words having a vowel preceding the *o*) form their plural with *s*. But many others take *es*. Some musical terms may also use the Italian form of the plural.

piano, pianos	echo, echoes	potato, potatoes
cello, cellos, celli	solo, solos	tomato, tomatoes

(See also "Variant Spellings," page 33.)

4. Some nouns ending in *f* or *fe* merely add *s;* some change *f* or *fe* to *ves* in the plural.

leaf, leaves	life, lives	half, halves	wolf, wolves
roof, roofs	safe, safes	gulf, gulfs	elf, elves

(See also "Variant Spellings," page 33.)

5. A few nouns have the same form for singular and plural. A few have irregular plurals.

ox, oxen	child, children	deer, deer	goose, geese
man, men	foot, feet	sheep, sheep	mouse, mice

6. Many words of foreign origin use two plurals; some do not. Always check in your dictionary.

alumna, alumnae	basis, bases	criterion, criteria
alumnus, alumni	bon mot, bons mots	datum, data
analysis, analyses	crisis, crises	thesis, theses
appendix, appendixes, appendices		focus, focuses, foci
beau, beaus, beaux		fungus, funguses, fungi
curriculum, curriculums, curricula		index, indexes, indices
memorandum, memorandums, memoranda		
tableau, tableaus, tableaux		

WARNING: Do not use the apostrophe to form the plural of nouns. (See P 24.)

II. VARIANT SPELLINGS

A variant or secondary spelling finds its way into a dictionary when lexicographers, reflecting up-to-the-minute usage, decide that an alternate spelling appears often enough in reputable sources to prevent its being looked upon as a misspelling. Reputable modern dictionaries contain hundreds of variant spellings. When you find two spellings of a word in your dictionary, you would be wise to use the one given in first position, an indication in most cases that it is the form commonly used. And, although we all know that consistency is not always a virtue, don't puzzle your reader by writing, for example, *useable* in one spot and *usable* a few lines later.

Remember that a variant spelling is not an exception: A secondary spelling, although listed as acceptable in a dictionary, in no way invalidates a general principle of spelling. We should here take note of some acceptable secondary spellings for words that exemplify some of the general principles covered in the preceding pages. Only a few of the available examples are given. In each case the first word of each pair is the spelling found in first position in most dictionaries.

1. Dropping or retaining final silent *e* (Sp 1):

   choosy/choosey, eyeing/eying, likable/likeable, lovable/loveable, movable/moveable, nosy/nosey, sizable/sizeable, usable/useable.

2. Doubling final consonant before a suffix (Sp 3):

Dictionaries show variant spellings for the *ed* and *ing* forms (and a few other derived forms) of dozens of verbs ending in single consonants preceded by single vowels. In general, the single-consonant spelling is usually found in American printing; some of the dictionaries label the double-consonant spelling a British preference. For words with two spellings for the *ed* form, the double-consonant spelling is also acceptable for the *ing* form.

> *biased/biassed, canceled/cancelled, counselor/counsellor, diagramed/diagrammed, equaled/equalled, marvelous/marvellous, modeled/modelled, totaled/totalled, traveler/traveller*

3. Plurals (Sp 6):

> *banjos/banjoes, buses/busses, cargoes/cargos, halos/haloes, hoofs/hooves, mottoes/mottos, taxis/taxies, wharves/wharfs, zeros/zeroes.*

III. SPELLING LIST

This list includes three hundred words frequently misspelled by high school and college students. The words are arranged for convenience in numbered groups of twenty, with each word repeated to show its syllabic division. Whether this list is used for individual study and review or in some kind of organized class activity, your method of studying should be the following: (1) Learn to pronounce the word syllable by syllable. Some of your trouble in spelling may come from incorrect pronunciation. (2) Copy the word carefully, forming each letter as plainly as you can. Some of your trouble may come from bad handwriting. (3) Pronounce the word carefully again. (4) On a separate sheet of paper write the word from memory, check your spelling with the correct spelling before you, and, if you have misspelled the word, repeat the learning process.

1

1. abbreviate	1. ab–bre–vi–ate
2. absence	2. ab–sence
3. accidentally	3. ac–ci–den–tal–ly
4. accommodate	4. ac–com–mo–date
5. accompanying	5. ac–com–pa–ny–ing
6. accomplish	6. ac–com–plish
7. accumulate	7. ac–cu–mu–late
8. achievement	8. a–chieve–ment
9. acknowledge	9. ac–knowl–edge
10. acquaintance	10. ac–quaint–ance
11. acquire	11. ac–quire
12. across	12. a–cross
13. aggravate	13. ag–gra–vate
14. all right	14. all right
15. always	15. al–ways

16. amateur
17. among
18. analysis
19. apparatus
20. apparently

16. am-a-teur
17. a-mong
18. a-nal-y-sis
19. ap-pa-ra-tus
20. ap-par-ent-ly

2

1. appearance
2. appreciate
3. appropriate
4. approximately
5. argument
6. arithmetic
7. arrangement
8. association
9. athletics
10. attendance
11. audience
12. auxiliary
13. awkward
14. barbarous
15. becoming
16. beginning
17. believing
18. beneficial
19. benefit
20. boundaries

21. ap-pear-ance
22. ap-pre-ci-ate
23. ap-pro-pri-ate
24. ap-prox-i-mate-ly
25. ar-gu-ment
26. a-rith-me-tic
27. ar-range-ment
28. as-so-ci-a-tion
29. ath-let-ics
30. at-tend-ance
31. au-di-ence
32. aux-il-ia-ry
33. awk-ward
34. bar-ba-rous
35. be-com-ing
36. be-gin-ning
37. be-liev-ing
38. ben-e-fi-cial
39. ben-e-fit
40. bound-a-ries

3

1. Britain
2. business
3. calendar
4. candidate
5. carburetor
6. category
7. cemetery
8. certain
9. changeable
10. characteristic
11. chosen
12. clothes
13. coming
14. commission
15. committed

41. Brit-ain
42. busi-ness
43. cal-en-dar
44. can-di-date
45. car-bu-re-tor
46. cat-e-go-ry
47. cem-e-ter-y
48. cer-tain
49. change-a-ble
50. char-ac-ter-is-tic
51. cho-sen
52. clothes
53. com-ing
54. com-mis-sion
55. com-mit-ted

16. committee	56. com-mit-tee
17. comparative	57. com-par-a-tive
18. compelled	58. com-pelled
19. competent	59. com-pe-tent
20. competition	60. com-pe-ti-tion

4

1. completely	61. com-plete-ly
2. compulsory	62. com-pul-so-ry
3. concede	63. con-cede
4. conceivable	64. con-ceiv-a-ble
5. conference	65. con-fer-ence
6. conferred	66. con-ferred
7. confidentially	67. con-fi-den-tial-ly
8. confidently	68. con-fi-dent-ly
9. conscience	69. con-science
10. conscientious	70. con-sci-en-tious
11. conscious	71. con-scious
12. consistent	72. con-sist-ent
13. continuous	73. con-tin-u-ous
14. controlled	74. con-trolled
15. controversial	75. con-tro-ver-sial
16. convenient	76. con-ven-ient
17. criticism	77. crit-i-cism
18. criticize	78. crit-i-cize
19. curiosity	79. cu-ri-os-i-ty
20. dealt	80. dealt

5

1. decided	81. de-cid-ed
2. decision	82. de-ci-sion
3. definitely	83. def-i-nite-ly
4. describe	84. de-scribe
5. description	85. de-scrip-tion
6. desirable	86. de-sir-a-ble
7. desperate	87. des-per-ate
8. dictionary	88. dic-tion-ar-y
9. difference	89. dif-fer-ence
10. dilapidated	90. di-lap-i-dat-ed
11. disappear	91. dis-ap-pear
12. disappoint	92. dis-ap-point
13. disastrous	93. dis-as-trous
14. discipline	94. dis-ci-pline
15. dissatisfied	95. dis-sat-is-fied

16. dissipate
17. divide
18. doesn't
19. dormitory
20. during

96. dis–si–pate
97. di–vide
98. does–n't
99. dor–mi–to–ry
100. dur–ing

6

1. efficient
2. eligible
3. eliminate
4. embarrass
5. eminent
6. emphasize
7. enthusiastic
8. environment
9. equipment
10. equipped
11. equivalent
12. especially
13. exaggerated
14. exceed
15. excellent
16. exceptionally
17. exhaust
18. existence
19. experience
20. explanation

101. ef–fi–cient
102. el–i–gi–ble
103. e–lim–i–nate
104. em–bar–rass
105. em–i–nent
106. em–pha–size
107. en–thu–si–as–tic
108. en–vi–ron–ment
109. e–quip–ment
110. e–quipped
111. e–quiv–a–lent
112. es–pe–cial–ly
113. ex–ag–ger–at–ed
114. ex–ceed
115. ex–cel–lent
116. ex–cep–tion–al–ly
117. ex–haust
118. ex–ist–ence
119. ex–pe–ri–ence
120. ex–pla–na–tion

7

1. extraordinary
2. extremely
3. familiar
4. fascinate
5. February
6. finally
7. foreign
8. forty
9. frantically
10. fraternities
11. fundamental
12. generally
13. government
14. grammar
15. grievous

121. ex–traor–di–nar–y
122. ex–treme–ly
123. fa–mil–iar
124. fas–ci–nate
125. Feb–ru–ar–y
126. fi–nal–ly
127. for–eign
128. for–ty
129. fran–ti–cal–ly
130. fra–ter–ni–ties
131. fun–da–men–tal
132. gen–er–al–ly
133. gov–ern–ment
134. gram–mar
135. griev–ous

16. guarantee
17. height
18. hindrance
19. humorous
20. hurriedly

136. guar-an-tee
137. height
138. hin-drance
139. hu-mor-ous
140. hur-ried-ly

8

1. imaginary
2. imagination
3. immediately
4. impromptu
5. incidentally
6. incredible
7. independence
8. indispensable
9. inevitable
10. influential
11. intelligence
12. intentionally
13. intercede
14. interesting
15. interpretation
16. interrupt
17. irresistible
18. knowledge
19. laboratory
20. led

141. im-ag-i-nar-y
142. im-ag-i-na-tion
143. im-me-di-ate-ly
144. im-promp-tu
145. in-ci-den-tal-ly
146. in-cred-i-ble
147. in-de-pend-ence
148. in-dis-pen-sa-ble
149. in-ev-i-ta-ble
150. in-flu-en-tial
151. in-tel-li-gence
152. in-ten-tion-al-ly
153. in-ter-cede
154. in-ter-est-ing
155. in-ter-pre-ta-tion
156. in-ter-rupt
157. ir-re-sist-i-ble
158. knowl-edge
159. lab-o-ra-to-ry
160. led

9

1. legitimate
2. liable
3. library
4. lightning
5. literature
6. livelihood
7. loneliness
8. maintain
9. maintenance
10. marriage
11. mathematics
12. meant
13. merely
14. miniature
15. mischievous
16. misspelled

161. le-git-i-mate
162. li-a-ble
163. li-brar-y
164. light-ning
165. lit-er-a-ture
166. live-li-hood
167. lone-li-ness
168. main-tain
169. main-te-nance
170. mar-riage
171. math-e-mat-ics
172. meant
173. mere-ly
174. min-i-a-ture
175. mis-chie-vous
176. mis-spelled

17. murmuring
18. mysterious
19. naturally
20. necessary

177. mur-mur-ing
178. mys-te-ri-ous
179. nat-u-ral-ly
180. nec-es-sar-y

10

1. neither
2. nevertheless
3. ninety
4. ninth
5. noticeable
6. nowadays
7. nuclear
8. obedience
9. oblige
10. obstacle
11. occasionally
12. occurred
13. occurrence
14. omission
15. omitted
16. opportunity
17. optimistic
18. original
19. outrageous
20. pamphlet

181. nei-ther
182. nev-er-the-less
183. nine-ty
184. ninth
185. no-tice-a-ble
186. now-a-days
187. nu-cle-ar
188. o-be-di-ence
189. o-blige
190. ob-sta-cle
191. oc-ca-sion-al-ly
192. oc-curred
193. oc-cur-rence
194. o-mis-sion
195. o-mit-ted
196. op-por-tu-ni-ty
197. op-ti-mis-tic
198. o-rig-i-nal
199. out-ra-geous
200. pam-phlet

11

1. parallel
2. parliament
3. particularly
4. partner
5. pastime
6. peaceable
7. performance
8. permissible
9. perseverance
10. perspiration
11. persuade
12. physically
13. picnicking
14. politics
15. possession

201. par-al-lel
202. par-lia-ment
203. par-tic-u-lar-ly
204. part-ner
205. pas-time
206. peace-a-ble
207. per-form-ance
208. per-mis-si-ble
209. per-se-ver-ance
210. per-spi-ra-tion
211. per-suade
212. phys-i-cal-ly
213. pic-nick-ing
214. pol-i-tics
215. pos-ses-sion

16. practically	216. prac-ti-cal-ly
17. preceding	217. pre-ced-ing
18. preference	218. pref-er-ence
19. preferred	219. pre-ferred
20. prejudice	220. prej-u-dice

12

1. preparation	221. prep-a-ra-tion
2. prevalent	222. prev-a-lent
3. privilege	223. priv-i-lege
4. probably	224. prob-a-bly
5. procedure	225. pro-ce-dure
6. proceed	226. pro-ceed
7. professor	227. pro-fes-sor
8. prominent	228. prom-i-nent
9. pronunciation	229. pro-nun-ci-a-tion
10. propaganda	230. prop-a-gan-da
11. psychological	231. psy-cho-log-i-cal
12. pursue	232. pur-sue
13. quantity	233. quan-ti-ty
14. realize	234. re-al-ize
15. really	235. re-al-ly
16. receive	236. re-ceive
17. recognize	237. rec-og-nize
18. recommend	238. rec-om-mend
19. reference	239. ref-er-ence
20. referred	240. re-ferred

13

1. regard	241. re-gard
2. religious	242. re-li-gious
3. remembrance	243. re-mem-brance
4. repetition	244. rep-e-ti-tion
5. representative	245. rep-re-sent-a-tive
6. respectfully	246. re-spect-ful-ly
7. respectively	247. re-spec-tive-ly
8. restaurant	248. res-tau-rant
9. rhythm	249. rhythm
10. ridiculous	250. ri-dic-u-lous
11. sandwich	251. sand-wich
12. satisfactorily	252. sat-is-fac-to-ri-ly
13. saxophone	253. sax-o-phone
14. schedule	254. sched-ule

15. secretary	255. sec-re-tar-y
16. seize	256. seize
17. sense	257. sense
18. separately	258. sep-a-rate-ly
19. sergeant	259. ser-geant
20. shining	260. shin-ing

14

1. siege	261. siege
2. significant	262. sig-nif-i-cant
3. similar	263. sim-i-lar
4. sincerely	264. sin-cere-ly
5. sophomore	265. soph-o-more
6. specifically	266. spe-cif-i-cal-ly
7. specimen	267. spec-i-men
8. speech	268. speech
9. strictly	269. strict-ly
10. studying	270. stud-y-ing
11. successful	271. suc-cess-ful
12. superintendent	272. su-per-in-tend-ent
13. supersede	273. su-per-sede
14. surprise	274. sur-prise
15. syllable	275. syl-la-ble
16. temperament	276. tem-per-a-ment
17. temperature	277. tem-per-a-ture
18. thorough	278. thor-ough
19. together	279. to-geth-er
20. tragedy	280. trag-e-dy

15

1. tries	281. tries
2. truly	282. tru-ly
3. twelfth	283. twelfth
4. unanimous	284. u-nan-i-mous
5. undoubtedly	285. un-doubt-ed-ly
6. unnecessarily	286. un-nec-es-sar-i-ly
7. until	287. un-til
8. useful	288. use-ful
9. usually	289. u-su-al-ly
10. various	290. var-i-ous
11. vegetable	291. veg-e-ta-ble
12. village	292. vil-lage
13. villain	293. vil-lain

14. Wednesday
15. weird
16. whether
17. wholly
18. women
19. writing
20. written

294. Wednes-day
295. weird
296. wheth-er
297. whol-ly
298. wom-en
299. writ-ing
300. writ-ten

PART II
Principles of Sentence Structure

COMPLETENESS

A complete sentence contains a subject and a verb as its essential nucleus, or core. Without a subject and a verb, there is no complete sentence. In addition, a sentence must be able to stand alone as an independent unit of communication. Therefore, a clause—which must contain, of course, a subject and a verb—introduced by a subordinating word is obviously not a complete sentence. It is a dependent unit and must be joined to some independent unit.

Incomplete sentences, or **sentence fragments,** are usually considered a serious error in writing. The error committed by punctuating a fragment as if it were a sentence is called a **period fault.**

The best thing to do with sentence fragments is to avoid them. And you can avoid them if you have a working knowledge of the grammatical make-up of the sentence and if you practice reasonable care in your writing. If you have repeatedly had fragments called to your attention, try this technique: When you reread and revise what you have written, read the sentences in a paragraph in reverse order. Start with your last sentence and work back to your first. This process, by breaking the tie between a fragment and the sentence that it depends on, makes any grammatically incomplete sentence reveal itself.

When you discover a fragment in your writing, any one of several possible corrections can be easily made. Sometimes you can attach the fragment to the preceding sentence by doing away with the fragment's capital letter and supplying the right punctuation. Or you can change the fragment to a subordinate clause and attach it to the main clause by means of the right connective. Or you can change the fragment to a separate sentence by supplying a subject or a verb or both.

The undesirable sentence fragments that inexperienced writers sometimes construct are almost always of the three types in the following illustrations. The rewritten version given for each fragment is not, of course, the only possible correction.

Sn 1. Do not punctuate as a sentence a subordinate clause standing by itself.

> **FRAGMENTS:** I customarily mow my own lawn. *Although I cannot say I enjoy the chore.*
>
> Environmentalists are alarmed about strip mining. *Which can leave ugly scars on the face of the earth.*
>
> **CORRECTED:** I customarily mow my own lawn, *although I cannot say I enjoy the chore.*
>
> Environmentalists are alarmed about strip mining, *which can leave ugly scars on the face of the earth.*

Sn 2. Do not punctuate as a sentence a verbal phrase standing by itself.

> **FRAGMENTS:** The delegates agreed upon a compromise wage scale. *Realizing that the strike could not go on indefinitely.*
>
> Glenn found an excuse to leave early. *Being, in spite of his bravado, a real coward.*
>
> We hope to go on to New York City. *Especially to visit the UN Building.*
>
> **CORRECTED:** The delegates agreed upon a compromise wage scale *because they realized that the strike could not go on indefinitely.*
>
> *Being, in spite of his bravado, a real coward,* Glenn found an excuse to leave early.
>
> We hope to go on to New York City. *We want especially to visit the UN Building.*

Sn 3. Do not punctuate as a sentence a noun followed by a phrase or subordinate clause but lacking a verb to go with it.

> **FRAGMENTS:** The committee should include Mrs. Tartar. *A tireless worker with many constructive ideas.*

I hope you will let me have my old job back. *A chance to show you that I have learned my lesson.*

You must play checkers with him. *A game of checkers being the old man's idea of the perfect way to spend an afternoon.*

Junior will require a special kind of tutor. *Someone who will realize how sensitive the child really is.*

CORRECTED: The committee should include Mrs. Tartar, *a tireless worker with many constructive ideas.*

I hope you will let me have my old job back *and give me a chance to show you that I have learned my lesson.*

You must play checkers with him. *A game of checkers is the old man's idea of the perfect way to spend an afternoon.*

Junior will require a special kind of tutor, *someone who will realize how sensitive the child really is.*

A few types of word groups, although lacking a complete subject-verb combination, are not objectionable fragments. They are accepted as legitimate language patterns. These are

1. Commands, in which the subject "you" is understood.

   Please be seated. Put your name on a slip of paper. Pass the papers to the left aisle.

2. Exclamations.

   What excitement! Only two minutes to go! Good Heavens, not a fumble? How terrible!

3. Bits of dialogue.

   "New car?" she asked. "Had it long?"
   "Picked it up last week," he replied.

4. Occasional transitions between units of thought.

   On with the story.
   And now to conclude.

You have very likely observed in your reading that experienced writers sometimes use sentence fragments, especially in narrative and descriptive writing. But they are skillful workers who are masters of the tools they are using, and when they use fragments they are consciously striving for a stylistic effect. You, as a beginning writer, must understand that such experimentation should be practiced only when you have mastered the fundamental forms of the sentence. For the time being, you may have enough of a problem showing that you can write clear, correct sentences. Later on, there will be plenty of time for experimenting.

Sn 4. Do not omit words that are needed for grammatical completeness or for exact meaning.

1. Auxiliary verbs. When compound verbs are of the same tense and number, the auxiliary is often not repeated with the second verb.

> **CORRECT:** The bushes *have been* trimmed and the leaves *raked.*

But if the same auxiliary does not fit both verbs, each auxiliary must be expressed.

> **INCOMPLETE:** The grass has been cut and the clippings put in lawn bags. [Clippings *has been* (?)]
> **CORRECT:** The grass has been cut and the clippings have been put in lawn bags.

2. Form of main verb. If compound auxiliaries take the same principal part of the verb, the main verb is sometimes not stated with the first auxiliary.

> **CORRECT:** I *should,* in fact I will, *offer* to lend him the money.

However, if the compound auxiliaries do not take the same principal part of the main verb, both forms of the verb should be expressed.

> **INCOMPLETE:** I never have and never will admire him. [Have *admire* (?)]
> **CORRECT:** I never have admired and never will admire him.

3. *That* introducing a noun clause. The conjunction *that* is often unexpressed before a noun clause.

> **CORRECT:** I hope [that] the examination will be short.

But if the subject of the noun clause could be misconstrued as being the object of the main verb, the *that* should be expressed to avoid even momentary confusion for the reader.

> CONFUSING: Grandfather suspected all county officials were crooks.
>
> I soon learned the Russian alphabet is different from ours.
>
> CORRECT: Grandfather suspected that all county officials were crooks.
>
> I soon learned that the Russian alphabet is different from ours.

4. Nouns with more than one modifier. The noun need not be stated with the first modifier if both modifiers refer to the same number.

> CORRECT: We visited the *main* and *one suburban* library.

But if one modifier refers to the singular and the other to the plural, both nouns should be expressed.

> INCOMPLETE: We visited the main and three suburban libraries.
>
> CORRECT: We visited the main library and three suburban libraries.
>
> INCOMPLETE: Because he always looks on the bright side of things, Grandpa has made his own, as well as others', lives pleasant.
>
> CORRECT: Because he always looks on the bright side of things, Grandpa has made his own life, as well as others' lives, pleasant.

PARALLEL STRUCTURE

When two or more parts of a sentence are similar in function, they should be expressed in the same grammatical construction; in other words, they should be made parallel. The principle of parallelism implies that, in a series, nouns should be balanced with nouns, adjectives with adjectives, prepositional phrases with prepositional phrases, clauses with clauses, and so forth. Effective parallelism in a sentence requires that coordinators—*and, but, or, not (only) . . . but (also)*—be properly used; that is, they join grammatical units that are alike because they represent units of thought that are balanced and equal.

The following sentence owes much of its clarity and effectiveness to the careful parallel arrangement: Two adjective clauses are joined with *and,* two adverbs with *but,* and three noun direct objects with *and.*

Anyone ‖ who studies world affairs *and*
‖ who remembers our last three
‖ wars will realize,   sadly *but*
‖ inevitably,

that another conflict will endanger ‖ the economic strength
of our nation,
the complacency of our
political institutions, *and*
the moral fiber of our people.

Sn 5. Use like grammatical forms for two or more sentence parts that are equal in function.

> **WEAK:** A park ranger is entrusted with the safety of tourists and also to protect wildlife. [The *and* joins a noun, *safety,* to an infinitive phrase.]
>
> **BETTER:** A park ranger is entrusted with the safety of tourists and the protection of wildlife.
>
> **WEAK:** Some friends warned me of the length of the course and how difficult it is. [The *and* joins a noun, *length,* and a noun clause.]
>
> **BETTER:** Some friends warned me of the length of the course and its difficulty.
>
> Some friends warned me that the course was long and difficult.
>
> **WEAK:** Most men play golf for exercise, pleasure, and so they can meet people. [The *and* ties an adverb clause to two nouns.]
>
> **BETTER:** Most men play golf for exercise, for pleasure, and for social contacts.
>
> **WEAK:** It was weeks before Mary could bring herself to get into a car, much less driving one.
>
> **BETTER:** It was weeks before Mary could bring herself to get into a car, much less drive one.
>
> **WEAK:** Some critics complained about the triteness of the plot and that the characters are stereotyped.
>
> **BETTER:** Some critics complained about the trite plot and the stereotyped characters.
>
> Some critics complained that the plot is trite and the characters are stereotyped.
>
> **WEAK:** The half-time entertainment was good: there were two marching bands, a glee club from Oakdale College, and the governor made a short speech.

> **BETTER:** The half-time entertainment was good: there were two marching bands, a glee club from Oakdale College, and a short speech by the governor.

Sn 6. Avoid using *and, but,* or *or* to tie an adjective clause to some structure other than an adjective clause.

> **WEAK:** She is a person with great talent *and who* should be encouraged.
>
> **BETTER:** She is a person who has great talent and who should be encouraged.
>
> She is a talented person who should be encouraged. [Here the series is avoided.]
>
> **WEAK:** I am taking Physics 388, a difficult course *and which* demands much time.
>
> **BETTER:** I am taking Physics 388, a difficult course that demands much time.
>
> I am taking Physics 388, which is difficult and demands much time.
>
> **WEAK:** We finally located a house large enough for our expanding family *but which* was fairly reasonably priced.
>
> **BETTER:** We finally located a house that was large enough for our expanding family but fairly reasonably priced.

SUBORDINATION

In the preceding section you learned that you should use similar grammatical forms to express ideas that perform similar functions in the sentence. But it is just as important to recognize those parts of the sentence that are *unequal* in force. One common fault among beginning writers is the habit of joining two independent clauses with *and, but, or, so,* or *and so* when a more nearly exact relationship between the two ideas could be pointed out. Related to this weakness is the habit of producing strings of short independent clauses, either as separate sentences or as longer sentences with coordinate connectives between the clauses.

Correct immature sentences of these types by determining the exact relationship between the parts of the sentence. To avoid excessive coordination, get in the habit of trying out various subordinate structures, especially adjective and adverb clauses; participial, infinitive, and absolute phrases; and appositives. The result will be writing that is more mature, more economical, and more expressive.

Sn 7. Avoid writing a compound sentence when one of the ideas is logically subordinate to the other.

> **WEAK:** I heard Bob's explanation, and I marveled at his cleverness.
>
> **BETTER:** When I heard Bob's explanation, I marveled at his cleverness.
>
> **WEAK:** You should cover the pipes with asbestos, and this will reduce heat loss.
>
> **BETTER:** If you cover the pipes with asbestos, you will reduce heat loss.
>
> You should cover the pipes with asbestos to reduce heat loss.
>
> **WEAK:** A young woman was sitting at the front desk, and she greeted us.
>
> **BETTER:** A young woman who was sitting at the front desk greeted us.
>
> A young woman sitting at the front desk greeted us.
>
> **WEAK:** The play was a critical success, but the producers made no profit.
>
> **BETTER:** Although the play was a critical success, the producers made no profit.
>
> **WEAK:** The children's favorite was a fat clown, and he was wearing a policeman's uniform.
>
> **BETTER:** The children's favorite was a fat clown wearing a policeman's uniform.
>
> **WEAK:** Mr. Barton is a former actor, and he directed the local pageant.
>
> **BETTER:** Mr. Barton, a former actor, directed the local pageant.

Sn 8. Avoid writing a series of short, one-clause sentences when some of the ideas are logically subordinate.

> **WEAK:** I thought I was too old to take up golf. Graham insisted that I try the game. I have enjoyed it very much.
>
> **BETTER:** Although I had thought I was too old to take up golf, I have enjoyed it very much since Graham insisted that I try the game.
>
> **WEAK:** My old Ford cost me only six hundred dollars. I bought it seven years ago. It still performs well for me.

> **BETTER:** My old Ford, which cost me six hundred dollars when I bought it seven years ago, still performs well for me.

Sn 9. Avoid writing a long sentence made up of a string of independent clauses when some of the ideas are logically subordinate.

> **WEAK:** Laboratory fees have to be paid by today or credit for the course is not given so I'm going right over to the bursar's office.
>
> **BETTER:** Because credit for the course is not given if laboratory fees are not paid by today, I'm going right over to the bursar's office.
>
> **WEAK:** I followed Lucy's advice and went to the Thrift Shop and found some serviceable second-hand furniture.
>
> **BETTER:** Following Lucy's advice, I found some serviceable second-hand furniture at the Thrift Shop.

ARRANGEMENT

Proper arrangement of the parts of your sentence will help to make your meaning immediately clear to your reader. Ordinarily you will have no trouble with the main parts—the subjects, the verbs, and the complements. But problems may arise with the placement of the modifiers.

Sn 10. Do not allow modifying words, phrases, and clauses to attach themselves to the wrong sentence unit.

> **POOR:** I wish every person in this class could know the man I'm going to talk about *personally*.
>
> I heard that Senator Jones had been shot *on the morning broadcast*.
>
> Robbins slipped and fell while catching the ball *on his back*.
>
> Dan now lives in a little shack on an island *that he made out of driftwood*.
>
> **BETTER:** I wish every person in this class could know *personally* the man I'm going to talk about.
>
> *On the morning broadcast* I heard that Senator Jones had been shot.
>
> While catching the ball, Robbins slipped and fell *on his back*.

Dan now lives on an island in a little shack *that he made out of driftwood.*

Sn 11. Place limiting adverbs so that they modify the units being limited.

Although usage sanctions a rather loose placing of some common adverbs, such as *only, nearly, almost, hardly,* better sentences result if they are placed close to the words they modify.

    LOOSE: This will *only* take five minutes.
            I *nearly* earned a hundred dollars last week.
    BETTER: This will take *only* five minutes. [*Only* limits *five,* not *take.*]
            I earned *nearly* a hundred dollars last week.

Sn 12. Place correlatives—*both . . . and, either . . . or, neither . . . nor, not (only) . . . but (also)*—immediately before the parallel units they connect.

    POOR: We sent invitations *both* to Webster *and* Jenkins.
            You must *either* promise me that you will attend *or* send a substitute.
            He *not only* gets along with young people *but also* with their parents.
    BETTER: We sent invitations to *both* Webster *and* Jenkins. [The parallel units are *Webster . . . Jenkins.*]
            You must promise me that you will *either* attend *or* send a substitute.
            He gets along *not only* with young people *but also* with their parents.

Sn 13. Avoid squinting modifiers. A squinting modifier is one that is placed between two sentence units, either of which could be modified.

    SQUINTING: Reading a book *frequently* can change the whole course of a man's life.
            Students who can type *normally* are put into an advanced class.
            He said *after the dinner* some color slides would be shown.
            Camping in the mountains *for the past twenty years* has been my favorite vacation.
    BETTER: Reading a book can *frequently* change the whole course of a man's life.

Students who can type are *normally* put into an advanced class.

He said some color slides would be shown *after the dinner.*

For the past twenty years camping in the mountains has been my favorite vacation.

Sn 14. Avoid split infinitives that call attention to themselves.

An adverbial modifier of an infinitive, particularly a modifier consisting of more than one word, should not be placed between the *to* and the root verb. The split infinitive is greatly overemphasized by some people as an error; still, it is usually avoided by careful writers.

POOR: It was my custom to *at least once a month* visit my grandmother.

BETTER: It was my custom to visit my grandmother *at least once a month.*

COMPARISONS

Sentences that make a comparison or a contrast offer a few difficulties that you should understand.

Sn 15. Use the comparative degree when the comparison is limited to two things; use the superlative degree when more than two things are involved.

Both Jane and Edwina sing well, but Jane has the *better* voice.

Which takes *more* time, your studies or your job?

January is the *worst* month of the year.

Sn 16. In general, use *er, est* to form the comparative and superlative degrees with short words and *more, most* with longer words.

When I was *younger,* I was *more apprehensive* about thunder and lightning.

This encyclopedia is the *newest* and the *most comprehensive.*

Bob drives *faster* and *more recklessly* than he should.

Remember that in present-day standard English we don't combine *er, est* with *more, most* in the same word. We don't say, for example, *more pleasanter, most loveliest.* (See also U 43.)

Sn 17. Be sure that you compare only those things that are capable of being compared.

> FAULTY: The damage done by the fire was more severe than the earthquake. [What is wrong with this sentence is that two unlike things, *damage* and *earthquake,* are being compared.]
>
> The influence of the statesman is more ephemeral than the artist.
>
> IMPROVED: The damage done by the fire was more severe than *the damage* done by the earthquake.
>
> The damage done by the fire was more severe than *that of* the earthquake.
>
> The influence of the statesman is more ephemeral than *the influence* of the artist.
>
> The influence of the statesman is more ephemeral than *that of* the artist.
>
> The influence of the statesman is more ephemeral than *the artist's.*

Sn 18. When you are using the comparative form in a comparison, use *any other* when it is necessary to exclude the subject of the comparison from the group.

The men's dormitory is larger than *any other* building on the campus. [If you were to say ". . . than any building on the campus," you would compare the men's dormitory to a group that *includes* the men's dormitory.]

Sn 19. When your sentence contains a double comparison, you should include all the words necessary to make the idiom complete.

> FAULTY: Glenn is *as* young if not younger *than* you.
>
> Jane is one of the best, if not the best, *cook* in town.
>
> BETTER: Glenn is *as* young *as* if not younger *than* you.
>
> Glenn is as young as you, if not younger.
>
> Jane is one of the best *cooks,* if not the best *cook,* in town.
>
> Jane is one of the best cooks in town, if not the best.

DANGLING MODIFIERS

In a well-constructed sentence any modifying phrase containing a participle, a gerund, or an infinitive (see "Verbals," pages 127–130) is attached to a word that it logically modifies. By this we mean that the noun or pronoun being modified could be a logical subject of the verb from which the verbal is derived.

> Being a stubborn child, Ted usually gets his way. [*Test:* Ted is a stubborn child.]
> After leaving the dentist's office, I bought my groceries. [*Test:* I left the dentist's office.]
> To qualify for the job, an applicant must be able to type. [*Test:* An applicant qualifies for the job.]

If the modifying unit attaches itself to a noun or pronoun that does not produce this logical subject-verb relationship, we say that the phrase dangles.

> After leaving the dentist's office, my groceries had to be bought. [*Test:* My groceries left the dentist's office.]

Although danglers are occasionally found in the writings of very good authors, a dangler is undesirable if it calls attention to itself, if it causes even momentary confusion, or if it gives a ludicrous meaning that the writer did not intend.

The easiest way to correct a dangler is to supply the word the phrase should modify and to place the phrase next to the word. Another way is to change the dangling phrase to a subordinate clause with a subject and a verb expressed.

Sn 20. Avoid dangling introductory participial phrases.

> **DANGLER:** *Stepping into the boat,* my camera dropped into the water. [Was the camera stepping into the boat? Of course not. The trouble here is that the word which the phrase should modify is not expressed in the sentence.]
>
> *Burned to a cinder,* I could not eat the toast. [The sentence sounds as if *I* were burned to a cinder. The word that the dangler should modify is *toast,* but this word is too far from the phrase to be immediately associated with it.]
>
> **BETTER:** Stepping into the boat, I dropped my camera into the water.

While I was stepping into the boat, my camera dropped into the water.

Burned to a cinder, the toast was inedible.

I could not eat the toast because it was burned to a cinder.

Sn 21. Avoid dangling introductory gerund phrases used as objects of prepositions.

DANGLER: *After driving all day,* the motel was a welcome sight. [Was the motel doing the driving? That is not what is meant, and yet that is what the sentence states.]

Upon graduating from high school, my father let me work in his office. [The sentence says that your father let you work in his office when *he,* not *you,* graduated from high school.]

Since breaking my leg, my neighbors have helped with my farm chores. [A logical sentence only if the neighbors broke the leg.]

BETTER: After driving all day, we welcomed the sight of the motel.

After we had driven all day, the motel was a welcome sight.

Upon graduating from high school, I was given a chance to work in my father's office.

After I had graduated from high school, my father let me work in his office.

Since breaking my leg, I have been helped with my farm chores by my neighbors.

My neighbors have helped with my farm chores since I broke my leg.

Sn 22. Avoid dangling introductory infinitive phrases.

DANGLER: *To enter the contest,* a box top must be sent with your slogan.

BETTER: To enter the contest, you must send a box top with your slogan.

If you want to enter the contest, a box top must be sent with your slogan.

When you enter the contest, you must send a box top with your slogan.

Sn 23. Avoid dangling elliptical clauses.

An elliptical clause is one in which some grammatically necessary word or words (the subject, and often part or all of the verb) are not stated but are understood. One type that must be used carefully is the adverbial "time" clause introduced by the subordinating conjunction *when* or *while*. The clause becomes a dangler when the understood subject of the clause is different from the subject of the main clause. The reader wrongly assumes that both clauses have the same subject, and the result can be a ridiculous meaning that the writer never intended.

> **DANGLER:** *When ten years old,* my father sold his farm and moved to Los Angeles. [Because the subject of the elliptical clause is not stated, the reader assumes that it was the father who was ten years old.]
>
> *While combing my hair this morning,* a man's face appeared at the window. [Was the face combing the hair?]
>
> **BETTER:** When I was ten years old, my father sold his farm and moved to Los Angeles.
>
> While combing my hair this morning, I saw a man's face at the window.
>
> While I was combing my hair this morning, a man's face appeared at the window.

PART III
Principles of Word Choice

USING VERBS CORRECTLY

I. PRINCIPAL PARTS

The differences in form between regular verbs (I *laugh*, I *laughed*, I have *laughed*) and irregular verbs (I *fall*, I *fell*, I have *fallen*) bring up occasional problems of word choice for even experienced speakers and writers. On pages 102–104 you will find an explanation of principal parts of verbs—the three forms that show the difference between regular verbs and irregular verbs—and also a list of the principal parts of many verbs that sometimes cause confusion.

To gain assurance in your use of verbs, you must remember how the past tense and the past participle are used:

1. The past tense is always a single-word verb; it is never used with an auxiliary.

> "I *ate* my lunch," but not "I *have ate* my lunch."

2. The past participle is never a single-word verb; it is used with the auxiliary *have* to form the perfect tenses or the auxiliary *be* to form the passive voice.

> "I *have done* the work" or "The work *was done*," but not "I *done* the work."

(The past participle is, of course, used as a single word when it is a modifier of a noun: the *broken* toy, the *worried* parents, some *known* criminals.)

U 1. Do not confuse the past tense and the past participle.

> Later their actions *became* [not *become*] offensive.

They *began* [not *begun*] to laugh at us.
She should not have *chosen* [not *chose*] that hat.
Yesterday the child *came* [not *come*] home.
I had *driven* [not *drove*] all day.
Have you ever *ridden* [not *rode*] a horse?
I *saw* [not *seen*] him staring at me.
The letter had been *torn* [not *tore*] in two.

U 2. Do not confuse regular and irregular verb forms.

He *blew* [not *blowed*] smoke in my face.
The children *built* [not *builded*] a fort.
Slowly they *crept* [not *creeped*] up the stairs.
A friend *lent* [not *lended*] me a dime.
The child *threw* [not *throwed*] a stone at the dog.

U 3. Do not use obsolete or dialectal verb forms in serious writing.

The child *burst* [not *busted*] out crying.
I *climbed* [not *clumb*] a tree for a better view.
You could not have *dragged* [not *drug*] me there.
The boy was nearly *drowned* [not *drownded*].
At the picnic I *ate* [not *et*] eight hot dogs.

U 4. Do not confuse the forms of certain verbs that look or sound almost alike but are quite different in meaning, such as *lie/lay, sit/set, rise/raise.*

Note that three of these troublesome verbs—*lay, set, raise*—in their ordinary uses take objects and the other three—*lie, sit, rise*—do not.

Please *lay* your books on the table.
Harry *laid* several logs on the fire.
The men have *laid* some boards over the puddle.

The old dog *lies* [not *lays*] on the grass.
Yesterday he *lay* [not *laid*] on the floor.
Your dress must have *lain* [not *laid*] on the floor all night.

She *sets* the plate in front of me.
Tom *set* out some food for the birds.
I had *set* the camera at a full second.

(*Set,* normally a transitive verb demanding an object, has a few intransitive uses: A hen *sets* on eggs. The sun *sets* in the west. The new cement has *set.* Your new jacket *sets* [*fits*] perfectly.)

> I usually *sit* in that chair.
> Yesterday he *sat* in my chair.
> I have *sat* at my desk all morning.

> At his command they *raise* the flag.
> The boy quickly *raised* his hand.
> He had *raised* the price of his old car.

> He *rises* when we enter the room.
> Everyone *rose* as the speaker entered the room.
> The water has *risen* a foot since midnight.

U 5. Refer to your dictionary for the correct form of a few verbs for which special meanings demand different principal parts.

Notice that for certain of the verbs in the list on pages 102–104 there are two past tense forms or two past participles, reflecting modern dictionary practice of recognizing alternate forms. For most of these the forms are interchangeable. Remember, however, that the form listed first is the one more commonly used.

For a few of these verbs, however, there are small differences in meaning.

1. Bear: The past participle *borne* is used in the active voice and in the passive when followed by a "by" prepositional phrase.

> She has *borne* six children.
> These burdens must be *borne* by all of us.

Born is used in other passive constructions relating to the fact of birth.

> He was *born* in New York.

2. Hang: *Hanged* is the usual form for one meaning, "to suspend by the neck until dead."

3. Pay: *Payed* is the past tense for a special meaning, "to let out (a line or cable) by slackening."

4. Shine: *Shined* is the form generally used for the transitive meaning "to cause to shine."

> Yesterday I *shined* [not *shone*] my shoes.

II. Tense, Voice, Mood

A. TENSE

U 6. Avoid a needless shift in tense between past and present.

> **SHIFT IN TENSE:** The puppy *hesitated* and *seemed* puzzled by the confusion, but finally, with much barking and tail-wagging, he *climbs* onto Susan's lap and *becomes* very friendly. Within ten minutes he *was* fast asleep.
>
> **IMPROVED:** The puppy hesitated and seemed puzzled by the confusion, but finally, with much barking and tail-wagging, he *climbed* onto Susan's lap and *became* very friendly. Within ten minutes he was fast asleep.

However, statements that are "timeless" (true in the present as well as the past) should be expressed in the present tense even when the rest of the sentence uses the past tense.

> **CORRECT:** That experience taught me that family ties *are* [not *were*] the most enduring.
>
> Dr. Allen reminded us that St. Bernard of Menthon, a tenth-century archbishop who founded mountain hospices for travelers, *is* [not *was*] the patron saint of mountain climbers.

U 7. Use the tense of an infinitive or a participle that shows the logical time relationship to that of the main verb.

1. Use the present tense of an infinitive unless the infinitive represents a time or condition earlier than that of the main verb. The present infinitive shows the same time as that of the main verb.

> **CORRECT:** I intend *to leave* soon.
>
> I intended *to leave* an hour ago.
>
> For years Alice has wanted *to become* a lawyer.
>
> I am sorry *to have missed* your earlier lecture. [The time represented by this infinitive precedes that of the main verb.]

2. Use the present participle to show action or condition occurring at the same time as that of the main verb.

CORRECT: *Being* an only child, Mark usually gets his own way.
Being an only child, Mark will probably get his own way.
Seeing the assembled guests, Elaine smiled warmly.
Being distrustful of Wall Street, Dad has never owned any common stock.

3. Use the past participle or the perfect participle to show action or condition occurring before the time of the main verb.

CORRECT: *Left* bankrupt by the market crash, Dad distrusts all brokers.
Confused by the heavy traffic, the old man stopped his car.
Having finished the placement test, you will then be interviewed.
Having been found guilty, the boy was sent to prison.

B. VOICE

In a sentence using an active form of the verb, the subject of the verb names the doer of the action or the thing that is in the condition described by the verb. The active voice is the natural one to use in most narrative and descriptive writing. The passive verb (see pages 113–114) is logically used, however, when the doer of the action is unknown or is of less interest than the receiver of the action.

U 8. Avoid a needless shift from active voice to passive voice.

WEAK: If you can learn how to use a thesaurus, it *will be found* quite helpful.
BETTER: If you can learn how to use a thesaurus, you *will find* it quite helpful.
WEAK: The girl testified that she had seen the car *being stolen* by the thief.
BETTER: The girl testified that she had seen the thief *stealing* the car.
WEAK: Although he calls himself a real man of the people, his delight in pomp and riches *is* frequently *revealed*.
BETTER: Although he calls himself a real man of the people, he frequently *reveals* his delight in pomp and riches.

U 9. Use the passive voice when the doer of the action is unknown or of no real importance.

Failure to use a passive verb when the context warrants its use can lead to a reliance upon a vague indefinite pronoun as the subject of an active verb form. (See U 21.)

> **WEAK:** I stopped at the next filling station, and *he gave* me the proper directions.
>
> **BETTER:** I stopped at the next filling station and *was given* the proper directions.
>
> **WEAK:** At the county assessor's office *they told* me that *they had misplaced* my folder.
>
> **BETTER:** At the county assessor's office *I was told* that my *folder had been misplaced.*

C. MOOD

Nearly every verb you use in making statements and asking questions is in the indicative mood. The imperative mood, used in making commands or requests, presents no real problem in modern usage. The subjunctive mood, however, offers a rich area of study for students of English language history and usage. (For the distinctive subjunctive forms, see pages 100–101.) Fortunately for the average speaker and writer, the subjunctive is so little used in present-day English that in only one sentence situation is its use general.

U 10. Use a subjunctive verb in an "if" clause to show that the statement is clearly contrary to fact.

> If I *were* [not *was*] you, I'd accept the offer.
> *Were* [not *Was*] that the case, we would all be happier.

It might be a good idea to remember the "If I *were* you" sentence as an isolated set pattern, since it is, in fact, the only situation in which the use of a verb other than the subjunctive calls attention to itself. Other subjunctive uses (most of them residual from older English) are encountered, especially at formal levels of usage, in sentences like these:

> **"WISH" CLAUSES:** John wishes that he *were* at least five inches taller.

RESOLUTIONS, DEMANDS: I move that Mr. Blair *be* appointed chairman.

I demand that the former treasurer *return* the money.

It is imperative that you *be* in the courtroom on time.

SET EXPRESSIONS: *Suffice* it to say

Peace *be* with you.

Far *be* it from me to

Be that as it may

For most sentence situations in which older English used subjunctive verbs, modern writers can, and usually do, choose either an indicative verb or a form using a modal auxiliary such as *may, might,* or *should.*

U 11. In giving directions, do not shift between imperative verbs and nonimperative forms.

WEAK: Before you drive across the desert, *check* the gas and oil, *see* that the tires are sound, and you *should have* plenty of water in the radiator.

BETTER: Before you drive across the desert, *check* the gas and oil, *see* that the tires are sound, and *have* plenty of water in the radiator.

Before you drive across the desert, you *should check* the gas and oil, *see* that the tires are sound, and *have* plenty of water in the radiator.

WEAK: The negative *should be left* in the fluid until the print is reasonably clear, but *don't leave* it there too long.

BETTER: *Leave* the negative in the fluid until the print is reasonably clear, but *don't leave* it there too long.

III. SUBJECT-VERB AGREEMENT

I earn	We earn
You earn	You earn
He earns	They earn

Examine the conjugation given and observe that in the present tense the third person singular form (*He earns*) differs from the third person plural (*They earn*). This change we call a change in number: *Singular number* means that only one thing is talked about; *plural number* means that more than one thing is talked about. Notice how verbs and nouns differ in this respect: The *s* ending on nouns is a plural marker, but with verbs it designates the third person singular form.

The following examples show how the number of the subject (one or more than one) affects the form of the verb. The verbs *have, do,* and *be* are important because they have auxiliary uses as well as main verb uses. *Be* is an exceptional verb; with it there is a change of form in the past tense as well as in the present tense.

Singular	Plural
She *walks* slowly.	They *walk* slowly.
Mother *seems* pleased.	My parents *seem* pleased.
Mary *has* a new dress.	All of the girls *have* new dresses.
He *has traveled* widely.	They *have traveled* widely.
She *does* her work easily.	They *do* their work easily.
Does he *have* enough time?	*Do* they *have* enough time?
He *is* a friend of mine.	They *are* friends of mine.
My brother *is coming* home.	My brothers *are coming* home.
His camera *was taken* from him.	Their cameras *were taken* from them.

The information given here leads to an important principle of good usage: The verb agrees in number with its subject. To help you avoid some common pitfalls, we shall examine a few situations that sometimes cause trouble in speech or writing.

U 12. Do not allow the number of the verb to be affected by words standing between the verb and its subject.

Determine the *real* subject of the verb. Remember that the number of the verb is not altered when the subject is modified by phrases using *in addition to, together with, as well as, with, along with,* and the like.

> Immediate *settlement* of these problems *is* [not *are*] vital.
> Continued *exposure* to loud noises *damages* [not *damage*] nerve cells of the ear.
> The *cost* of replacing the asbestos shingles with shakes *was* [not *were*] considerable.
> *Tact* as well as patience *is* [not *are*] required.
> *Mr. Sheldon,* together with several other division heads, *has* [not *have*] decided to resign.

U 13. Use singular verbs with indefinite pronoun subjects like *either, neither, each, one,* **and compounds like** *someone, no one, everyone, somebody.*

> Only *one* of these suggestions *was* [not *were*] discussed.
> *Each* of the plans *has* [not *have*] its virtues.
> *Neither* of my parents *speaks* [not *speak*] French.

None may take either a singular verb or a plural verb, depending upon whether the writer wishes to emphasize "not one" or "not any" of the group.

> *None* of us *is* [or *are*] perfect.

U 14. Make the verb agree with its subject even when the subject follows the verb.

Be especially careful to find the real subject in sentences starting with *there* or *here.*

> Behind the shed *were* some gnarled apple *trees.* [*Trees were.*]
> He handed us a paper on which *was scribbled* a *warning.* [*Warning was scribbled.*]
> There *seems* to be little *time* left. [*Time seems.*]
> There *seem* to be too many *players* on the field. [*Players seem.*]
> Here *comes* the delivery *van* now. [*Van comes.*]
> Here *come* the three noisy *children* from next door. [*Children come.*]

U 15. With a collective noun subject, use a singular verb when the subject refers to a unit. Use a plural verb when the subject refers to the individuals of the group.

Words like *number, all, rest, part, some, more, most, half,* and so forth, are singular or plural, depending on the meaning intended. Words of this type will sometimes have modification that will give a clue as to the number intended. When the word *number* is a subject, it is considered singular if it is preceded by *the* and plural if it is preceded by *a.*

> The *audience is* very enthusiastic tonight.
> The *audience are returning* to their seats. [Notice pronoun *their.*]
> The *band is playing* a rousing march.
> Now the *band are putting* away their instruments. [Again note *their.*]
> *Most* of the book *is* blatant propaganda.

Most of my friends *are* happy about the election.
All is ready for the reception.
All are eager to leave now.
The *rest* of the lecture *was* dull.
The *rest* of the cars *are* on sale.
The *number* of accidents *is* increasing.
A *number* of the officers *are* resigning.

U 16. Use singular verbs with plural subjects of amount, distance, and so on, when the nouns are used as singular units of measurement.

A hundred *dollars was* once *paid* for a single tulip bulb.
Thirty *miles seems* like a long walk to me.
Seven *years* in prison *was* the penalty he had to pay.

U 17. When the subject is a relative pronoun, refer to the antecedent of the pronoun to determine the proper number (and person) of the verb.

He told a joke *that was* pointless. [*Joke was.*]
He told several jokes *that were* pointless. [*Jokes were.*]
I paid the expenses of the trip, *which were* minimal. [*Expenses were.*]
Jack is one of those boys *who enjoy* fierce competition.

The last example, sometimes called the "one of those . . . who" sentence, is particularly troublesome. Generally we find a plural verb used. Recasting the sentence to read "Of those boys who enjoy fierce competition, Jack is one" shows that the logical antecedent of *who* is the plural noun *boys*. However, usage is divided. And notice that a singular verb must be used when the pattern is altered slightly, as follows: "Jack is the only *one* of my friends *who enjoys* fierce competition."

Because a relative pronoun subject nearly always has an antecedent that is third person singular or third person plural, we are accustomed to pronoun–verb combinations like these: A boy *who is* . . ., Boys *who are* . . ., A man *who knows* . . ., Men *who know* . . . . But in those occasional sentences in which a relative pronoun subject has an antecedent that is first or second person, meticulously correct usage calls for subject–verb combinations like the following:

I, *who am* in charge here, should pay the bill. [*I . . . am.*]
They should ask me, *who know* all the answers. [*I . . . know.*]

You, *who are* in charge here, should pay the bill. [*You . . . are.*]
They should ask you, *who know* all the answers. [*You . . . know.*]

U 18. Use plural verbs with most compound subjects joined by *and*.

A little *boy* and his *dog were playing* in the yard.
Sitting near us *were* Mrs. *Locke* and her three *grandchildren.*

But the verb should be singular if the subjects joined by *and* are thought of as a single thing, or if the subjects are considered separately, as when they are modified by *every* or *each.*

The *sum* and *substance* of this argument *is* peace. [One thing.]
Every *man* and every *woman is asked* to help. [Considered separately.]

U 19. Use singular verbs with singular subjects joined by *or* or *nor*.

Either a *raincoat* or an *umbrella is* advisable.
Neither *he* nor his *assistant is* ever on time.
Was either *China* or *India* represented at the conference?

In some sentences of this pattern, especially in questions like the last example, a plural verb is sometimes used, both in casual conversation and in writing. In serious and formal writing, the singular verb is considered appropriate.

If the subjects joined by *or* or *nor* differ in number, the verb agrees with the subject nearer to it.

Neither the *mother* nor the two *boys were* able to identify him.
Either the *players* or the *coach is* responsible for the defeat.

USING PRONOUNS CORRECTLY

I. Reference and Agreement

A pronoun is a word that substitutes for a noun or another pronoun. The word for which a pronoun stands is called its antecedent.

I invited *Joan,* but *she* could not attend. [*She* substitutes for *Joan. Joan* is the antecedent of *she.*]
Because *Joan and Mary* were on vacation, I did not see *them.* [The antecedent of *them* is the plural unit *Joan and Mary.*]

I have lost *my* wristwatch.
One of the boys lost *his* wristwatch.
Two of the boys lost *their* wristwatches.

In order to use pronouns effectively and without confusing your reader, you must follow two basic principles:

1. You must establish a clear, easily identified relationship between a pronoun and its antecedent.

2. You must make the pronoun and its antecedent agree in person, number, and gender.

U 20. Be sure that every personal pronoun you use has a definite and easily located antecedent.

Your reader should not be made to look through several sentences for the antecedent of a pronoun, nor should he be asked to manufacture an antecedent for it. Avoid using a pronoun that refers to the possessive form of a noun. When you discover in your writing a pronoun with no clear and unmistakable antecedent, your revision, as many of the following examples demonstrate, will often require rewriting to remove the faulty pronoun from your sentence.

FAULTY: A strange car followed us closely, and *he* kept blinking his lights at us.

IMPROVED: A strange car followed us closely, and the driver kept blinking his lights at us.

FAULTY: If a man is a sports fan, should his wife become interested in *them*?

IMPROVED: If a man likes sports, should his wife become interested in them?

If a man is a sports fan, should his wife become interested in sports?

FAULTY: Because I have always been interested in machines, I intend to make *it* my life work. [*It* cannot refer to *machines*. Nor can "machines" be considered a "life work."]

IMPROVED: Because I have always been interested in machines, I intend to make mechanics [*or* engineering] my life work.

FAULTY: The committee's first task was to set up a schedule, but *it* met too late to accomplish much this year.

IMPROVED: The first task of the committee was to set up a schedule, but it met too late to accomplish much this year.

U 21. In serious writing avoid using the indefinite *you* or *they,* forms that may be appropriate in informal speech and writing.

> **FAULTY:** In Alaska *they* catch huge king crabs.
>
> **IMPROVED:** In Alaska huge king crabs are caught. [Often the best way to correct an indefinite *they* or *you* sentence is to use a passive verb.]
>
> **FAULTY:** Before the reform measures were passed, *you* had few rights.
>
> **IMPROVED:** Before the reform measures were passed, people had few rights.
> Before the reform measures were passed, one had few rights.
>
> **FAULTY:** At the placement office *they* told me to get three recommendations.
>
> **IMPROVED:** A clerk at the placement office told me to get three recommendations.
> At the placement office I was told to get three recommendations.

U 22. Avoid using a pronoun that could refer to either of two antecedents.

> **FAULTY:** Bob told Jim that *he* was getting bald. [Which one was getting bald?]
>
> **IMPROVED:** "You are getting bald," said Bob to Jim. [In sentences of this type, the direct quotation is sometimes the only possible correction.]

U 23. Avoid the "it-says" introduction when giving the substance of spoken or written material.

This loose use, although common in informal talk, is objectionable in serious writing.

> **FAULTY:** *It* says on the bottle that the chemical will kill weeds but not grass.
> *It* said on the morning news program that a bad storm is coming.
>
> **IMPROVED:** The directions on the bottle state that the chemical will kill weeds but not grass.
> According to the morning news program, a bad storm is coming.

At this point you should be reminded that *it* without an antecedent has some uses that are completely acceptable in both formal and informal English. One of these is in the delayed subject or object pattern. (See page 120.) Another is its use as a kind of filler word in expressions having to do with weather, time, distance, and so forth.

> *It* is fortunate that you had a spare tire.
> I find *it* difficult to believe Ted's story.
> *It* is cold today; *it* snowed last night. *It* is twelve o'clock; *it* is almost time for lunch.
> How far is *it* to Phoenix?

U 24. Avoid vague or ambiguous reference of relative and demonstrative pronouns.

> **FAULTY:** Only twenty people attended the lecture, *which* was due to poor publicity.
>
> The suspect was arrested after police spotted him driving a van on the San Francisco peninsula *that* he had purchased in Idaho.
>
> Good writers usually have large vocabularies, and *this* is why I get poor grades on my themes.
>
> **IMPROVED:** Because of poor publicity, only twenty people attended the lecture.
>
> The suspect was arrested after police spotted him on the San Francisco peninsula driving a van that he had purchased in Idaho.
>
> I get poor grades on my themes because my vocabulary is inadequate; good writers usually have large vocabularies.

A special situation relates to the antecedent of the pronouns *which, this,* and *that.* In a sentence such as "The children giggled, *which* annoyed the teacher" or "The children giggled, and *this* annoyed the teacher," the thing that annoyed the teacher is not the *children* but "the giggling of the children" or "the fact that the children giggled." This kind of reference to a preceding idea rather than to an expressed noun is unobjectionable provided that the meaning is instantly and unmistakably clear. But you should avoid sentences like the following. In the first one, the reader is hard pressed to discover exactly what the *which* means; and in the second he must decide whether the antecedent is the preceding idea or the noun immediately preceding the *which:*

> **FAULTY:** Hathaway's application was rejected because he spells poorly, *which* is very important in an application letter.
>
> The defense attorney did not object to the judge's concluding remark, *which* surprised me.
>
> **IMPROVED:** Hathaway's application was rejected because he spells poorly; correct spelling is very important in an application letter.
>
> I was surprised that the defense attorney did not object to the judge's concluding remark.

U 25. Use the form of a pronoun that agrees with its antecedent in person, number, and gender.

The following chart classifies for you the three forms of each personal pronoun on the basis of person, number, and gender.

Singular	*Plural*
1ST PERSON	
[the person speaking] *I, my, me*	[the persons speaking] *we, our, us*
2ND PERSON	
[the person spoken to] *you, your, you*	[the persons spoken to] *you, your, you*
3RD PERSON	
[the person or thing spoken of] *he, his, him* *she, her, her* *it, its, it*	[the persons or things spoken of] *they, their, them*

A singular antecedent is logically referred to by a singular pronoun; a plural antecedent requires a plural pronoun.

> My neighbor is mowing *his* lawn.
> My neighbors are mowing *their* lawns.
> The managers expect us to address *them* respectfully.
> A person is respected if *he* does *his* best work.
> Whoever used a coathanger to get into my locked car knew what *he* was doing.
> Local 714 of the Metal Workers' Union has purchased a waterfront campsite for the use of *its* members.

U 26. Use singular pronouns, in most cases, to refer to *each,* *either, neither, one, everyone, someone, no one, anyone, every-* *body, somebody,* **and** *nobody,* **indefinites that are usually felt to be singular.**

> Everybody has *his* faults and *his* virtues. [Not *their* faults and *their* virtues.]
> England expects every man to do *his* duty. [Not *their* duty.]
> Everyone has *his* own idea of what duty is. [Not *their* own idea.]
> I suspect that each of us tries *his* best to do what *he thinks* is right. [Not *their* best to do what *they think.*]

The primary difficulty with these words is that they suggest a group instead of an individual in the group. Hence in some situations we find plural pronouns referring to them. In a sentence like "No one noticed the accident, for *their* attention was focused on the stage performance," a singular pronoun would be unnatural. In the occasional sentence where a singular pronoun would give a confused meaning, you will have to use a plural pronoun or revise the sentence entirely.

U 27. Determine the logical number of the antecedent when you use a pronoun referring to a collective noun or to a compound unit. (See U 15, U 18, and U 19.)

> My afternoon class has already been given *its* final examination.
> My afternoon class are slow about getting *their* themes in on time.
> Both she and her daughter have changed the color of *their* hair.
> Either Tom or Floyd will bring *his* camera.

U 28. Do not use *you* **to refer to an antecedent in the third person.**

Misuse of *you* develops when the writer, forgetting that he has established the third person in the sentence, shifts the structure and begins to talk directly to the reader.

> **FAULTY:** In a large university a *freshman* can feel lost if *you* have grown up in a small town.
> If a *person* really wants to become an expert golfer, *you* must practice every day.
>
> **IMPROVED:** In a large university a freshman can feel lost if *he* has grown up in a small town.
> If a person really wants to become an expert golfer, *he* must practice every day.

When the context is such that a shift from third person to second person is natural and logical, the shift should be made not within a single sentence but between larger units, such as sentences or paragraphs.

U 29. When two singular antecedents differ in gender or if the antecedent is a single word that could include both sexes, it has been customary to use the singular masculine pronoun forms to refer to the antecedent.

Those who consider this usage discriminatory often use the *he or she* forms.

> Every man and woman must do *his* [or *his or her*] share of the work.
> Any graduate student, if *he* [or *he or she*] is interested, may attend the lecture.

Although it is sometimes desirable to use the *he or she* forms to emphasize the fact that an antecedent can include both masculine and feminine, a piling up of *he or she's, his or her's,* and *him or her's* in a single sentence or in related sentences is wordy and cumbersome. If you discover such a proliferation developing in something you are writing, remember that you can usually avoid the problem by changing the antecedent to a plural noun and referring to it with *they, their,* and *them.*

II. CASE

In rule U 25 a chart classifies for you the forms of the personal pronouns on the basis of person, number, and gender. For each pronoun the three forms that are listed—first person singular, *I, my, me;* third person plural, *they, their, them,* and so on—illustrate the three case forms. *I* and *they* are nominative, *my* and *their* are possessive, and *me* and *them* are objective, for example.

The way you use these pronouns in everyday language, in sentences such as "Two of *my* books have disappeared; *they* cost *me* twenty dollars, and *I* must find *them*," for instance, shows you that the case form depends upon the use of the word within the sentence.

The only words in modern English that retain distinctions between nominative and objective case forms are a few pronouns. With nouns these two forms are identical, and the correct use of the distinctive form, the possessive, requires only a knowledge of how the apostrophe is used. (See P 20.)

Here are the pronouns arranged according to their case forms. The first eight are the personal pronouns; notice that with *you* and *it* the only distinctive form is the possessive. The last two pronouns, which we shall examine separately from the personal pronouns, are used only in questions and in subordinate clauses.

Nominative	Possessive	Objective
I	my, mine	me
you	your, yours	you
he	his, his	him
she	her, hers	her
it	its, its	it
we	our, ours	us
you	your, yours	you
they	their, theirs	them
who	whose	whom
whoever	whosever	whomever

The possessive case is used to show possession. Two possible trouble spots should be noted.

U 30. Distinguish between the two possessive forms of the personal pronouns.

The preceding chart shows two possessive forms for the personal pronouns. The first form for each pronoun is used as a *modifier* of a noun. The second form is used as a nominal; in other words, it fills a noun slot, such as the subject, the complement, or the object of a preposition.

> This is *your* umbrella; *mine* has a white handle.
> Mary found *my* books, but one of *hers* is still missing.
> *Their* team was faster, but the final victory was *ours*.

U 31. Use an apostrophe in the possessive forms of the indefinite pronouns but not in those of the personal pronouns.

Remember that *it's* is a contraction meaning *it is*. The possessive pronoun is *its*.

> It now becomes *everybody's* duty.
> It's still *anyone's* game.
> You will ride in someone *else's* car.

These seats are *ours* [not *our's*]. *Yours* [not *Your's*] are in the next row.
It's [*It is*] obvious that the car has outworn *its* [possessive] usefulness.

The rules governing the uses of the other two cases are simple.

**U 32. Use the nominative case when the pronoun fulfills one
of three functions:**

1. As a subject: *I* know that *he* is honest.
2. As a subjective complement: This is *she* speaking.
3. As an appositive of a nominative noun: *We* children ate the
ice cream.

**U 33. Use the objective case when the pronoun fulfills one of
four functions:**

1. As an object of a verb or verbal: I enjoyed meeting *them.*
John gave *me* the key.
2. As an object of a preposition: No one except *me* knew the
answer.
3. As the subject of an infinitive: The policeman ordered *me* to
halt.
4. As an appositive of an objective noun: Two of *us* children ate
the ice cream.

We need not examine in detail every one of these applications.
As one grows up using the English language, he or she learns that
such usages as "*Them* arrived late" or "I spoke to *she*" do not
conform to the system of the language. Instead, we should examine the trouble spots where confusion may arise. For the personal
pronouns, care must be exercised in the following situations:

**U 34. When the pronoun follows *and* (sometimes *or*) as part
of a compound unit, determine its use in the sentence
and choose the appropriate form.**

The temptation here is usually to use the nominative, although the
last example below shows a trouble spot in which the objective
case is sometimes misused. Test these troublesome constructions by
using the pronoun by itself and you will probably discover which
form is the correct one.

> The man gave Sue and *me* some candy. [Not Sue and *I.* Both words
> are indirect objects. Apply the test. Notice how strange "The
> man gave . . . *I* some candy" sounds.]
> Send your check to either my lawyer or *me.* [Not "to . . . *I.*"]

Have you seen Bob or *her* lately? [Direct objects require the objective case.]

Just between you and *me,* the lecture was a bore. [Never say "between you and *I*." Both pronouns are objects of the preposition *between*. If this set phrase is a problem with you, find the correct form by reversing the pronouns: Would you ever say "between I and you?"]

Mrs. Estes took *him* and *me* to school. [Not *he* and *I* or *him* and *I*. Both pronouns are direct objects.]

Will my sister and *I* be invited? [Not *me*. The subject is *sister and I*.]

U 35. In comparisons after *as* and *than,* when the pronoun is the subject of an understood verb, use the nominative form.

He is taller than *I* [*am*]. I am older than *he* [*is*].

Can you talk as fast as *she* [*can talk*]? No one knew more about art than *he* [*did*].

Sentences like these nearly always call for nominative case subjects. Occasionally the meaning of a sentence may demand an objective pronoun. Both of the following sentences are correct; notice the difference in meaning.

You apparently trust Mr. Alton more than *I*. [The meaning is ". . . more than I (trust Mr. Alton.")]

You apparently trust Mr. Alton more than *me*. [The meaning here is ". . . more than (you trust) me."]

U 36. In most situations, use the nominative form for a pronoun used as a subjective complement.

The specific problem concerns such expressions as *It's me* or *It is I, It was they* or *It was them*. Many people say *It's me,* but they would hesitate to say *It was her, It was him, It was them,* instead of *It was she, It was he, It was they*. However, this is a problem that does not arise often in the writing of students. The following are examples of correct formal usage:

It is *I*. It could have been *he*. Was it *she*? Was it *they* who called?

U 37. Use the form of an appositive pronoun that is the same case as that of the word it refers to.

Notice particularly the first three examples below. The usage employing *we/us* as an appositive modifier preceding a noun is a real trouble spot.

We boys were hired. [The unit *We boys* is the subject and requires the nominative.]

Two of *us* boys were hired. [The object of a preposition requires the objective case.]

Mr. Elder hired *us* boys. [Not *we boys* for a direct object.]

Two boys—you and *I*—will be hired. [In apposition with the subject.]

Mr. Elder will hire two boys—you and *me*. [In apposition with the object.]

The only other pronouns in standard modern English that have distinctive nominative/objective forms are *who/whom* and *whoever/whomever*. The rules that apply to the personal pronouns apply to these words as well: In subject position *who/whoever* should be used; in direct object position *whom/whomever* should be used, and so forth. (These pronouns, it should be noted, are never used as appositives.)

The special problem in the application of the case rules to these words comes from their special use as interrogatives and as subordinating words. These words, because they serve as signal words, always stand at the beginning of their clauses. To locate the grammatical function of the pronoun within its clause, you must examine the clause to determine the normal subject-verb-complement positioning.

U 38. In formal contexts, use *whom* when it is an object of a verb or a preposition, even though it stands ahead of its subject and verb.

Whom did he marry? [If you are troubled by this sort of construction, try reading the sentence so that the object comes after the verb, where it usually comes: "Did he marry *whom*?"]

He is a boy *whom* everyone can like. [*Whom* is the object of *can like*.]

Wilson was the man *whom* everybody trusted. [Everybody trusted *whom*.]

She is the girl *whom* Mother wants me to marry. [Object of the verbal *to marry*.]

Whom was she speaking to just then? [To *whom* was she speaking?]

U 39. When *who(m)* or *who(m)ever* begins a subordinate clause that follows a verb or a preposition, remember that the use of the pronoun *within its own clause* determines its case form.

Do you know *who* sent Jane the flowers? [*Who* is the subject of *sent*, not the direct object of *do know*.]

No one knows *who* the intruder was. [*Who* is the subjective complement in the noun clause.]

No one knows *whom* the mayor will appoint. [The objective form *whom* is used because it is the direct object of *will appoint*. The direct object of *knows* is the whole noun clause.]

I will sell the car to *whoever* offers the best price. [The whole clause, *whoever offers the best price*, is the object of the preposition *to*. A subject of a verb must be in the nominative case.]

U 40. When the pronoun subject is followed by a parenthetical insertion like *do you think, I suspect, everyone believes, we know*, **and so on, use the nominative form.**

Who do you think *is* their strongest candidate? [*Who* is the subject of *is*. The *do you think* is merely parenthetical.]

Jenkins is the one *who* I suspect *will make* the best impression. [Determine the verb that goes with the pronoun. If you are puzzled by this type of sentence, try reading it like this: "Jenkins is the one *who will make* the best impression—I suspect."]

But if the pronoun is not the subject of the verb, the objective form should be used.

Mr. Bass is the suitor *whom* we hope Portia will accept. [*Whom* is the direct object of *will accept*.]

USING MODIFIERS CORRECTLY

An adjective is a word that describes or limits a noun or pronoun. An adverb modifies a verb, an adjective, or another adverb. Many adverbs end in *ly*, such as *happily, beautifully, extremely*, and the like. (But some adjectives, *lovely, likely, deadly, neighborly, homely*, for instance, also end in *ly*.) Some adverbs do not end in *ly*, and these happen to be among the most frequently used words in speech and writing: *after, always, before, far, forever, here, not, now, often, quite, rather, soon, then, there, too*.

Some adverbs have two forms, one without and one with the *ly*, including *cheap, cheaply; close, closely; deep, deeply; high, highly; late, lately; loud, loudly; quick, quickly; slow, slowly; wide, widely*. With some of these pairs the words are interchangeable; with most they are not. The idiomatic use of this group of adverbs is a complex matter; no rules can be made that govern every situation. We can, however, make a few generalizations that reflect present-day practice:

1. The shorter form of a few of these—*late, hard,* and *near,* for example—fill most adverbial functions because the corresponding *ly* forms have acquired special meanings.

We must not stay *late*.	I have not seen him *lately* [recently].
I studied *hard* last night.	I *hardly* [scarcely] know him.
Winter is drawing *near*.	I *nearly* [almost] missed the last flight.

2. The *ly* form tends toward the formal, with the short form lending itself to more casual, informal speech and writing.

It fell *close* to the target.	You must watch him *closely*.
They ate *high* off the hog.	He was *highly* respected.
Drive *slow!*	Please drive more *slowly*.
	He *slowly* removed his glasses.
Must you sing so *loud?*	He *loudly* denied the charges.
We searched far and *wide*.	She is *widely* known as an artist.

3. Because the short form seems more direct and forceful, it is often used in imperative sentences.

Hold *firm* to this railing.
Aim *high* and slightly to the left.
Stay *close* to me.

4. The short form is often the one used when combined with an adjective to make a compound modifier preceding a noun.

a *wide*-ranging species	The species ranges *widely*.
a *slow*-moving truck	The truck approached *slowly*.

Some words can be used either as adjectives or as adverbs, as the following examples will show.

	Adverbs	*Adjectives*
close	She came *close*.	That was a *close* call.
far	Don't go too *far*.	He went on a *far* journey.
fast	She talks too *fast*.	She's a *fast* thinker.
hard	Hit it *hard*.	That was a *hard* blow.
late	She usually arrives *late*.	She arrived at a *late* hour.
straight	He went *straight* to bed.	I can't draw a *straight* line.

U 41. Do not misuse an adjective for an adverb.

I did *well* [not *good*] in my test. [Modifies the verb *did*.]

This paint adheres *well* [not *good*] to concrete. [Modifies the verb *adheres.*]

Almost [not *Most*] every student owns a car. [Modifies the adjective *every.*]

Today my shoulder is *really* [or *very*—not *real*] sore. [Modifies the adjective *sore.*]

We left the room *really* [or *very*—not *real*] fast. [Modifies the adverb *fast.*]

This rain has been falling *steadily* [not *steady*] for a week.

The champion should win his first match *easily* [not *easy*].

You'll improve if you practice *regularly* [not *regular*].

She wants that prize very *badly* [not *bad*].

U 42. Do not misuse an adverb for an adjective subjective complement.

The most common verb to take the subjective complement is *be;* fortunately, mistakes with this verb are nearly impossible. A few other verbs, like *seem, become, appear, prove, grow, go, turn, stay, remain,* when they are used in a sense very close to that of *be,* take subjective complements. This complement must be an adjective, not an adverb.

> The house *seems empty.* [House *is* empty.]
> Their plans *became apparent.* [Plans *were* apparent.]
> The work *proved* very *hard.* [Work *was* hard.]

The adjective subjective complement is also used with another group of verbs, the so-called verbs of the senses. These are *feel, look, smell, sound, taste.*

> You shouldn't feel *bad* [not *badly*] about this.
> His cough sounds *bad* [not *badly*] this morning.
> How *sweet* [not *sweetly*] the air smells today.
> This blouse will look *good* [not *well*] with your new slacks.
> Notice how *different* [not *differently*] your voice sounds on the tapes.

The verb *feel* is involved in two special problems. In the first place, it is often used with *good* and *well.* These two words have different meanings; one is not a substitute for the other. When used with the verb *feel, well* is an adjective meaning "in good health." The adjective *good,* when used with *feel,* means "filled with a sense of vigor and excitement." Of course, both *well* and *good* have other meanings when used with other verbs. In the second place, the expression "I feel badly" has been used so widely, especially in spoken English, that it should not be considered an error in usage. Many careful writers, however, prefer the adjective, with the result that "feel bad" is usually found in formal written English.

U 43. Do not combine the two forms (*more* + *er*, *most* + *est*) in forming the comparative and superlative degrees. (See also Sn 16.)

> After Al worked on my motorcycle, it sounded *quieter* [not *more quieter*].
> Please drive *slower* [not *more slower*].
> Please drive *more slowly* [not *more slower*].

U 44. Do not compare or intensify adjectives that represent absolute qualities.

Be especially careful with *unique* ("being the only one"). Avoid using *very*, *more*, or *most* with it.

> He occupies a *unique* [not *very unique*] position in our government.
> She manages a *unique* [not *the most unique*] restaurant in town.
> I can't imagine a *more nearly ideal* [not *more ideal*] vacation spot.
> Your engineers submitted the *most nearly exact* [not *most exact*] specifications.
> Our marching files should be *more nearly straight* [not *straighter*].

Purists recommend avoiding such uses, arguing that there are no degrees of uniqueness, exactness, straightness, and so forth. General usage, however, has pretty well established both forms.

USING PREPOSITIONS CORRECTLY

U 45. Use the exact preposition for the meaning intended.

Many words, especially verbs and adjectives, give their full meaning only when modified by a prepositional phrase. Choosing the proper preposition can occasionally bring up a problem even for native speakers of English. In most cases the meaning of the preposition dictates a logical idiom: to sit *on* a couch, to walk *with* a friend, to lean *against* a fence, and so on. For some more abstract concepts, however, the acceptable preposition may seem to have been selected arbitrarily. Here are a few examples of different meanings with different prepositions:

agree *to* a proposal, *with* a person, *on* a price, *in* principle.
argue *about* a matter, *with* a person, *for* or *against* a proposition.
compare *to* to show likenesses, *with* to show differences [sometimes
   similarities].
correspond *to* a thing, *with* a person.
differ *from* an unlike thing, *with* a person.
live *at* an address, *in* a house or city, *on* a street, *with* other people.

NOTE: Any good modern dictionary will provide information about and examples of correct usage of prepositions.

U 46. Avoid unnecessary or repeated prepositions.

Examples like the following, although acceptable at colloquial levels, are improved for serious contexts if written without the words in brackets:

I met [up with] your uncle yesterday.
We keep our dog inside [of] the house.
Our cat, however, sleeps outside [of] the house.
The package fell off [of] the speeding truck.
The garage is [in] back of the cottage.

Avoid especially the needless preposition at the end of a sentence or the repeated preposition in adjective clauses and in direct or indirect questions:

Where is your older brother *at?*
He is one of the few people *to* whom I usually feel superior *to.* [Use
   one or the other, but not both.]
To what do you attribute your luck at poker *to?*

Placing an idiomatically necessary preposition at the end of a sentence has been grossly, and incorrectly, emphasized as an error. The end of the sentence is often the natural position for a preposition, and with one type of restrictive adjective clause the preposition *must* stand at the end; for example, "That is a problem that I never worry *about.*" The beginning writer should remember, however, that when he has a choice between the "hanging" preposition and the "buried" preposition, the latter placement will give a more formal tone to the sentence.

CORRECT: How many of these candidates did you vote for?
   He plays the harmonica, a skill he is inordinately
   proud of.
FORMAL: *For* how many of these candidates did you vote?

He plays the harmonica, a skill *of* which he is inordinately proud.

U 47. When the two words of a compound unit require different prepositions, express both prepositions.

INCOMPLETE: The child shows an *interest* and *talent for* music. [interest . . . *for* (?)]

CORRECT: The child shows an interest *in* and talent *for* music.

INCOMPLETE: I am sure that Ms. Lewis would both *contribute* and *gain from* a summer workshop.

CORRECT: I am sure that Ms. Lewis would both contribute *to* and gain *from* a summer workshop.

When the same preposition is idiomatically correct with both units, it need not be stated with the first unit.

CORRECT: We were alternately *repelled* and *fascinated by* the snake charmer's act.

A GLOSSARY OF USAGE

For many of the entries in the following list, the other forms suggested are those usually preferred in standard formal English, the English appropriate to your term papers, theses, term reports, examination papers in all your courses, and to most of the serious papers written for your English classes. Many of the words or expressions in brackets, marked "not," are appropriate enough in informal conversation and in some informal papers.

Some of the entries are labeled "colloquial," a term you should not think of as referring to slang, to forms used only in certain localities, or to "bad" English. The term applies to usages that are appropriate to informal and casual *spoken* English rather than to formal written English. However, the expressions marked "substandard" should be avoided at all times.

A, an. Use *a* when the word immediately following it is sounded as a consonant; use *an* when the next sound is a vowel sound: *a, e, i, o,* or *u* (a friend, an enemy). Remember that it is the consonantal or vowel *sound,* not the actual letter, that determines the choice of the correct form of the indefinite article: *a* sharp curve, *an* S-curve; *a* eulogy, *an* empty house; *a* hospital, *an* honest person; *a* united people, *an* uneven contest.

Ad. Clipped forms of many words are used informally, such as *ad* (*advertisement*), *doc* (*doctor*), *exam* (*examination*), *gent* (*gentleman*), *gym* (*gymnasium*), *lab* (*laboratory*), *math* (*mathematics*), *prof* (*professor*). Formal usage requires the long forms.

Aggravate. In standard formal English the word means "make more severe," "make worse." Colloquially it means "annoy," "irritate," "exasperate."

> Walking on your sprained ankle will aggravate the hurt. [*Informal:* All criticism aggravates him.]

Ain't. Substandard for *am not, are not, is not, have not.*

> Am I not [not *Ain't I*] a good citizen?
> The command hasn't [not *hain't* or *ain't*] been given yet.
> They are not [not *ain't*] going either.

All the farther, all the faster, and the like. Generally regarded as colloquial equivalents of *as far as, as fast as,* and the like.

> This is as far as [not *all the farther*] I care to go.
> That was as fast as [not *all the faster*] he could run.

A lot of. See *Lots of.*

Alright. This spelling, like *all-right* or *allright,* although often used in advertising, is generally regarded as very informal usage. The preferred form is *all right.* In strictly formal usage, *satisfactory* or *very well* is preferred to *all right.*

> Very well [not *All right*], you may report to the infirmary.
> The members agreed that the allocation of funds was satisfactory [not *all right*].

Among, between. *Among* is used with three or more persons or things, as in "Galileo was among the most talented men of his age," or "The estate was divided among his three sons." *Between* usually refers to two things, as in "between you and me," "between two points," "between dawn and sunset."

Amount, number. Use *number,* not *amount,* in reference to units that can actually be counted: the *amount* of indebtedness; the *number* of debts.

And etc. Because *etc.* (*et cetera*) means "and so forth," *and etc.* would mean "and and so forth." You should not use *etc.* to replace some exact, specific word, but if you do use it, be sure not to spell it *ect*. And remember that *etc.* requires a period after it.

Anyplace, anywheres. Colloquial and dialectal forms for *anywhere*. Similar colloquial forms are *anyways* for *anyhow, everyplace* for *everywhere, no place* or *nowheres* for *nowhere, someplace* or *somewheres* for *somewhere*.

> I looked for my books everywhere. They must be hidden somewhere.

As, like. See *Like, as, as if.*

As to whether. *Whether* is usually enough.

Awful, awfully. Like *aggravate*, these words have two distinct uses. In formal contexts, they mean "awe-inspiring" or "terrifying." Often in conversation and sometimes in writing of a serious nature, *awful* and *awfully* are mild intensifiers, meaning "very."

Because. See *Reason is because.*

Because of. See *Due to.*

Being that, being as how. Substandard for *because* or *since*.

Beside, besides. These two prepositions are clearly distinguished by their meanings. *Beside* means "at the side of" and *besides* means "in addition to."

> Lucy sits beside me in class.
> Did anyone besides you see the accident?

Between. See *Among.*

But what, but that. Colloquial for *that*.

> Both sides had no doubt that [not *but what*] their cause was just.

Can, may. *Can* suggests ability to do something. *May* is the preferred form when permission is involved.

> Little Junior can already count to ten.
> May [not *Can*] I borrow your pencil?

Can't hardly, couldn't hardly, can't scarcely, couldn't scarcely. Substandard for *can hardly, could hardly, can scarcely, could scarcely*. These are sometimes referred to as double negatives.

> They could hardly [not *couldn't hardly*] hear his shout for help.
> He could scarcely [not *couldn't scarcely*] walk when they found him.

Caused by. See *Due to.*

Complected. Dialectal or colloquial for *complexioned.*

> Being light-complexioned [not *light-complected*], Sue must avoid prolonged exposure to sunlight.

Contact. Used as a verb meaning "to get in touch with," this word, probably because of its association with sales-promotion writing, annoys enough people to warrant caution in its use in serious writing.

Continual, continuous. A fine distinction in meaning can be made if you remember that *continual* means "repeated regularly and frequently" and that *continuous* means "occurring without interruption," "unbroken."

Could(n't) care less. This worn-out set phrase used to indicate total indifference is a colloquialism. A continuing marvel of language behavior is the large number of people who insist on saying "I could care less" when they obviously mean the opposite.

Could of, would of, might of, ought to of, and so on. Substandard for *could have, would have,* and so on.

Couple. Colloquial in the sense of *a few, several.*

> The senator desired to have a few [not *a couple*] changes made in the bill.

Criteria. The singular noun is *criterion;* the plural is *criteria* or *criterions. Criteria* uses a plural verb, and such combinations as "a criteria," "one criteria," and "this criteria" are incorrect.

Data. Originally the plural form of the rarely used Latin singular *datum, data* has taken on a collective meaning so that it is often treated as a singular noun. "This data has been published" and "These data have been published" are both correct, the latter being the use customarily found in scientific or technical writing.

Different from, different than. *Different from* is generally correct. Many people object to *different than,* but others use it, especially when a clause follows, as in "Life in the Marines was different than he had expected it to be."

> Their customs are different from [not *different than*] ours.
> Life in the Marines was different from what he had expected it to be.

Disinterested, uninterested. Many users of precise English deplore the tendency to treat these words as loose synonyms, keeping a helpful distinction between *disinterested* ("impartial," "free from bias or self-interest") and *uninterested* ("lacking in interest," "unconcerned"). Thus we would hope that a referee would be disinterested but not uninterested.

Due to, caused by, because of, owing to. *Due to* and *caused by* are used correctly after the verb *to be,* as "His illness was caused by a virus." "The flood was due to the heavy spring rains." Many people object to the use of *due to* and *caused by* adverbially at the beginning of a sentence, as in "Due to the heavy rains, the streams flooded." "Caused by the storm, the roads were damaged." It is better to use either *because of* or *owing to* in similar situations. Note in the examples what variations are possible. *Due to* is also used correctly as an adjective modifier immediately following a noun, as "Accidents due to excessive speed are increasing in number."

> The streams flooded because of the heavy rains.
> The flooding of the streams was due to the heavy rains.
> The floods were caused by the rapid melting of the snow.

Emigrate, immigrate. To *emigrate* is to *leave* one region to settle in another; to *immigrate* is to *enter* a region from another one.

Enthuse. Colloquial or substandard, depending on the degree of a person's aversion to this word, for *be enthusiastic, show enthusiasm.*

> The director was enthusiastic [not *enthused*] about his new program.

Everyplace. See *Anyplace.*

Farther, further. Careful writers observe a distinction between these two words, reserving *farther* for distances that can actually be measured.

> Tony can hit a golf ball farther than I can.
> We must pursue this matter further.

Fewer, less. *Fewer* refers to numbers, *less* to quantity, extent, degree.

> Fewer [not *Less*] students are taking courses in literature this year.
> Food costs less, but we have less money to spend.

Figure. Colloquial for *consider, think, believe, suppose.*

> He must have thought [not *figured*] that nobody would see him enter the bank.

Fine. Colloquial, very widely used, for *well, very well.*

> The boys played well [not *just fine*].

Had(n't) ought. *Ought* does not take an auxiliary.

> You ought [not *had ought*] to apply for a scholarship.
> You ought not [not *hadn't ought*] to miss the lecture.

Hardly. See *Can't hardly.*

Healthy, healthful. *Healthy* means "having health," and *healthful* means "giving health." Thus a person or an animal is healthy; a climate, a food, or an activity is healthful.

Immigrate. See *Emigrate.*

Imply, infer. Despite the increasing tendency to use these words more or less interchangeably, it is well to preserve the distinction: *Imply* means "to say something indirectly," "to hint or suggest," and *infer* means "to draw a conclusion," "to deduce." Thus you *imply* something in what you say and *infer* something from what you hear.

Incredible, incredulous. An unbelievable *thing* is incredible; a disbelieving *person* is incredulous.

In regards to. The correct forms are *in regard to* or *as regards.*

Inside of. *Inside* or *within* is preferred in formal writing.

> We stayed inside [not *inside of*] the barn during the storm.

Invite. Slang for *invitation.*

> They will be sent an invitation [not *invite*] to join us in a peace conference.

Irregardless. Substandard or humorous for *regardless.*

> The planes bombed the area regardless [not *irregardless*] of consequences.

Is when, is where. The *is-when, is-where* pattern in definitions is clumsy and should be avoided. Write, for example, "An embolism is an obstruction, such as a blood clot, in the bloodstream," instead of "An embolism is where an obstruction forms in the bloodstream."

Kind, sort. These words are singular and therefore should be modified by singular modifiers. Do not write *these kind, these sort, those kind, those sort.*

> I cannot wear this kind [not *these kind*] of shoes.
> Who could believe that sort [not *those sort*] of arguments?

Kind of, sort of. Colloquial for *somewhat, in some degree, almost, rather.*

> They felt somewhat [not *sort of*] depressed.

Kinda, sorta, kind of a, sort of a. Undesirable forms.

Learn, teach. *Learn* means "to acquire knowledge"; *teach* means "to give or impart knowledge."

> Mrs. Brown taught [not *learned*] me Spanish.

Leave. Not to be used for *let.*

> Let [not *Leave*] me carry your books for you.

Less. See *Fewer.*

Let. See *Leave.*

Let's us. The *us* is superfluous, since *let's* means *let us.*

Like, as, as if. The use of *like* as a conjunction (in other words, to introduce a clause) is colloquial. It should be avoided in serious writing.

> As [not *Like*] I warned you earlier, the path is dangerous.
> You must walk as if [not *like*] there were snipers in every tree.
> Do as [not *like*] I tell you.

Line. Often vague and redundant, as in "What do you read *in the line of* books?" "Don't you enjoy fishing and other sports *along that line?*" It is better to say, more directly, "What kind of books do you read?" "Don't you enjoy fishing and sports like that?"

Lots of, a lot of. Colloquial in the sense of *many, much.*

> Many [not *Lots of*] families lost everything during the depression.
> The storms caused us much [not *lots of*] trouble that spring.
> This year you have much [not *a lot*] to be thankful for.

Mad. Colloquially it is often used to mean *angry.* In formal English it means *insane.*

> Why was she angry [not *mad*] because I did not make my bed?

May. See *Can.*

Media. A plural noun, currently in vogue to refer to all mass communicative agencies. The singular is *medium.* Careful writers and speakers avoid the use of *media* as a singular noun, as in "Television is an influential media." Even more objectionable is the use of *medias* as a plural.

Might of. See *Could of.*

Most. Colloquial for *almost.* At the formal level it is the superlative form of *much* and *many* (*much, more, most; many, more, most*).

Almost [not *Most*] all of my friends work during the summer.

Nauseated, nauseous. A misdirected sense of delicacy might explain the widespread use of *nauseous* for *nauseated.* Precise users of the language know that *nauseated* means "suffering from nausea" and that *nauseous* means "causing nausea."

Nohow. This emphatic negative is substandard.

Not all that. A basically meaningless substitute for *not very* or *not really;* it can easily become a habit.

The movie was not very [not *not all that*] amusing.

Nowheres, no place. See *Anyplace.*

Number. See *Amount.*

Of. See *Could of.*

Off of. Dialectal or colloquial for *off.*

She asked me to get off [not *off of*] my high horse.

OK. This form calls attention to itself in serious writing. It is appropriate only to business communications and casual speech or writing. Modern dictionaries offer several permissible forms: *OK, O.K.,* and *okay* for the singular noun; *OK's, O.K.'s,* and *okays* for the plural noun; and *OK'd, OK'ing, O.K.'d, O.K.'ing, okayed,* and *okaying* for verb forms.

Ought. See *Had(n't) ought.*

Ought to of. See *Could of.*

Owing to. See *Due to.*

Party. Colloquial in the sense of *man, woman, person.*

Sir, a man [not *party*] came in to see you this morning.

Plenty. Colloquial for *very, extremely, fully. Plenty* is a noun, not an adjective or an adverb.

Filmore's shooting during the second half was extremely [not *plenty*] good.

Quote, unquote. Although these words may be needed in the oral presentation of quoted material, they have no use in written material, in which quotation marks or indentation will set off the quoted material from the text proper.

Real, really. The use of *real,* which is an adjective, to modify another adjective or an adverb is colloquial. In formal contexts *really* or *very* should be used.

> We had a really [not *real*] enjoyable visit.
> The motorcycle rounded the corner very [not *real*] fast.

Reason is because, reason is due to, reason is on account of. In serious writing a *reason is* clause is usually completed with *that,* not with *because, due to,* or *on account of.*

> The reason they surrendered is that [not *because*] they were starving.
> The reason for my low grades is that I have poor eyesight [not *is on account of my poor eyesight*].

Same. The use of *same* as a pronoun, often found in legal or business writing, is inappropriate in most other types of writing.

> I received your report and look forward to reading it [not *the same*].

Scarcely. See *Can't hardly.*

So, such. These words when used as exclamatory intensifiers are not appropriate in a formal context. Sentences like the following belong in informal talk: "I am *so* tired." "She is *so* pretty." "They are having *such* a good time."

Some. Colloquial for *somewhat, a little.*

> The ailing senator was reported as being somewhat [not *some*] better this morning.

Somewheres, someplace. See *Anyplace.*

Sort. See *Kind.*

Such. See *So.*

Suppose to. See *Use to.*

Sure. *Sure* is correctly used as an adjective: "We are not sure about his plans." "He made several sure investments." *Sure* is colloquial when used as an adverbial substitute for *surely, extremely, certainly, indeed, very, very much.*

> The examination was surely [not *sure*] difficult.

Certainly [not *Sure*], your objections will be considered by the court.

Sure and. See *Try and.*

Suspicion. *Suspicion* is a noun; it is not to be used as a verb in place of *suspect.*

No one suspected [not *suspicioned*] the victim's widow.

Swell. Not to be used as a general term of approval meaning *good, excellent, attractive, desirable,* and so on.

Teach. See *Learn.*

That there, this here, those there, these here. Substandard for *that, this, those, these.*

Them. Substandard when used as an adjective.

How can you eat those [not *them*] parsnips?

Try and, sure and. *Try to, sure to* are the preferred forms in serious writing.

We shall try to [not *try and*] make your visit a pleasant one.
Be sure to [not *sure and*] arrive on time.

Type. Colloquial when used as a modifier of a noun. Use *type of* or *kind of.*

I usually don't enjoy that type of [not *type*] movie.

Uninterested. See *Disinterested.*

Use to, suppose to. Although these incorrect forms are difficult to detect in spoken English, remember that the correct written forms are *used to, supposed to.*

Want in, want off, want out. Colloquial and dialectal forms for *want to come in, want to get off, want to go out.* Inappropriate in serious writing.

Ways. Colloquial for *way,* in such expressions as, "It is just a short distance [not *ways*] up the canyon." "We do not have a long way [not *ways*] to go."

What. Substandard when used for *who, which,* or *that* as a relative pronoun in an adjective clause.

His raucous laugh is the thing that [not *what*] annoys me most.

When, where clauses. See *Is when, is where.*

Where at. The *at* is unnecessary. Undesirable in both speech and writing.

Where [not *Where at*] will you be at noon?
Where is your car? [Not *Where is your car at?*]

-wise. The legitimate function of this suffix to form adverbs like *clockwise* does not carry with it the license to concoct such jargon as "Entertainmentwise this town is a dud" or "This investment is very attractive long-term–capital-gains ·wise."

Without. Not to be used as a conjunction instead of *unless.*

He won't lend me his car unless [not *without*] I fill the gas tank.

Worst way. Not acceptable for *greatly, very much, exceedingly,* and similar words.

She wanted very much [not *the worst way*] to be liked and respected.

Would of. See *Could of.*

PART IV

An Outline of the Essential Grammar of the Sentence

PARTS OF SPEECH

A **noun** is a word that names something, such as a person, a place, a thing, a quality, or an idea. A noun is called a common noun and is not capitalized if it names just any member of a group or class (*man, city, school, relative*); it is called a proper noun and is capitalized if it names a particular individual in a group or class (*Albert Lawson, Toledo, Horace Mann Junior High School, Aunt Louise*).

Most nouns have two forms to show whether the noun is naming one thing (singular number) or more than one thing (plural number, which adds *s* or *es* to the singular): one *coat*, two *coats*; a *lunch*, several *lunches*. Proper nouns are pluralized only rarely, and there are some common nouns that have no plural form: *honesty, courage, ease, hardness,* for example.

Nouns are easily recognized because they often follow one of the articles *the, a,* or *an.* Sometimes adjectives come between articles and the nouns that follow them, but a noun will still answer the question "What?" after an article.

Another aid in the recognition of nouns is an understanding of suffixes. A suffix is a unit added to the end of a word or word base, making a derived form. (A similar unit added to the beginning of a word is called a prefix.) Thus, to the adjective *kind* we add a prefix to derive another adjective, *unkind,* and a suffix to derive the nouns *kindness* and *unkindness.* An awareness of how suffixes are used adds to more than your ability to recognize parts of speech: Your spelling will improve and your vocabulary will expand as well.

Hundreds of nouns have distinctive suffix endings. The definitions of some suffixes are rather difficult to formulate, but you can quite readily grasp the meanings of most of them: *ness,* for instance, means "quality or state of" (thus *firmness* means "the state or quality of being firm"); *or, er* show the agent or doer of something (an *investor* is "one who invests"). Here are some of the common suffixes that form nouns:

> age [break*age*]; ance, ence [resist*ance,* insist*ence*]; dom [king*dom*]; hood [child*hood*]; ion [prevent*ion*]; ism [national*ism*]; ment [move*ment*]; ness [firm*ness*]; or, er [invest*or,* los*er*]; ure [expos*ure*].

A **pronoun** is a word that substitutes for a noun. There are several classes of pronouns, but the following are the most important:

1. Personal, used to substitute for definite persons or things: *I, me, you, he, him, she, her, it, we, us, they, them.*

2. Demonstrative, used to substitute for things being pointed out: *this, that, these, those.*

3. Indefinite, used to substitute for unknown or unspecified things: *each, either, neither, anyone, somebody, everybody,* and so on.

4. Intensive or reflexive, the "self" words used to add emphasis [You *yourself* must decide] or to name the receiver of an action when the doer is the same as the receiver [John fell and hurt *himself*]: *myself, yourself, himself, herself, itself, ourselves, yourselves, themselves.*

5. Possessive, used to substitute for things that are possessed: *mine, yours, his, hers, its, ours, theirs.*

6. Interrogative, used to substitute for unknown things or persons in direct questions and in noun clauses: *who, which, what,* and their *-ever* compounds.

7. Relative, used in adjective clauses to substitute for the noun or pronoun being modified by the clause: *who, which, that.*

A **verb** is a word that expresses action, existence, or occurrence by combining with a subject to make a statement, ask a question, or give a command. One easy way for you to identify a word as a verb is to use the following slot test:

> Let's _____ [something].

Any word that will function in this position is a verb: Let's *leave*. Let's *buy* some popcorn. Let's *be* quiet. This test works only with what is called the basic present form of the verb, not with forms that have endings added to them or that show action taking place in the past: Let's *paint* the car (not Let's *painted* the car).

An **adjective** is a word that describes or limits, that is, modifies or gives qualities to, a noun. The positions adjectives occupy within the sentence are (1) preceding a noun in any of the noun positions within the sentence (The *small* child left. He is a *small* child. I saw the *small* child. I gave it to the *small* child.); (2) following a describing (linking) verb and modifying the subject (The child is *small*. Mary looked *unhappy*. We became *upset*.); and, less often, (3) directly following the noun (He provided the money *necessary* for the trip. The hostess, *calm* and *serene*, entered the hall).

Certain characteristics of form and function help us recognize adjectives. There are several suffixes that, when added to roots or other words, form adjectives. Here again, an understanding of the meaning of a suffix can save extra trips to the dictionary. For instance, in the hundreds of adjectives ending in *able* (*ible*), the suffix means "capable of" or "tending to"; thus *usable* means "capable of being used" and *changeable* means "tending to change."

> able, ible [read*able,* irresist*ible*]; al [internation*al*]; ant, ent [resist*ant,* diverg*ent*]; ar [lun*ar*]; ary [budget*ary*]; ful (meaning *ful*); ic, ical [cosm*ic,* hyster*ical*]; ish [fool*ish*]; ive [invent*ive*]; less [blame*less*]; ous [glamor*ous*]; y [greas*y*]

(One word of warning: Many other words in English *end* with these letters, but you can easily see that they are not employing the suffix. T*able,* ferm*ent,* arr*ive,* d*ish,* pony, for instance, are not adjectives.)

Nearly all adjectives, when they are used in comparisons, can be strengthened or can show degree by changing form or by using *more* and *most:*

> *great* trust, *greater* trust, *greatest* trust.
> *sensible* answer, *more* sensible answer, *most* sensible answer.

The second of these (*greater* trust, *more* sensible answer), called the comparative degree, compares two objects; the *est* or *most* form, called the superlative degree, distinguishes from among three or more.

There are other classes of words that modify nouns, although they differ somewhat in form and use from the true adjectives. However, on the basis of *function,* we can classify as adjectives all words that precede nouns and limit their meaning, including articles, numerals, and possessives (*an* apple, *the* weather, *my three* roommates); modifiers that can be used also as pronouns (*these* people, *some* friends, *all* workers); and nouns when they modify other nouns (*basketball* players, *summer* days, *crop* failures).

However, many words can be used as adjectives or as pronouns; the position of a word within the sentence determines which part of speech it is.

> Many [*adjective*] friends of mine [*pronoun*] believed this [*adjective*] story.
> Many [*pronoun*] of my [*adjective*] friends believed this [*pronoun*].

The **adverb** is another modifier, a word that modifies anything except a noun or pronoun. Most adverbs modify verbs (He returned *soon*); others modify adjectives and other adverbs (The *very* old man walked *quite* slowly); and some modify whole sentences (*Consequently,* we refused the offer).

Adverbs tell certain things about the verb, the most common being

Manner:	John performed *well.* We worked *hard.* The child laughed *happily. Gladly* would I change places with you.
Time:	I must leave *now.* I'll see you *later. Soon* we shall meet *again.*
Frequency:	We *often* go on picnics, *sometimes* at the lake but *usually* in the city park.
Place:	*There* he sat, alone and silent. *Somewhere* we shall find peace and quiet.
Direction:	The policeman turned *away.* I moved *forward* in the bus.
Degree:	I could *scarcely* hear the speaker. I *absolutely* refuse to believe that story.

Adverbs of a subclass called intensifiers modify adjectives or adverbs but not verbs: a *very* good meal, his *quite* surprising reply, *too* often, *somewhat* reluctantly, and so on.

A **preposition** is a word that introduces a phrase and shows the relationship between its object and some other word in the sentence. Notice that many prepositions show a relationship of space or time. Here are some words commonly used as prepositions; those in the last column are called "group prepositions."

about	beside	inside	through	according to
above	besides	into	throughout	because of
across	between	like	till	by way of
after	beyond	near	to	in addition to
against	by	of	toward	in front of
around	down	off	under	in place of
at	during	on	until	in regard to
before	except	out	up	in spite of
behind	for	outside	upon	instead of
below	from	over	with	on account of
beneath	in	since	without	out of

Every preposition has an object; with its object and any modifiers the preposition makes a prepositional phrase. You can easily illustrate the function of prepositions by constructing sentences like the following:

After lunch I conferred *with* the owner *of* the building. [Objects: *lunch, owner, building.*]

Two *of* the motions were seconded *by* a delegate *from* Detroit. [Objects: *motions, delegate, Detroit.*]

Because of the noise made *by* the workmen *in* the room *above* my office, I usually go *into* one *of* the other offices when I talk *on* the telephone. [Objects: *noise, workmen, room, office, one, offices, telephone.*]

In spite of my warning, the boy rushed *out of* the house and stood *in front of* the parked truck. [Objects: *warning, house, truck.*]

A **conjunction** is a connective that joins words, phrases, and clauses. One type, the **coordinating conjunction,** ties together units that are equal grammatically. This process, called compounding, can be applied to any parts of the sentence—subjects, verbs, modifiers, complements, phrases, and clauses. The three common coordinating conjunctions are *and, but,* and *or;* others are *nor, for, yet,* and pairs of words, called **correlatives:** *not (only) . . . but (also), either . . . or, neither . . . nor.*

Tom *and* I heard your answer. [Compound subjects.]

We looked far *and* wide *but* found no clues. [Compound verbs and adverbs.]

For dessert you may choose *either* pie *or* cake. [Compound direct objects with correlative conjunctions.]

I had reviewed the material, *but* I did poorly on the test. [Compound independent clauses.]

Subordinating conjunctions are words like *that, if, whether, because, while, although* that introduce subordinate clauses. (See "Subordination: Dependent Clauses," pages 121, 124–126.)

An **interjection,** of little importance and rare use in most writing but traditionally called a part of speech, is a word used independently of the rest of the sentence to produce an exclamatory effect: *Oh!, Gracious!,* and so on.

FORMS OF THE VERB

I. Conjugation

English verbs can change their form depending upon three things:

1. The person or thing represented by the subject, whether it is the speaker (I *believe*), the one spoken to (You *believe*), or a third person or thing spoken about (He—*or* She, *or* John, *or* My brother—*believes*).

2. The number of the subject, whether it represents one thing (The boy *works*) or more than one thing (The boys *work*).

3. The time represented in the statement, whether it applies to the present moment (I *like* him) or to some other time (I *liked* him).

You should learn the most important of these forms, the ones that occur in nearly every sentence you speak or write. And the best way to observe these forms is with a chart or arrangement called a conjugation. The one given for you here is not a complete conjugation. It shows only distinctive samples, not the complete listing, of the passive voice and the subjunctive mood forms. Three verbs, *earn, grow,* and *be,* are illustrated. *Be* is shown because it is highly irregular in its forms and functions. The personal pronoun subjects are included in this partial conjugation to show how verbs change form to indicate person and number.

INDICATIVE MOOD, ACTIVE VOICE

PRESENT TENSE

Singular	*Plural*
I earn, grow, am	We earn, grow, are
You earn, grow, are	You earn, grow, are
He earns, grows, is	They earn, grow, are

PAST TENSE

I earned, grew, was   We earned, grew, were
You earned, grew, were   You earned, grew, were
He earned, grew, was   They earned, grew, were

FUTURE TENSE

I shall earn, grow, be   We shall earn, grow, be
You will earn, grow, be   You will earn, grow, be
He will earn, grow, be   They will earn, grow, be

PRESENT PERFECT TENSE

I have earned, grown, been   We have earned, grown, been
You have earned, grown, been   You have earned, grown, been
He has earned, grown, been   They have earned, grown, been

PAST PERFECT TENSE

I had earned, grown, been   We had earned, grown, been
You had earned, grown, been   You had earned, grown, been
He had earned, grown, been   They had earned, grown, been

FUTURE PERFECT TENSE

I shall have earned, grown, been   We shall have earned, grown, been
You will have earned, grown, been   You will have earned, grown, been
He will have earned, grown, been   They will have earned, grown, been

NOTE: Observe that in the indicative mood all verbs in the third person singular of the present tense end in *s* (earn*s*, grow*s*, teache*s*, i*s*, ha*s*). Whereas most nouns add *s* (or *es*) to form the plural (see Sp 6), an *s* ending of a verb shows a singular form.

PASSIVE VOICE

The passive verb, which is formed with the auxiliary verb *be* and the past participle of the main verb, has singular and plural forms in all three persons. Here are the third person plural passive forms of the verb *earn* in the six tenses: They *are earned,* They *were earned,* They *will be earned,* They *have been earned,* They *had been earned,* They *will have been earned.*

SUBJUNCTIVE MOOD

As they apply to present-day English usage, verbs (except *be*) have only one subjunctive form—the third person singular present—that differs from the indicative forms. *Be* must be considered separately; it has eight distinctive subjunctive forms. The subjunctive forms that differ from the indicative are printed below in heavy type:

PRESENT TENSE

Singular	*Plural*
I earn, grow, **be**	We earn, grow, **be**
You earn, grow, **be**	You earn, grow, **be**
He **earn, grow, be**	They earn, grow, **be**

PAST TENSE

Singular	*Plural*
I earned, grew, **were**	We earned, grew, were
You earned, grew, were	You earned, grew, were
He earned, grew, **were**	They earned, grew, were

IMPERATIVE MOOD

SINGULAR AND PLURAL: (You) *earn, grow, be.*

II. USES OF THE SIX TENSES

In general, the tenses are used as follows:

PRESENT: Action occurring at the present moment: He *earns* a good salary.

PAST: Action occurring at a definite time before the present moment: Last year he *earned* a good salary.

FUTURE: Action occurring at some time beyond the present moment: Next year he *will earn* a good salary.

PRESENT PERFECT: Action continuing to the present moment: So far this year he *has earned* ten thousand dollars.

PAST PERFECT: Action continuing to a fixed moment in the past: Before leaving for college, he *had earned* ten thousand dollars.

FUTURE PERFECT: Action continuing to a fixed moment in the future: By next Christmas he *will have earned* ten thousand dollars.

III. PRINCIPAL PARTS

The conjugation shows you that the two verbs *earn* and *grow* differ in form in all tenses except the present tense and the future tense. This difference illustrates regular verbs and irregular verbs, the two groups into which all English verbs can be classed. The regular class is much the larger of the two groups. *Earn* is a regular verb and *grow* is an irregular verb.

We customarily make use of three distinctive forms, called the principal parts of the verb, to show the difference between the two classes. The principal parts are (1) the *base* or infinitive, the "name" of the verb, used in the present tense; (2) the *past,* the form used in the simple past tense; and (3) the *past participle,* the form used in the three perfect tenses.

On the basis of these three forms we classify verbs as being regular or irregular. With all regular verbs the past and the past participle are alike, formed simply by the addition of *ed* to the base form (or only *d* if the base word ends in *e*). The irregular verbs are more complicated because for nearly all of them the past tense and the participle are not spelled alike. The verb *be* is completely irregular. The conjugation shows you that, unlike any other verb in the language, it has three forms (*am, is, are*) in the present tense and two forms in the past tense (*was, were*). Its past participle is *been.*

The following list gives the principal parts that account for most of the verb form errors found in speaking and writing. The principal parts are listed in the customary order: base form (the infinitive without the "to"), the past tense, and the past participle. For those marked *, see U 5.

Base	Past	Past Participle
be	was	been
bear	bore	borne
		born*
beat	beat	beaten
		beat*
become	became	become
begin	began	begun
bite	bit	bitten
		bit*
blow	blew	blown
break	broke	broken

bring	brought	brought
build	built	built
burst	burst	burst
buy	bought	bought
catch	caught	caught
choose	chose	chosen
climb	climbed	climbed
cling	clung	clung
come	came	come
creep	crept	crept
deal	dealt	dealt
dive	dived	dived
	dove*	
do	did	done
drag	dragged	dragged
draw	drew	drawn
drink	drank	drunk
drive	drove	driven
drown	drowned	drowned
eat	ate	eaten
fall	fell	fallen
flee	fled	fled
fling	flung	flung
fly	flew	flown
forbid	forbade	forbidden
	forbad*	
forget	forgot	forgotten
		forgot*
freeze	froze	frozen
give	gave	given
go	went	gone
grow	grew	grown
hang	hung	hung
	hanged*	hanged*
hide	hid	hidden
		hid*
know	knew	known
lay	laid	laid
lead	led	led
lend	lent	lent
lie	lay	lain
lose	lost	lost
pay	paid	paid
	payed*	

plead	pleaded	pleaded
	pled*	pled*
raise	raised	raised
ride	rode	ridden
ring	rang	rung
rise	rose	risen
run	ran	run
see	saw	seen
seek	sought	sought
send	sent	sent
set	set	set
shake	shook	shaken
shine	shone	shone
	shined*	shined*
show	showed	shown
		showed*
shrink	shrank	shrunk
	shrunk*	shrunken*
sing	sang	sung
	sung*	
sink	sank	sunk
	sunk*	
slay	slew	slain
speak	spoke	spoken
spend	spent	spent
steal	stole	stolen
sting	stung	stung
stink	stank	stunk
	stunk*	
swear	swore	sworn
sweep	swept	swept
swim	swam	swum
swing	swung	swung
take	took	taken
teach	taught	taught
tear	tore	torn
throw	threw	thrown
wear	wore	worn
weep	wept	wept
write	wrote	written

Another change in form for both regular and irregular verbs—the addition of *ing* to the base form—produces the present participle. One of its important uses is explained in the next section.

IV. AUXILIARY VERBS

In some tenses the verb is a single word (He *grew*) and in other tenses the whole verb consists of two words (He *has grown*) or even three (He *will have grown*). In these three examples the main idea of the action is found in the forms of *grow*, but we get help in understanding the exact time of the action from *has* and *will have*. Words of this kind are called helping verbs—or, more technically, auxiliary verbs.

In addition to the "time" auxiliaries *have*, *will*, and *shall*, other auxiliaries are used to give exact meanings to verbs. *Be* is an important auxiliary. As noted in the conjugation, it combines with the past participle to form the passive verb forms. It is also the auxiliary used with the *ing* form (the present participle) of the main verb to produce what is called the progressive form. As an illustration, if someone asks you about the current activity in your English class, you would probably not reply, "Right now we *review* parts of speech." Instead, you would say, "Right now we *are reviewing* parts of speech," to show that the action is not fixed in an exact moment of time but is a continuing activity. This very useful type of verb occurs in all six tenses: We *are reviewing;* we *were reviewing;* we *shall be reviewing;* we *have been reviewing;* we *had been reviewing;* we *shall have been reviewing.*

Another type of auxiliary verb includes *may, might, must, can, could, would,* and *should.* These words are called modal auxiliaries, and they are used the way *will* and *shall* are used: I *should study* this weekend; I *should have studied* last weekend.

Variations of some modals and "time" auxiliaries make use of *to* in the verb phrase. Here are examples of some that you use and hear regularly:

> I *have to leave* [= *must leave*] early.
> You *ought to apologize* [= *should apologize*].
> Mr. Bright *used to be* a teacher.
> You *were supposed to be* here on time.
> I *am to leave* soon for Chicago.
> I *am going to leave* soon for Chicago.

Have and *be* are not used exclusively as auxiliaries; they are also two of our most commonly used main verbs:

> I *have* a new car. [Main verb.]
> I *have* bought a new car. [Auxiliary.]

He *is* a good speaker. [Main verb.]
He *is* becoming a good speaker. [Auxiliary.]

FIVE BASIC SENTENCE PATTERNS

A sentence is an orderly arrangement of words that makes sense. You may be surprised to learn that, in spite of the apparent complexity of English sentences, there are only a few *basic* patterns into which words can arrange themselves and still make sense. We shall examine five basic sentence patterns, which you should think of as the simplest units of communication. These five basic patterns are used to make more complicated sentences, most of which are combinations of basic sentences or well-defined and orderly alterations of them.

Each of the five basic sentence types is distinguished from the others by the function of the verb and the nature of the complement (or completer) required by the verb. Verbs are classified as transitive or intransitive. *Trans*itive verbs *trans*fer the action of the verb to a receiver. Compare these two sentences:

> The first batter [*subject*] hit [*transitive verb*] the ball [*receiver of the action*].
> He [*subject*] sprinted [*intransitive verb*] to first base.

Hit is transitive because the statement is incomplete without the noun *ball,* the receiver of the action. *Sprinted* is intransitive because no action is transferred to a following noun.

The complement is the unit, such as *ball* in the example above, that must be added to many subject-verb combinations to give completeness to the statement.

Sentence Pattern 1 is the only basic sentence that does not require a complement.

SAMPLE SENTENCE: Children run.

This pattern can be represented as follows: S—Vi, with the *S* standing for subject and the *Vi* standing for intransitive verb, or the kind of verb in which no action is performed upon or transferred to anything. Pattern 1 sentences nearly always contain modifiers:

Sometimes the neighborhood children run happily down the street.

Notice that the material associated with the verb is all adverbial: *sometimes* (When?), *happily* (How?), *down the street* (Where?). All of these, of course, add to the total meaning of the verb, but the important characteristic of a Pattern 1 sentence is that there is no noun answering the question "What?" of the verb. The lack of a noun answering the question "What?" after the verb is the best way to recognize an intransitive verb.

In some Pattern 1 sentences the purpose of the statement is essentially to say that the subject exists. Usually some adverbial material is added to show the place or the time of the existence:

> Your friends *are* in the front hall.
> The dedication *will be* much later.

In most of them, however, some activity takes place:

> My roommate *sings* beautifully.
> Jackson Creek *flows* into the Platte River.

The normal order of the modern English sentence places the subject before the verb. We sometimes begin Pattern 1 sentences, however, with adverbial modification, with the verb preceding the subject.

> Behind the house *stood* [verb] an old *mill* [subject].
> Here *is* [verb] my late *theme* [subject].

A very common type of sentence with an inverted subject-verb arrangement uses the word *there* preceding the verb.

> There *are* [verb] ten *chairs* [subject] in this room.
> Suddenly there *came* [verb] a *cry* [subject] for help.

In **Sentence Pattern 2** sentences the verb names some activity and the subject is, of course, the doer of that activity, as it is in many Pattern 1 sentences. But in a Pattern 2 sentence the subject and the verb, even with the addition of adverbial material, are insufficient to produce a satisfying statement because the activity named in the verb is performed *upon* something. This kind of verb is called a transitive verb, for which we shall use the symbol *Vtr*.

> **SAMPLE SENTENCE:** Children play games.

The complement (completer) required with a transitive verb is the **direct object,** for which we shall use the symbol *DO*. It names the receiver of the action—in other words, a transitive verb *trans*fers the action to an object. The direct object is always a noun or a noun equivalent, such as a pronoun, and we find it by asking the question "What?" of the transitive verb:

> I broke my *glasses*. [What names the activity? *Broke* is the verb. Who did the action? *I* is the subject. What was broken? *Glasses* is the direct object.]
> Someone threw *stones* at us. [What was thrown? *Stones* is the direct object.]

We can represent this sentence pattern as follows:

$$\text{S} - \text{Vtr} - \text{DO}$$
$$\text{[children]} \quad \text{[play]} \quad \text{[games]}$$

Another helpful representation is as follows: $N_x - Vtr - N_y$. N stands for a noun or a noun equivalent such as a pronoun. The small letters x and y show that the nouns refer to separate things: *I* and *glasses* are obviously not one and the same, nor are *someone* and *stones*.

With one special kind of verb there is a problem of distinguishing between a direct object and an object of a preposition. Notice these two sentences:

> Harry jumped off the box.
> Harry took off his raincoat.

The first sentence is Pattern 1. *Off* is a preposition, *box* is the object of the preposition, and the prepositional phrase is used as an adverbial modifier, because it tells *where* Harry jumped. The second sentence is Pattern 2. The verb, with its adverbial modifier *off*, is the equivalent of the transitive verb *remove*. *Raincoat* is the direct object.

There is another way to distinguish between the adverbial use and the prepositional use of such a word as *off* in the above examples. When the word is a vital adverbial modifier of the verb, it can, in most cases, be used in either of two positions: immediately following the verb or following the direct object— "Harry took off his raincoat" or "Harry took his raincoat off." But when the word is a preposition, the alternate position is not possible. "Harry jumped the box off" is non-English.

Here are some other examples of this kind of verb with adverbial modifier. Notice that in each case you can easily find a transitive verb synonym for the combination:

give up [relinquish] his rights.
leave out [omit] the second chapter.
put out [extinguish] the fire.
make over [alter] an old dress.
make up [invent] an excuse.

Under **Sentence Pattern 3** we include two closely related kinds of sentences. The purpose of the first type is to say that the subject is the same thing as something else, in other words, to rename the subject.

SAMPLE SENTENCE: The child is a genius.

The noun or pronoun that renames the subject is called a **subjective complement** (*SC* in the example), because it completes the verb and renames the subject. The special type of intransitive verb that is used in Pattern 3 sentences is called the link or linking verb (*Vlk* in the example).

$$\text{S—Vlk—SC}$$
$$\text{[child]} \quad \text{[is]} \quad \text{[genius]}$$

Or we can also represent this sentence as follows:

$$N_x\text{—Vlk—}N_x$$

Both of the noun elements in the sentence refer to the same thing, in contrast to the situation in Pattern 2 sentences, which we charted, you remember, as N_x—Vtr—N_y to show that the two nouns refer to separate things.

In the second type of Pattern 3 sentence the subjective complement is an adjective (*Adj* in the example); it relates to the subject as a describer rather than as a renamer.

SAMPLE SENTENCE: The child is clever.

$$\text{S—Vlk—SC}$$
$$\text{[child]} \quad \text{[is]} \quad \text{[clever]}$$
$$\text{N—Vlk—Adj}$$

There are comparatively few verbs that have the linking function. We can conveniently think of them in three closely related groups:

1. *Be,* the most commonly used linking verb, and a few others meaning essentially the same thing: *seem, appear, prove, remain, continue,* and so forth.

My roommate *is* a very good student.
The speaker *seemed* unhappy.
He *remained* a rebel.
The weather *continued* warm.

2. *Become,* and a few others like it: *turn, grow, work, get, wear,* and so forth.

Later he *became* an accountant.
The weather *turned* colder.
I *grew* weary of his talking.

3. A few verbs referring to the senses, *look, smell, taste, feel, sound,* which can be followed by adjective subjective complements that describe the condition of the subject. Ability to recognize this kind of N—Vlk—Adj sentence pattern will help you understand a few troublesome usage problems—to understand why, for instance, many careful writers insist on "feel bad" rather than "feel badly." (See U 42.)

Mr. Smith *is looking* stronger.
These cookies *taste* good.
I *feel* bad about the election results.

It is important to remember that most linking verbs can be used for other purposes; they are not always linking verbs. Notice in the following sentences how the different meanings of the verbs result in different sentence patterns (*Adv* stands for adverb):

Lucy *appeared* in the doorway. [S—Vi—Adv. Pattern 1.]
Lucy *appeared* worried. [S—Vlk—SC. Pattern 3.]

The watchman *sounded* the alarm. [S—Vtr—DO. Pattern 2.]
Your proposal *sounds* workable. [S—Vlk—SC. Pattern 3.]

The child *is growing* rapidly. [S—Vi—Adv. Pattern 1.]
Mother *grows* delicious tomatoes. [S—Vtr—DO. Pattern 2.]
I *am growing* dissatisfied. [S—Vlk—SC. Pattern 3.]

The road *continues* north to Clarkston. [S—Vi—Adv. Pattern 1.]
You *should continue* your education. [S—Vtr—DO. Pattern 2.]
Relations between us *continue* strained. [S—Vlk—SC. Pattern 3.]

Pattern 4 sentences contain two complements, the indirect object and the direct object. The direct object, the receiver of the action, answers the question "Who?" or "What?" after the transitive verb. The **indirect object** answers a question such as "To whom (or which)?" or "For whom (or which)?" of the verb.

Thus in the sentence "She sang a lullaby" we have a Pattern 2 sentence, but in "She sang the children a lullaby" we have a Pattern 4. *IO* stands for indirect object in the examples.

SAMPLE SENTENCE: The child gives the parents pleasure.

$$S—Vtr—IO—DO$$

We can also chart this pattern as follows:

$$N_x—Vtr—N_y—N_z$$

By this method we get an important structural clue: All three of the noun elements refer to different things.

A typical verb for Pattern 4 is *give,* as in "The clerk gave me a refund." You can easily see why the two complements are used here: The sentence mentions the thing that is given (*refund,* the *DO*) and also the person to whom the *DO* is given (*me,* the *IO*). Although the *IO* usually names a person, it can name a nonhuman thing, as in "We gave your *application* a careful reading."

Other verbs that commonly are used this way and therefore can create Pattern 4 structures are *allow, assign, ask, tell, write, send, show, pay, grant,* and so on. Nearly all sentences using these verbs can make essentially the same statement by using a prepositional phrase, the preposition usually being *to* or *for.* When the prepositional phrase is actually present in the sentence, it is a Pattern 2 sentence.

> I sent him the money. [Pattern 4; *him* is an indirect object.]
> I sent the money to him. [Pattern 2; *him* is an object of a preposition.]
> Mother bought us some taffy. [Pattern 4.]
> Mother bought some taffy for us. [Pattern 2.]

Pattern 5, like Pattern 3, consists of two closely related types of sentences. There are two complements in Pattern 5 sentences. The one closer to the verb is the direct object, and the second one is the **objective complement,** which we can define as a noun that *renames* the direct object or an adjective that *describes* the direct object. The objective complement is represented as *OC* in the example.

SAMPLE SENTENCES: The parents consider the child a genius.
The parents consider the child clever.

$$S—Vtr—DO—OC$$

In our method of representing sentences to show the parts of speech and the reference of the noun elements, these sentences would appear this way:

$$N_x \quad - \quad Vtr \quad - \quad N_y \quad - \quad N_y$$
[parents] [consider] [child] [genius]
$$N_x \quad - \quad Vtr \quad - \quad N_y \quad - \quad Adj$$
[parents] [consider] [child] [clever]

The reference of the two nouns following the verb is a key to the difference between a Pattern 5 sentence and a Pattern 4 sentence: In a Pattern 4 sentence the two noun complements refer to separate things, but in a Pattern 5 sentence they refer to the same thing.

> Mother made us some fudge. [Pattern 4; *us* and *fudge* refer to separate things.]
> This experience made John an activist. [Pattern 5; *John* and *activist* refer to the same thing.]

Because the objective complement renames or describes the direct object, we can use a handy ear test to help us recognize this pattern: The insertion of *to be* between the complements will give us acceptable English idiom.

> We appointed Jones [to be] our spokesman.
> I thought this action [to be] unnecessary.

Sometimes the word *as* is used between the direct object and the objective complement.

> We appointed Jones as our spokesman.

There are a few expressions in which the adjective objective complement is so important to the meaning of the verb that we can have the objective complement placed next to the verb, preceding the direct object:

> He set free [OC] the caged animals [DO].
> *Usual order:* He set the caged animals free.

The following verbs are among those most commonly used in Pattern 5 sentences: *elect, appoint, name, call, consider, find, make, think,* and so on.

Summary

PATTERN 1:   S—Vi
PATTERN 2:   S—Vtr—DO
             $(N_x—Vtr—N_y)$

PATTERN 3: S—Vlk—SC
$(N_x—Vlk—N_x)$
$(N—Vlk—Adj)$

PATTERN 4: S—Vtr—IO—DO
$(N_x—Vtr—N_y—N_z)$

PATTERN 5: S—Vtr—DO—OC
$(N_x—Vtr—N_y—N_y)$
$(N_x—Vtr—N_y—Adj)$

ALTERATIONS OF BASIC SENTENCE PATTERNS

Any extended piece of writing made up exclusively of basic sentences would be so monotonous that reading it would be overwhelmingly dreary. You should think of the basic sentences not as models for your writing but as rudimentary units of communication, important because they are the structures from which amplified sentences develop.

Three important alterations of basic sentences result in (1) sentences using passive verbs, (2) sentences in the form of questions, and (3) sentences that are negative rather than positive.

I. PASSIVE VOICE

The conjugation in Section I of "Forms of the Verb" shows how the passive verb is formed: the auxiliary verb *be,* in all six tenses, is used with the past participle of the verb.

The passive voice serves a real purpose in effective communication. It should be used when the *doer* of the action is unknown or is of secondary interest in the statement. In such a situation the writer, wishing to focus attention on the *receiver* of the action, places that unit in the emphatic subject position. The passive verb form makes this arrangement possible. Thus, instead of some vague expression such as "Some unknown person had tampered with the carburetor," we can say, "The carburetor *had been tampered* with."

Since only transitive verbs have passive forms, the basic patterns that can be altered to passive versions are Patterns 2, 4, and 5. When the idea of a Pattern 2 sentence is expressed with a passive verb, there will be no complement in the sentence:

ACTIVE VOICE: Children play games.
PASSIVE VOICE: Games are played [by children].

If the doer of the action is expressed in a sentence using a passive verb, the doer must occur as the object of the preposition *by*.

When a Pattern 4 sentence is altered to a passive construction, the indirect object that followed the active verb becomes the subject of the passive verb:

ACTIVE VOICE: Children give the parents pleasure.
PASSIVE VOICE: The parents are given pleasure [by the children].

Here the passive verb is followed by a complement, *pleasure,* which we shall call a direct object in spite of the fact that it follows a passive verb.

Notice also how a Pattern 5 sentence can be given a different kind of expression by means of a passive verb, with the direct object becoming the subject:

ACTIVE VOICE: The parents consider the child a genius.
The parents consider the child clever.
PASSIVE VOICE: The child is considered a genius [by the parents].
The child is considered clever [by the parents].

Here also the passive verb requires a complement (*genius, clever*), which, because it renames or describes the subject, is called a subjective complement.

II. QUESTIONS

People who grow up using the English language are usually not aware that most questions are quite different from statements in the grammatical arrangement of the parts of the sentence. We should note these differences, particularly since they are the basis for an understanding of certain usage problems.

The normal sentence has the subject first, followed by the verb, which is followed by the complement, if any. With questions, however, other arrangements may occur. The most effective method of showing these new structures is to contrast the structure of a statement with that of a question. We must, first of all, recognize the fact that there are two kinds of questions.

Question Answered by "Yes" or "No." With a "Yes" or "No" question, if the verb is *be* in the simple present or past tense, the subject and verb always reverse positions. This arrangement also is sometimes used with *have* in the present tense.

STATEMENT: John is happy.   You have some money.
QUESTION: Is John happy?   Have you some money?

With all other verbs an auxiliary must be used, and the subject comes between the auxiliary and the main verb. (If there is more than one auxiliary, the subject comes after the first auxiliary.) If the statement is in the present or past tense and does not already have an auxiliary, the auxiliary *do* is used. *Have* in the present tense may use the "do" form also. Notice the subject–verb positions in the following typical sentences:

Will John be present? [Contrast this with the structuring of the underlying statement: John will be present.] Have you seen him lately? Had you met him earlier? Will the work be completed soon? Is he being difficult? Were you studying hard last night? May I leave early? Should I have been flattered? Did you have a good time? Do you have a new car? [or] Have you a new car?

Question Answered by Information. A request for information cannot be answered with a "Yes" or a "No." This kind of question makes use of certain words called interrogatives: pronouns (*who, whom, what, which, whoever, whatever*); adjectives (*what, which, whose, whatever, whichever*); and adverbs (*when, where, why, how*). With questions using these words the subject–verb arrangement is the same as it is with the "Yes"/"No" questions. But in addition, the interrogative word, or the unit modified by the interrogative, always stands at the beginning to signal the fact that a question, not a statement, is forthcoming. Thus we may find an arrangement of sentence parts quite different from that of a statement; we can have complements and objects of prepositions standing before the subject. Notice the structure of these related statements and questions:

My brother paid the bill.
Who paid the bill? [Normal arrangement, since the interrogative pronoun *Who* is the subject.]

You studied *geometry* last night.
What did you study last night? [*What* is the direct object.]

You saw *Elsie* at the party.
Whom did you see at the party? [*Whom* is the direct object.]

She is *Mother's cousin.*
Who is she? [*Who* is the subjective complement.]

You bought *a sports car.*
What kind of car did you buy? [*Kind,* the direct object, is modified by the interrogative adjective *what.*]

She is *forty years old.*
How old is she? [*Old,* the subjective complement, is modified by the interrogative adverb *how.*]

You called *Bob* a *thief.*
Who called Bob a thief? [*Who* is the subject.]
Whom did you call a thief? [*Whom* is the direct object.]
What did you call Bob? [*What* is the objective complement.]

When the interrogative unit is the object of a preposition, two versions of the question are often possible: The entire prepositional phrase may stand at the beginning or the interrogative may stand at the beginning with the preposition in its usual position. (See U 46.)

The speaker was referring *to the mayor.*
To whom was the speaker referring? [*Whom* is the object of the preposition.]
Whom was the speaker referring to? [*Whom* is still the object of the preposition.]

III. NEGATIVES

The basic method of changing a positive sentence to a negative is by using the adverb *not* or its contraction *n't.* Negatives are like questions in that the arrangement of the sentence parts depends on the presence or absence of an auxiliary. And as with questions, *be* and *have* must be considered separately.

1. If the main verb is *be* in the present tense or past tense, the *not* follows the verb.

I am *not* happy about this.
He is *not* [*isn't*] a friend of mine.
They were *not* [*weren't*] able to attend.

2. With other verbs in the present or past tense the auxiliary *do,* followed by the negator, is used.

I do *not* [*don't*] consider him reliable.
He does *not* [*doesn't*] play golf.
They did *not* [*didn't*] reply.

3. If the verb (including *be*) already has an auxiliary, the

negator follows the auxiliary. When there are two or more auxiliaries, the *not* follows the first one.

> We could *not* [*couldn't*] be happier.
> They will *not* [*won't*] return this week.
> You have *not* [*haven't*] heard the last of this.
> We may *not* have heard him correctly.
> This light ought *not* to have been left on.

4. When *have* in the present tense is the main verb, two negative forms are possible:

> I have *not* [*haven't*] enough money with me.
> I do *not* [*don't*] have enough money with me.

COORDINATION: THE COMPOUND SENTENCE

On the basis of the number and kinds of clauses they contain, we classify sentences as **simple, compound, complex,** and **compound-complex.** A **clause** is a combination of words containing a subject and a verb. From this definition it would seem that a sentence and a clause may be identical, and in a way that is true. The kind of clause that can stand by itself as a sentence is the independent clause. Conversely, every group of words, to be called a grammatically complete sentence, must contain at least one independent clause.

Every sentence that has been used to this point to illustrate basic sentences has been a **simple** sentence, meaning that the sentence is made up of only one independent clause. We shall now examine two other kinds of sentences, both of which involve the process called compounding, whereby grammatically equal parts are placed together. In the first kind, two or more equal units stand side by side within a simple sentence. In the other kind, two independent clauses are joined to form one sentence.

All sentence units can be compounded; that is, a sentence may contain two or more subjects, verbs, complements, or modifiers joined by a coordinating conjunction. The three common coordinating conjunctions for this use are *and, but,* and *or;* other coordinators are *nor, for,* and *yet.* Sometimes the equal grammatical relationship is pointed out by the use of pairs of words, called correlatives: *not (only) . . . but (also), either . . . or, neither . . . nor.*

You *and* I know the answer. [Compound subjects.]

My favorite desserts are cake *and* pie. [Compound subjective complements.]

I studied long *and* hard *but* failed the test. [Compound verbs and adverbs.]

I found the lecture *and* the discussion neither interesting *nor* instructive. [Compound direct objects and objective complements.]

Compounding is often used with two (sometimes more than two) independent clauses, resulting in a sentence called the **compound** sentence. Any of the coordinating conjunctions and any of the correlatives mentioned above can be used to join two independent clauses. In the compound sentence the presence or absence of one of these coordinators is the basis for a problem in punctuation, a problem so important that you must be able to recognize the compound sentence and must know that it can occur in either of two patterns (see P 1, P 16, P 17):

1. The two clauses are joined by a coordinating conjunction. The normal punctuation is a comma before the conjunction.

I had reviewed the material, but I did poorly on the test.

It is important to distinguish this sentence from a nearly synonymous version using a compound verb: "I had reviewed the material but did poorly on the test." In this version the sentence is not a compound sentence because there is no separate subject for the second verb. It is a simple sentence and in usual practice would be written without a comma.

2. The two independent clauses are *not* joined by a coordinating conjunction. Sometimes in this kind of compound sentence the two independent clauses stand side by side with no word tying them together:

No one had warned me; I was completely unaware of the difficulty.

Sometimes the second clause begins with an adverbial unit that serves as a loose tie between the clauses:

The evidences of perjury are conclusive; therefore we find you guilty.

For the time being I use a motorcycle; later I plan to buy a car.

Since adverbial units like *therefore* and *later* are not coordinating conjunctions, the use of a comma in this type of sentence is inappropriate. The important thing to remember is that when the independent clauses are joined by a coordinating conjunction, we normally use a comma. When there is no coordinating conjunction, the comma will not suffice; the customary mark is the semicolon.

SUBORDINATION: DEPENDENT CLAUSES

The **complex sentence** is made up of one independent clause and at least one dependent clause.

A **dependent,** or **subordinate,** clause is a unit containing a subject and a verb, but this group of words cannot stand alone as a sentence. Rather, it functions *within* the sentence as a single part of speech—a noun, an adjective, or an adverb. To illustrate this relationship, examine the following very common type of noun clause:

Mr. Allen announced *that he had resigned.*

The group of words *that he had resigned* is, first of all, a clause because it contains a subject *he* and a verb *had resigned.* It is a dependent clause because its meaning is clear and complete only by reference to the whole independent clause. In other words, because it is used within the sentence as a single part of speech—in this case, as a noun—it depends on something else in the sentence for its complete meaning. And it is a noun clause because it is the direct object of the main verb *announced,* and the unit filling a direct object slot—whether it is a single word or a group of related words—is always a noun unit. (Compare "Mr. Allen announced his *resignation.*" What is announced? *Resignation* is the direct object. By the same process you can see that *that he had resigned* is also a direct object and thus a noun unit.)

Remember this important fact: A dependent clause, whether noun, adjective, or adverb, includes the word that introduces it. In the example above, "he had resigned" could stand alone as a complete sentence. But "*that* he had resigned" obviously depends on something else to be meaningful.

I. THE NOUN CLAUSE

Noun clauses are used in the sentence where nouns are used. You will find that most noun clauses are used as subjects, as direct objects, as subjective complements, as objects of prepositions, or as appositives. Notice in the following sentences how noun clauses are used just as single nouns are used in these sentence positions:

His *story* is very convincing. [Noun as subject.]
What he told us is very convincing. [Noun clause as subject.]

He believes *anything*. [Indefinite pronoun as direct object.]
He believes *whatever is told to him*. [Noun clause as direct object.]

This is his *report*. [Noun as subjective complement.]
This is *what he told me*. [Noun clause as subjective complement.]

Give it to the *janitor*. [Noun as object of preposition.]
Give it to *whoever opens the door*. [Noun clause as object of preposition.]

One common noun clause use is as a delayed subject. The signal for this construction is the word *it* standing in subject position, with the meaningful subject being a noun clause following the verb:

It is unfortunate *that you were delayed*. [Although the clause follows the verb, it is the real subject and therefore is a noun clause. The meaning of the sentence is "That you were delayed is unfortunate."]

A related noun clause use puts *it* in the direct object slot with a noun clause following an objective complement. This use, which is encountered less frequently than the delayed subject, gives us a clause that we can call a delayed direct object:

I consider it unlikely *that he will resign*.

Another possible position for the noun clause is that of the **appositive.** The appositive is a noun unit inserted into a sentence to *rename* another noun that usually immediately precedes the appositive. A simple example occurs in the following sentence:

Senator Jones, *a dedicated environmentalist,* objected.

Since any noun unit can be used as an appositive, noun clauses sometimes function in this position. Some noun clause appositives are separated from the first noun by at least a comma, sometimes by a heavier mark:

There still remains one mystery: *how the thief knew your name*. [The noun clause renames the preceding noun *mystery*.]

A rather special type of noun appositive clause, subordinated by *that* and following such nouns as *fact, belief, hope, statement, news, argument,* and so on, is usually not set off by any mark of punctuation:

> You cannot deny the fact *that you lied under oath.*
> Your statement *that the boss is stupid* was undiplomatic.

Since an appositive is a renamer, it represents a reduced form of a Pattern 3 sentence in which a subject and a noun subjective complement are joined by a form of *be.* The writer of the sentence "Senator Jones, a dedicated environmentalist, objected" could have written two simple sentences, the second one repeating a noun used in the first:

> Senator Jones objected.
> Senator Jones [or *He*] is a dedicated environmentalist.

Instead, the writer incorporated the renaming noun unit as an appositive in the first sentence. If you think of the appositive as a renamer of the preceding noun (the two nouns could be joined by a form of *be*), you have a handy test to help you recognize any noun appositive use.

> There still remains one mystery: *how the thief knew your name.*
> [Test: The mystery *is* how the thief knew your name.]
> You cannot deny the fact *that you lied under oath.*
> [Test: The fact *is* that you lied under oath.]
> Your statement *that the boss is stupid* was undiplomatic.
> [Test: The statement *is* that the boss is stupid.]

The subordinating words that serve to introduce noun clauses are conjunctions (*that, if, whether*); pronouns (*who, whom, what, which, whoever, whatever, whichever*); adjectives (*whose, which, what*); and adverbs (*when, where, why, how*). Remember that the subordinating word always stands at or near the beginning of the clause. Thus it is useful as a signal that the clause it introduces is not an independent clause. If the subordinating word is one of the three conjunctions, the word order of the clause will not be affected. Remember also that the conjunction *that* is quite commonly not expressed in a noun clause:

> I hope [*that*] you are mistaken.

The other subordinating words that introduce noun clauses have two functions to perform: They not only are the signs of subordination but also are used within the clause as pronouns or as modifiers. You often find, therefore, in noun clauses that a complement or an object of a preposition, because it is a subordinating pronoun or a unit having a subordinating modifier attached to it, will be out of its usual position—it will precede the subject and verb.

> I wonder *who he is.* [The clause is a noun clause because it is the direct object of *wonder.* Within the clause *who* is the subjective complement.]
> I wonder *whom Mary is feuding with now.* [*Whom* is the object of the preposition *with* within the noun clause.]
> I wonder *what John will do.* [*What* is the direct object of *will do* within the noun clause.]

You have probably already noticed that the pronouns, adjectives, and adverbs that subordinate noun clauses are essentially the same words that are used in questions. The two uses are alike in the important respect that they always stand at the beginning of the clause. The two uses differ in that as interrogatives the words bring about the subject-verb inversion, whereas in noun clauses the subject-verb positioning is the normal one.

> *Whom* will the mayor appoint? [This sentence is a direct question; it calls for an answer. *Whom* is the direct object of the main verb.]
> I wonder *whom* the mayor will appoint. [This sentence is a statement, not a direct question. Notice that a question mark is not required. *Whom* is the direct object within the noun clause.]

II. THE ADJECTIVE CLAUSE

An adjective clause modifies or limits or points out a noun or pronoun. The normal position for an adjective clause is immediately following the noun or pronoun it modifies.

> He bought one of those houses *that have just been built in Westwood.*
> This car is one *that will save you money.*
> I like a youngster *who has plenty of initiative.*
> The boss hired Chet Black, *whom he had known in Omaha.*
> This is Chatham Hall, *which is the oldest building on the campus.*

The subordinating words that connect adjective clauses to the words they modify are called **relatives.** Notice how the relative is a substitute for the noun or pronoun being modified:

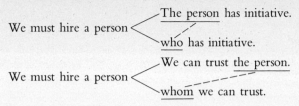

Nearly all of the adjective clauses that you write or speak will use *who, whom, that, which, whose, where, when,* or *why* as the subordinating word. Like the functioning subordinating words of noun clauses, these words are used within the adjective clause as pronouns (subject, complement, object of preposition), adjectives, or adverbs.

> The man *who tries* will succeed. [*Who* is the subject of *tries*.]
> This is the book *that I borrowed.* [*That* is the direct object of *borrowed.*]
>
> They are the people ⎫
> *with whom I lived.* ⎪
> ⎬ [*Whom* is the object of the preposition.]
> They are the people ⎪
> *whom I lived with.* ⎭
>
> We met Miss Jones, *whose garden you admired.* [*Whose* modifies *garden,* the direct object of *admired.*]

The words *where, when,* and *why* introduce adjective clauses in combinations meaning "place where," "time when," and "reason why."

> You saw the house *where I was born.* [House where—place where.]
> We married on the day *when I received my degree.* [Day when—time when.]
> Give me one reason *why you cannot go.* [Reason why.]

These clauses are logically called adjective clauses because they immediately follow nouns that require identification, and the clauses give the identifying material. Notice that "the house *where I was born*" is just another way of saying "the house *in which I was born.*" If you look for the place-where, time-when, reason-why combinations, you will not confuse this type of adjective clause with other kinds of dependent clauses that may use the same subordinating words.

In adjective clauses the relative word is often omitted, but clauses of this type should cause you no difficulty. You can readily understand the relative word that has been omitted.

The house *I live in*	The food *we eat*
The house *that I live in*	The food *that we eat*
The book *I am studying*	The man *you saw*
The book *that I am studying*	The man *whom you saw*
The time *you fell down*	The place *I live*
The time *when you fell down*	The place *where I live*

If you remember a few points about the form, function, and positioning of adjective clauses and noun clauses, you should have little difficulty in distinguishing between them. Although certain kinds of noun clauses in apposition may, at first glance, look like adjective clauses, a few simple tests clearly show the difference:

The news *that you brought us* is welcome. [Adjective clause.]
The news *that Bob has recovered* is welcome. [Noun clause.]

If you remember that an adjective clause is a *describer* and an appositive noun clause is a *renamer,* you can see that in the first sentence the clause describes, in fact identifies, the noun *news,* but it does not actually tell us what the news is. In the second sentence the clause does more; it tells us what the news is. Remember the *be* test discussed in the section on noun clauses. "The news is *that you brought us* . . ." does not make sense, but "The news is *that Bob has recovered* . . ." does; therefore the second clause is a noun clause in apposition. Another test that can be applied to these two types of sentences is based on the fact that in adjective clauses, but not in noun clauses, *which* can be substituted for *that.* "The news *which* you brought us . . ." is understandable English; the clause, in this case, is an adjective clause. But since we can't say "The news *which* Bob has recovered . . . ," this time the clause is a noun clause; it cannot be an adjective clause.

III. THE ADVERBIAL CLAUSE

Adverbial clauses may occur before, after, or within main clauses, but they can be distinguished from other kinds of clauses because, like simple adverbs, they describe the action of the main clause by telling certain things about it. Like adverbs, adverbial clauses may modify verbs, adverbs, or adjectives. The uses of adverbial clauses, together with some of their most common conjunctions (structural signals or signs of subordination), are listed here with examples.

1. Time (*when, before, after, since, while, until, as*).

   She left *before I could recognize her*. You must not talk *while you eat*. You may leave *when I tell you to*. *After the bell rings*, no one enters. I haven't seen him *since we left school*. He shouted *as I drove by*.

2. Manner (*as, as if, as though*).

   They write *as if they knew something*.
   Please do the work *as you have been instructed*.

3. Place (*where, wherever*).

   We parted *where the paths separated*.
   I shall meet you *wherever you want me to*.

4. Result (*that, so that*).

   He was so late *that he missed the lecture*.
   It rained all night, *so that the garden flowers were ruined*.

5. Cause (*because, since, as*).

   Since we could not pay the fine, we could not drive the car.
   She quit school *because her mother was ill*.

6. Purpose (*that, in order that*).

   They died *that their countrymen might live*.
   They came to America *in order that they might have freedom of speech*.

7. Condition (*if, unless, provided that, on condition that*).

   Stop me *if you have heard this before*.
   He will not give his talk *unless we pay his expenses*.
   I shall go *provided that you will drive carefully*.
   If I were you, I would accept the offer.
   If you had told me earlier, I could have helped.

Certain kinds of conditional clauses can occur in an alternate arrangement. The *if* is not used; instead, a subject-verb inversion signals the subordination. Sentences like the last two examples sometimes take this form:

   Were I you, I would accept the offer.
   Had you told me earlier, I could have helped.

8. Concession (*although, though, even if*).

   Although he is quite small, he plays basketball very well.
   Our car is dependable *even if it is old*.

9. Comparison (*than, as*).

> Gold is heavier *than iron* (*is*).
> Your dress is as new *as hers* (*is*).
> This theme is better *than any other one in class* (*is*).

Notice that adverb clauses may modify adjectives and adverbs as well as verbs.

> The lesson was so difficult *that we could not finish it.* [Modifies *so.*]
> We are sorry *that we were delayed.* [Modifies *sorry.*]

We have described sentences as being simple, compound, or complex, based on the kinds of clauses making them up. When we add one or more dependent clauses to a compound sentence, we have a **compound-complex** sentence.

> All of us worked until we were exhausted, and I can report that the campaign material we prepared will be really effective. [The first independent clause contains the adverbial clause *until we were exhausted.* The second independent clause has for its direct object the noun clause *that the campaign material we prepared will be really effective,* the subject of which is modified by the adjective clause (*that*) *we prepared.*]

SUBORDINATION: PHRASES

A **phrase** is a group of related words that does *not* contain a subject and a verb in combination. Like the subordinate clause, the phrase is used in the sentence as a single part of speech.

Many of the sentences that you have studied thus far have shown the common modifying uses of the **prepositional phrase,** which consists of a preposition (see pages 97–98), a noun or pronoun used as its object, and any modifiers of the object. Most prepositional phrases are used as adjectives or adverbs.

> Most *of my friends* live *in the East.* [The first phrase is used as an adjective to modify the pronoun *most;* the second is used as an adverb to modify *live.*]

Much less commonly, a prepositional phrase is used as a noun:

> *Before lunch* will be the best time for the meeting. [The phrase is the subject of the verb *will be.*]
> She waved to us from *inside the phone booth.* [The phrase is the object of the preposition *from.*]

Another very important kind of phrase makes use of a verbal. A **verbal** is a word formed from a verb but used as a different part of speech. There are three kinds of verbals: the gerund, the participle, and the infinitive.

I. THE GERUND PHRASE

A **gerund** is recognized by the ending *ing,* either on the simple form (*studying*) or on an auxiliary (*having studied, being studied, having been studied*). Before one of these units can be called a gerund, however, it must be used as a *noun* within the sentence:

> *Studying* demands most of my time. [Subject.]
> He enjoys *studying.* [Direct object.]
> My main activity is *studying.* [Subjective complement.]
> You won't pass the course without *studying.* [Object of preposition.]

Not all gerund uses are as simple as those illustrated above. The single-word gerund use is uncomplicated. "He enjoys *studying*" and "He enjoys *football*" are alike in their structure; the only difference is that in one the direct object is a word formed from a verb and in the other it is a regular noun. But gerunds (like the participles and infinitives that we shall look at shortly) have a verb quality that nouns do not have: They can take their own adverbial modifiers *and complements.* A gerund phrase, therefore, is a gerund plus its modifiers and/or complements.

As in basic sentences, the kind of complement in a verbal phrase is determined by the kind of verb from which the verbal is derived. Thus the gerund, participial, or infinitive form of a transitive verb must be followed by a direct object (sometimes used with an indirect object or an objective complement), and the verbal form of a linking verb must be followed by a subjective complement. The following examples will help to clarify this important point. In each of the examples the phrase is a gerund phrase because it is used as the direct object of the main verb.

> He enjoys *walking in the snow.* [The gerund has no complement. Compare "He walks in the snow."]
> He enjoys *building model airplanes.* [*Airplanes* is the direct object of the gerund *building.* Compare "He builds model airplanes."]
> He enjoys *being helpful.* He enjoyed *being elected treasurer.* [*Helpful* is the subjective complement of the gerund *being; treasurer* is the subjective complement of the passive gerund *being elected.* Compare "He is helpful" and "He was elected treasurer."]

He enjoyed *telling us the good news.* [*Us* is the indirect object and *news* the direct object of the gerund *telling.* Compare "He told us the good news."]

He enjoyed *making our vacation pleasant.* [*Vacation* is the direct object and *pleasant* the objective complement of the gerund *making.* Compare "He made our vacation pleasant."]

II. THE PARTICIPIAL PHRASE

The **participle** is identical in form with the four gerund forms; in addition there are the past participle (*studied*) and a progressive form (*having been studying*). The difference between the participle and the gerund is one of use: Whereas the gerund is always used as a noun (subject, direct object, renaming subjective complement, object of preposition), the participle is used as an adjectival modifier.

The *injured* bird clung to the *swaying* branch. [The past participle *injured* modifies the noun *bird;* the present participle *swaying* modifies the noun *branch.*]

The participial phrase, consisting of the participle plus its modifiers and/or complements, can be used at the beginning of the sentence, at the end of the sentence, or within the sentence immediately following the noun or pronoun it modifies.

Having once been a football coach, Bill could explain the play to us. [The phrase modifies *Bill. Coach* is the subjective complement of the participle *having been.* Compare "Bill had once been a football coach."]

We left at intermission, *having found the play exceedingly dull.* [The phrase modifies *We. Play* is the direct object and *dull* the objective complement of the participle *having found.* Compare "We had found the play exceedingly dull."]

The police removed the man *creating the disturbance,* and the lecture was resumed. [The phrase modifies *man. Disturbance* is the direct object of the participle *creating.* Compare "The man created the disturbance."]

The **absolute phrase** is a special kind of participial phrase, different from the standard participial phrase in both form and function. Within the absolute phrase the participle follows a noun or pronoun that is part of the phrase. The phrase adds to the meaning of the whole sentence, but it does not directly modify any noun or pronoun in the sentence. The absolute phrase is a versatile structure capable of many variations and widely used in modern prose writing to point out subtle relationships underlying ideas within a sentence.

> *The rain having started,* we abandoned our tents.
> The police recovered eight of the paintings, *three of them badly damaged.*

III. THE INFINITIVE PHRASE

An **infinitive** is a verbal consisting of the simple stem of the verb, generally preceded by *to,* called the sign of the infinitive. The infinitive can use auxiliaries to show tense and voice: *to study, to have studied, to be studying, to have been studying, to be studied, to have been studied.*

An infinitive phrase consists of an infinitive plus its modifiers and/or complements. Infinitive units are used as nouns, as adjectives, and as adverbs.

> *To leave the party early* will be impossible. [The infinitive phrase is used as the subject. *Party* is the direct object of the infinitive.]
> It will be impossible *to leave the party early.* [In this very common pattern the infinitive is called the delayed subject; hence it is used as a noun. The signal word for this construction is *it;* although it precedes the verb, the true subject is the infinitive. Compare the similar noun clause use.]
> I wanted *to give Chalmers another chance.* [The infinitive phrase is the direct object of *wanted.* Within the phrase *Chalmers* is the indirect object and *chance* the direct object of the infinitive. Compare "I gave Chalmers another chance."]
> My plan is *to become an active precinct worker.* [The infinitive phrase is used as a noun, since it is a subjective complement that renames the subject *plan.* Within the phrase *worker* is the subjective complement of the infinitive. Compare "I became an active precinct worker."]
> The test *to be taken tomorrow* is not difficult. [The infinitive is used as an adjective modifying *test.*]
> I am happy *to make your acquaintance.* [The infinitive phrase is used as an adverb modifying the adjective *happy.*]
> *To be sure of a good seat,* you should arrive early. [The infinitive phrase is used as an adverb modifying *should arrive.*]

Infinitive phrases sometimes include their own subjects. Notice that a pronoun used as the subject of an infinitive is in the objective case:

> We wanted *her to resign.*
> We know *him to be a good referee.*

The infinitive without the *to* may form a phrase that is used as the direct object of such verbs as *let, help, make, see, hear,* and *watch.*

> The teacher let *us leave early.*
> I helped *my neighbor paint the fence.*

The infinitive without *to* is also sometimes used as the object of a preposition such as *except, but,* or *besides.*

> He could do nothing except *resign gracefully.*

PART V

Essay Tests, Paragraphs, Essays, and Research Papers

TAKING ESSAY TESTS

There are a number of reasons why people write—to order milk, to register a complaint, to say "I love you because . . . ." All of these reasons are important, and all require a certain style and clarity of expression, but all are a little outside the scope of your immediate, ultimately practical needs at this moment. You are, after all, a student, and you have certain writing problems forced upon you by the nature and progress of your education. In many courses essay tests, reports, compositions, and long papers based on research and study are regularly required, so regularly that a good part of academic survival depends on knowing how to manage these writing assignments successfully.

To help you learn to handle required writing—essay tests, essays, and longer papers and reports—the following sections deal with each of these assignments, providing step-by-step instructions for performing them. We start with essay tests because they tend to be the shortest and, because of time constraints, the most closely organized form of writing you will be called on to produce. In later sections we shall deal with expository essays and longer papers.

There are two reasons for starting with essay-test responses. The first reason, suggested above, is that writing an answer to a specific question forces you to focus attention on a single topic and to marshal your materials in a well-organized, concise statement that includes, despite its limited length, all the important information relating to the question. Second, many essay-test questions can best be answered in a well-developed paragraph. The paragraph, the next unit of composition larger than the sentence, will be an integral part of everything that you write. Writing paragraphs provides excellent practice in organization and expression and is the next logical step in your study of composition.

SOME SUGGESTIONS FOR PREPARATION

It ought to go without saying that the most important step in preparing for an essay test is to *study the material*. As a general rule studying requires that you attend class, read assignments, and take notes on lectures, discussions, and outside assignments. An occasional review of these notes is an excellent way to keep the materials fresh in your mind.

As you read assignments in the text and in outside readings, you will find it useful to prepare a brief outline of each chapter. In this outline list the main ideas and the supporting points and illustrations for each section. Note useful bits of information (dates, names, facts, anecdotes, illustrations, definitions, equations, quotations, and so on) that are used to develop these supporting points. This information may serve as ammunition in writing answers to questions on the material.

With some students the accepted way to study is to do minimum levels of work during the term and then cram massive amounts of studying into the last few days. Since this cramming requires that you ingest large and potentially harmful doses of coffee, amphetamines, and other stimulants, and since material learned quickly is forgotten quickly, a system of regular, manageable doses of work has much to recommend it.

FINAL PREPARATION

You should begin your final preparation a few days before the test to give yourself ample time to organize and synthesize the materials. Your preparations might include the following steps:

Step 1. Make an overview or survey of the materials you have covered for the test. Look for periods, trends, theories, and general conclusions. Try to pinpoint important concepts and basic ideas in the materials.

Step 2. Write a series of questions encompassing the major items you have located. Cover broad areas of material. Try to concentrate on questions that begin with words such as *trace, outline,* and *discuss.* In five or six broad-scope questions of your own, try to cover all the possible questions that the teacher may ask. If you have covered all the material in your own questions, you will not be surprised by any questions on the exam.

Step 3. Read your outline, notes, and other materials, looking for answers to the questions you have composed. As you read and review, make lists or outlines of the answers that you can commit to memory and use as guides during the test. Practice writing out answers that are difficult for you.

Step 4. Review the outlines and materials and the answers to your questions the afternoon before the test. Then put the whole thing aside and get a good night's rest.

QUESTIONS AND RESPONSES

Train yourself to do two things when you are given the test:
First:
    Read the whole test all the way to the end.
    Determine the point value of each question.
    Determine which questions you know the most about.

In a typical essay test of five or six questions, different point values may be assigned to different questions. On a six-question test of 100 points it is not uncommon to find four questions worth twenty points each and two questions worth ten points each. It's clear that answering two ten-point questions perfectly is not worth as much as answering two twenty-pointers perfectly. Handle the important questions first. In a typical essay test of five or six questions, it's also not uncommon for the teacher to give certain options: Answer any two of questions 1–3 and two from 4–6. When such options are presented, be very sure that you understand what your choices are. When the options allow you to eliminate questions, be sure to answer the questions about which you know most. This advice sounds like a very elementary consideration, but many students begin to answer questions without any preparation and assessment. You can hurt your performance if you begin to write before weighing the questions and your knowledge.
Second:
    Make careful preparation before you write.

When you have decided which questions to answer, follow these simple preparatory steps to organize yourself and your material before answering each question:

Step 1. Collect what you know about the question. Recall your outlines and notes. Bring to mind the practice answers you wrote in the review exercises. Make notes on these on a sheet of paper. Try to remember as much material as you can.

Step 2. Decide exactly what the question asks for and what overall statement you are able to make *and* support in response to the question. Before you write, construct a definite statement, an idea or concept you intend to develop in writing your answer. This point, or main idea, will come out of the materials you reviewed in Step 1.

Step 3. Carefully select supporting materials, examples, explanations, and other data that will serve to establish and clarify the main idea. You may have pulled together a considerable amount of information in your quick mental review. Not all of this material will fit exactly the statement you are making; not all of it will be especially effective in your answer. Select materials that will establish and reinforce your point as effectively as possible within the constraints of time and space that bear on you.

(These three steps, expanded a bit, will also be useful in writing longer papers.)

Now that you have looked at the basic steps in writing essay-test answers, or any paragraph, for that matter, let us examine each of these steps in greater detail. Assume that you have read the test carefully, selected your questions, and are now ready to start on the questions you'll answer first.

Note that you don't always answer question #1 first; you should work first on the question you can answer best. Taking your best shot first will give you the best point accumulation and will loosen you up for the other questions.

Step 1 says that you should recollect all that you know about the question. Go back over your notes mentally. Jot down key words, phrases, and ideas on scratch paper. Collect all you know about the subject area and list it as it comes to mind. Don't try to be selective or discriminating at this stage. The basic need is for a large collection of data from which to select information and illustrations for your answer. It is important to jot down whatever comes to mind because even an insignificant item can trigger a memory of something important.

Let us set up a brief example and follow it through these three steps. Suppose that you pick up a test and find on it a problem such as this:

> Discuss the character and personality of F. Scott Fitzgerald's Jay Gatsby in *The Great Gatsby*.

You have read the book, done the work, and completed the review. Now jot down some information on Gatsby.

> Gatsby lived in the Twenties. Lived in West Egg. Very rich, well-established families lived in East Egg. Everyone lived lavishly. Played polo. Gave parties. Employed maids, butlers, chauffeurs. Gatsby lived as high as others, but was not from a "proper" family. People wondered who Gatsby was, where he got his money, what, if anything, he did for a living. He was darkly handsome. Rich. Owned an enormous, wonderfully elegant house. Drove beautiful cars. Loved Daisy for years, though she married Tom. Gave lavish parties. Seldom attended parties. Had friends among shady or criminal elements. Protected Daisy when she hit a woman with car. Was very awkward, almost shy, when meeting Daisy again after some years.

There is much more in the way of details and information that could be drawn together, but this list is long enough to serve as an example. Let's move to Step 2.

In Step 2 there are two things to accomplish. First, you must determine *what* the question asks. Second, you must establish what you can say in *direct* response to it.

The first problem involves your ability as a reader. Read the question and pick up its instruction words. You know the general subject area; now you need to find out what you must do or say about that subject area.

In the example mentioned for Step 1, Jay Gatsby is the subject; more specifically, the subject is the character and personality of Jay Gatsby. Your instruction is to discuss that subject area.

Here is a list of common instruction words and what they are probably asking you to do:

1. List, name, identify.

These words require short-answer responses that can be written in one or two complete sentences. Do exactly what the question asks; don't try to expand the scope of the question.

> **EXAMPLE:** Name the presidents who served in the military prior to becoming president.

The word *identify* suggests that you ought to mention the two or three most important facts about a person or subject area, not any facts that come to mind. You would thus identify Eisenhower as a military commander and U.S. President, not as a West Point graduate who played golf.

2. Summarize, trace, delineate.

An instruction to summarize asks that you give an overview, or a capsule version of the subject.

> **EXAMPLE:** Summarize Senator Smith's position on amnesty.

An answer to this question would provide a three- or four-sentence statement of the main points of Smith's position. The words *trace* and *delineate* usually ask that you describe the steps or process that brought some event to pass.

> **EXAMPLE:** Trace the steps that led to President Nixon's resignation.

The response here would require that you mention and describe the five or six major events or decisions that led to Mr. Nixon's act.

3. Define.

The instruction *define* usually asks that you establish the term within a class and then differentiate it from the other members of the class. "A parrot is a bird" establishes the word *parrot* in a class, and "found in the tropics and capable of reproducing human speech" is an attempt at differentiation. You should be careful to add enough elements of differentiation to eliminate other members of the class. For instance, since the myna is also a tropical bird capable of reproducing speech, you must complete your definition of *parrot* by specifying such items as size, color, and habitat.

4. Analyze, classify, outline.

These command words imply a discussion of the relationships that exist between a whole and its parts. *Analyze* asks that you break an idea, a concept, a class down to its integral parts.

> **EXAMPLE:** Analyze the various political persuasions that exist within the Republican party.

This question asks that you look at the party and identify the various categories of political belief ranging from right to left. *Classify* asks that you position parts in relation to a whole.

> **EXAMPLE:** Classify the following parts of an automobile as to location in engine, steering, or drive shaft:
> 1. Ball joint.
> 2. Piston ring.
> 3. Pinion gear.

Outline requires that you break an idea or concept into its parts and show how the parts support and reinforce each other. Whether you arrange your sentences in the form of a whole paragraph or in a listing of main headings and subheadings, your outline must show how the idea or concept is made up of smaller parts and how these parts relate to the idea and to each other.

> **EXAMPLE:** Outline Senator Smith's position on amnesty for draft evaders.

This problem requires that you state the position and its supporting points.

5. Discuss, explain, illustrate.

This type of command word is probably the most general of all the possible directions for essay tests. The request here is that you expose, in detail, the idea, concept, or process in question. Single simple sentences will not suffice to answer such instructions. You must provide all pertinent information and write enough so that your reader has no questions, no gaps left in his information, when he has finished reading. Often such questions can be answered by making a statement of the idea or process and providing examples to illustrate your statements. In fact, if the instruction is "illustrate," examples are required.

> **EXAMPLE:** Discuss the effects of depriving a child of physical affection in the first three years of its life.

The answer could be given by making a statement or statements of the effects and giving examples of each.

6. Compare, contrast.

A question may ask you to compare, to contrast, or to do both. Technically, comparison is a listing of like qualities, contrast a listing of unlike qualities. To develop a comparison/contrast, establish categories and show how the subjects are alike or not alike in each category.

> **EXAMPLE:** Compare the military abilities of Grant and Sherman.
> Contrast the military abilities of Grant and Sherman.

> Compare *and* contrast the military abilities of Grant and Sherman.

In terms of strategy Grant may have been equal to Sherman. In terms of ability to motivate men Grant may have been superior. The questions ask for a discussion of similarities and differences in these abilities.

7. Evaluate, criticize.

This type of question is probably the most difficult to answer because it requires that you know what is correct or best or ideal and that you assess the assigned topic against that ideal. So you must know the subject *and* the ideal equally well.

> **EXAMPLE:** Evaluate Eisenhower as a leader in foreign affairs.

The question is, then, "What are the characteristics of a leader in foreign affairs and how does Eisenhower measure up in each of these categories?"

Read a test question very carefully to determine what the teacher is asking. In order to make this determination, you must break the question into two parts: the instructions and the subject area.

Essay questions may be posed in many ways; they may have long introductions or fuzzy statements or confusing requests. But when you get the question clear in your mind, you will find two basic elements: (1) the instructions (*List, Name, Discuss, Evaluate,* and so on), and (2) the subject (*The qualities of Fitzgerald's prose, The reasons the Democrats won the election,* and so on).

Look at these parts long and hard (two full minutes if you have twenty minutes for the question). Be sure that you understand each part. You won't get much credit for *evaluation* when the instruction word is *name*. You won't get anything if the test item asks for the character and personality of Jay Gatsby and you respond with the qualities of U.S. culture in 1920. *Answer the question on the test, not the question you wish were on the test.*

A WORD ON DEADWOOD

One of the grand old skills students tend to develop is the ability to say nothing in a couple of pages. You ought to avoid this sort of production, because it is too easily discounted by most teachers. Half a page of direct, concise, well-organized answers will always produce better grades than two pages of baloney.

So far, then, you have done the following:

1. Collected in your memory and then put down on a small sheet of scratch paper a set of facts and ideas about the general subject area. (When you first read a question, you do this subconsciously anyway. We're just suggesting that you formalize the procedure.)

2. Determined both the subject and the instructions of the question.

The example question asks:

Instructions	*Subject*
Discuss	Gatsby's character and personality

The instructions are clear. The subject is fairly specific. You have a collection of general data that turns out to mention Gatsby and the Twenties. The next move (the second part of Step 2) is to decide exactly what you can say on this subject.

Examine your materials. Run through your notes mentally. Make one more quick search through your memory. Now decide on the best statement to make.

Look at the example question and the collection of facts and ideas. Three groups of material emerge when you examine the information closely (page 135):

1. Facts or impressions of the era.
2. Gatsby's unknown family, unknown source of money, status as *nouveau riche*.
3. Gatsby's enduring, devoted love for Daisy.

Of these three groups, the first is not important except as background, but the second and third bring out important ideas about Gatsby's personality.

1. He was *nouveau riche,* possibly made his money illegally, lived extravagantly.
2. He loved Daisy wildly for many years. Although she married Tom, Gatsby continued to pursue her.

Two specific statements or ideas that seem to illustrate Gatsby's personality have emerged. All that remains is to combine the two into one statement that captures both ideas. In this example, the overall statement might read like this:

Gatsby, a newly rich man who lived extravagantly, loved Daisy and tried to win her back from her husband, Tom.

Let us review the process one more time.

1. Read the question and begin to jot down information about the general subject.

2. Ascertain precisely what the question asks and what the specific subject is.

3. Review the collected materials and whatever else comes to mind and form a statement in response to the question.

Having now formulated your basic statement in response, you can move to Step 3, which will suggest ways to make the response. Follow this procedure for Step 3.

1. Read your basic statement.

2. Examine your collection of materials for illustrations and examples that support the statement.

Then write the answer to the question.

Let's look again at the sample test item:

> Discuss the character and personality of Jay Gatsby.

and the basic response:

> Gatsby, a newly rich man who lived extravagantly, loved Daisy and tried to win her back from her husband, Tom.

Now select from the materials you collected a few pertinent points to support the elements of the statement. What materials support the assertion that he was newly rich and extravagant?

The notes on the Twenties are not too useful, but his wild parties, his cars, and his enormous, opulent mansion illustrate his wealth and extravagance. Doubts about family and source of wealth, plus occasional references to underworld characters, will serve to illustrate his *nouveau riche* status.

His love for Daisy can be illustrated by his search for her, the parties he gave to attract her, his attempts to get her to leave Tom, and his following of her life for many years through newspaper stories. (Note that this last item is not in the original list. As you work, you will think of new materials.)

Take these materials, then, and use them to write your essay response. Do not include any comments or illustrations that are off the subject—the statement—you have established. Offer sufficient development and illustration, but do not pad your answer with extraneous material.

Writing the Answer

You now have before you, on a piece of scratch paper:
1. A basic idea.
2. Supporting data for materials.

These are for use in writing your answer. You have developed *content*. Now you need to concentrate on the form of the answer. Obviously, your answer ought to be written in grammatically correct complete sentences. Beyond that, the best answers come in well-developed paragraphs.

The Paragraph. In its form, a paragraph may be described as a single sentence or a group of related sentences that begins on a new line and usually has the last line unfilled. The first sentence of the paragraph may be indented, or it may begin flush left, block style, with extra space between the paragraphs, as in many business letters. In its function, a paragraph is defined as the expression of a single idea that is stated in a topic sentence and developed by a pattern of sentences that supply appropriate supporting data. Let us examine the topic sentence and consider some orders of paragraph development.

The Topic Sentence. A good paragraph is an expression of a complete idea, and that idea is probably best expressed in a complete sentence placed first or second in the paragraph. Two good things happen when you put your basic idea at the beginning of the paragraph:
1. You tell the reader what the paragraph is going to say.
2. You establish a control for development, assuring that you will not depart from the basic idea of the paragraph.

In the sample essay-test answer developed above, a topic sentence that restates the basic statement to show the writer's intended interpretation might read like this:

> Jay Gatsby, Fitzgerald's hero, let his love for Daisy drive him to acquire wealth by questionable means and pursue her to all imaginable lengths.

The rest of the paragraph might be developed as follows:

> Gatsby allied himself with shady characters and became magnificently wealthy. He used this wealth to buy a wonderfully elegant house, beautiful cars, and all sorts of luxuries. He often gave lavish parties, apparently wishing to attract Daisy to them so that he could win her love. His love had maintained itself for years, and he followed her life through newspaper clippings. He loved her so

much that he protected her when she ran down and killed a woman with his car. His great love led him to a tragic death at the hands of the woman's husband.

PATTERNS FOR PARAGRAPHS

The instructions in the essay-test questions discussed in the previous section suggest specific patterns for the presentation of the supporting materials in the answers. In planning a paragraph in response to a test problem using the command word *trace,* for instance, you would logically arrange the details in some kind of time order or space order. Every directive word you have studied implies some pattern of orderly development of the answer, and these patterns correspond to methods of organization for the paragraphs of longer essays. You will find it useful to familiarize yourself with some of these methods of presentation.

COMPARISON / CONTRAST

When you are asked to compare, to contrast, or to compare and contrast two or more people, ideas, attitudes, or objects, you are being asked to examine items that fall within the same general group or class and, after this examination, to point out ways in which the items are similar and dissimilar. Common test questions read like these:

> Compare the attitudes of General Patton and Bertrand Russell toward war and the maintenance of a standing army.
> Compare the effects of heroin and marijuana on the human body.
> Compare orange juice and lemon juice in respect to taste, Vitamin C content, and usefulness in cooking.

Note that in each question there is a large class that includes the subjects of the comparison:

> Patton and Russell were both famous people who held carefully developed attitudes toward war. [If one had no attitude on war, the comparison couldn't be made.]
> Heroin and marijuana are both drugs, both acting on the human body.
> Orange juice and lemon juice are citrus products.

The point of comparison/contrast is that the items share certain qualities but can be separated or distinguished by other qualities that they do not share. The identification of these like and unlike qualities is the aim of comparison/contrast.

In an article on the relative merits of sports cars and sports sedans, an auto magazine studied two small, low-priced cars, the Chevrolet Vega and the Triumph Spitfire, in an effort to help potential buyers choose between them. Obviously, because they are *cars,* both vehicles fall within the same large class. But they are alike, and not alike, in certain ways that are important. These similarities and differences constitute comparison/contrast.

The writing of a comparison/contrast permits two different orders of development. The first order is useful when only a few characteristics are discussed; the second presents a clearer picture when numerous items are important.

PATTERN 1: List in order all the qualities of the Vega and then, in the same order, all the qualities of the Spitfire. This method forces the reader to make his own judgments on the items listed.

VEGA

Engine type	In-line 4 cylinder
Transmission type	4-speed manual
Brakes	Disc/drum
Price	$3,818
Length	175.4"
Weight	2,880 lbs.
Horsepower	85
Body type	Sedan

SPITFIRE

Engine type	In-line 4 cylinder
Transmission type	4-speed manual
Brakes	Disc/drum
Price	$3,985
Length	155.2"
Weight	2,105 lbs.
Horsepower	57
Body type	Roadster

A properly constructed comparison/contrast paragraph based on this pattern would simply record the facts *in the order listed* in complete sentences. No other observations would be necessary. The reader would be left to draw his own conclusions about the data supplied.

PATTERN 2: List the areas for both cars—engine type, transmission, and so on—that are alike, then those that are not alike, discussing both cars in relation to each item. This order provides a focused comparison and helps the reader to draw conclusions concerning the data presented.

LIKE QUALITIES

Engine type	In-line 4 cylinder
Transmission type	4-speed manual
Brakes	Disc/drum
Price	$3,800+

UNLIKE QUALITIES

Length	175.4″ to 155.2″
Weight	2,880 lbs. to 2,105 lbs.
Horsepower	85 to 57
Body type	Sedan—Roadster

Here is a possible version of such a paragraph:

Two small cars, the Triumph Spitfire and the Chevy Vega, both falling into the $3,800+ price range, compare in several features. They use the same type of engine, an in-line 4 cylinder, and the same type of transmission, 4-speed manual. The brakes on both cars are the increasingly popular disc/drum arrangement that has proved its capabilities on many cars. But they differ in size; the Vega is 175.4 inches long, the Spitfire 155.2. The Spitfire is lighter, 2,105 compared to 2,880 pounds. The Spitfire has much the smaller engine, developing 57 horsepower to the Vega's 85. But the body type is the most important point of contrast; the Spitfire is an open car, a roadster, what Europeans call a Spider. The Vega is an enclosed sedan with a hard top and windows that close all around. And it is this final difference that is the point of choice for most drivers. Those who prefer enclosed comfort will choose the Vega, but those who want to feel the wind in their faces will choose the Spitfire.

DEFINITION

We have all read definitions; they are the subject matter of dictionaries, which we are accustomed to using to find the meaning of an unfamiliar word. But definition, as a process, is also a useful device in writing; it can serve to establish meaning for words, concepts, and attitudes. You have often written paragraphs of definition on tests and in essays. On tests, you might find instructions such as these:

> Define *sonata-allegro form* and give examples of it in twentieth-century music.
>
> Define *conservatism* as it is used in American politics.
>
> Define a *boom-vang* and say how it is used in sailing.

The correct responses to such instructions are paragraphs of definition. Such paragraphs ought to follow the same rules of presentation and development that the dictionary does. Let us examine two dictionary-type definitions and discover the pattern used in forming them.

> Basketball is a game played by two five-player teams on a rectangular court having a raised basket at each end. Points are scored by tossing a large round ball through the opponent's basket.
>
> Football is a game played with an oval-shaped ball by two eleven-player teams defending goals at opposite ends of a rectangular field. Points are scored by carrying or throwing the ball across the opponent's goal or by kicking the ball over the crossbar of the opponent's goal post.

These two definitions concern games familiar to most of us. Notice that they both follow the same pattern.

First, they identify both words as games. Second, they specify:

1. The number of teams.
2. The number of players on each team.
3. The type of playing area.
4. The way in which scoring occurs.
5. The shape of the ball.

The examples illustrate the classic pattern of definition: The first step is to classify the word within a class or group; the second step is to differentiate the word from other members of its class.

> Football is a game . . . . Establishes in a class.
> played by two teams
> of 11 players each
> on a rectangular field.   Differentiates from
> Scoring occurs by crossing   other games.
>   opponent's goal in a special way.

When you write a paragraph of definition, follow the same method: Classify the term, then distinguish it from other members of its class.

However, your paragraph of definition ought to offer more than just the basic points of differentiation. You should also provide illustrations, examples, and comparisons of the term being defined to terms that might be familiar to your reader. This additional information helps your reader understand and assimilate the information you are offering. The process is often called extending the definition. Examine the following paragraph defining football and note how basic definition and extension are combined to make an effective presentation.

> On any Saturday or Sunday afternoon in the fall of the year, hundreds of thousands of Americans betake themselves to stadiums, and millions more hunker down before television sets to witness the great American spectator sport, football. In simplest form, a definition of football states that it is a game played on a large field by two teams of eleven players and that scoring is accomplished by carrying or throwing an oval ball across the opponent's goal line or by kicking the ball between two uprights called goal posts. But such literal definition scarcely does justice to the game or to its impact on Americans. For it is more than a game or a sport; it is a happening, a spectacle, a ritual that is almost a religious experience for its devotees. The game catches them with its color: a beautiful green field surrounded by crowds dressed in a galaxy of hues, teams uniformed in the brightest shades ever to flow from the brush of deranged artists. It holds these fans with its excitement: the long pass, the touchdown run, the closing-minutes drive to victory. But above all the game seems to captivate them with its violence, with dangers vicariously experienced, with a slightly veiled aura of mayhem. This element of danger draws casual viewers and converts them into fanatic worshippers of the great American cult-sport, football.

Finally, a word of warning about constructing definitions: A fundamental rule is that a definition must not be circular. A useful definition does not define a term by using a related form of the term itself. To define the word *analgesic* by saying that it causes analgesia means nothing unless the reader knows that *analgesia* means absence or removal of pain. To define *conservatism* as a philosophy that attempts to conserve old values doesn't really add much to a reader's understanding. So then the rule:

Do not construct circular definitions; that is, do not use in the definition a form of the word being defined.

ANALYSIS

Chemists analyze compounds to isolate and identify their components. Economists analyze the financial data of the nation to determine the factors contributing to recessions. Sports commentators analyze games to explain the strengths leading to a victory.

Analysis is the act of breaking down a substance or entity into its component parts. It is possible to analyze a football team and point out the various positions: ends, tackles, guards, and the rest. An army can be broken down into infantry, artillery, and engineers. A piano is made up of parts: keys, strings, sounding board, and so on.

A paragraph of analysis provides information derived from this act of breaking down into parts, usually by listing, defining, and explaining the parts of the whole in question. As an example, take the elements or characteristics that make up that rarest of animals, the good driver.

> The good driver possesses
>   1. Technical competence.
>   2. Physical skills.
>   3. Sound judgment.
>   4. Emotional stability.

A paragraph analyzing the qualities of a good driver might read like this:

> Every American over fourteen years of age wants to drive, does drive, or just stopped driving because his or her license was revoked. Not every American, in fact only a very few Americans, can be counted in the ranks of good drivers. Good drivers must possess technical competence in the art of driving. They must know the simple steps, starting, shifting, and braking, and the highly sophisticated techniques, feathering the brakes and the power slide, for example. In addition they must possess physical skills, such as exceptional eye-hand coordination, fast reflexes, outstanding depth perception, and peripheral vision. They must also possess good judgment. What speed is safe on a rain-slick highway? How far can a person drive without succumbing to fatigue? What are the possible mistakes that the approaching driver can make? And besides the answers to these questions and the technical and physical skills listed above, good drivers must possess steel nerves to cope with that potentially lethal emergency that one day will come to everyone who slips behind the wheel of a car. Only with these qualities can a

person be called a good driver and be relatively sure of returning home in one piece.

A suggestion about analysis: When you divide or break down an entity into its elements, be sure that you establish parallel categories. It is not proper in analyzing a car in terms of its major systems to list

1. Frame.
2. Body.
3. Drive train.
4. Engine.
5. Piston ring.

Although the first four items could possibly be called major systems in an automobile, piston rings are a small part of a large system, the engine, and cannot be included in a list of major systems.

The rule for analysis is
Keep categories parallel.

PROCESS ANALYSIS

A process paragraph is a form of analysis that studies the steps involved in an action or sequence of actions. The most common sort of process analysis is the recipe: To make a rabbit stew, first catch a rabbit, and so forth. Instructions for building stereo receivers or flying kites or cleaning ovens are all process analyses. In addition to instructions, process analysis can be used to trace the steps involved in a historical event. Such analysis would be required to answer an essay-test question that begins with the words *trace* or *delineate.*

The following example, giving instructions in building a child's sandbox such as you might construct for a younger brother or sister, illustrates a process paragraph.

A sandbox is an ideal place for a three-year-old to while away an afternoon. A few hours spent constructing one will be an investment that will return hours of peace and quiet to anyone saddled with a youngster. The first step is site-selection. Choose a spot in semishade (you don't want the little darling to get sunstroke) at some distance from the house. Be sure that the spot is level and free of stones, so that Johnny (or Sue) doesn't scrape a finger while digging. Remove all the grass and roots from an area 6' x 8' to make the place flat and smooth. Next, nail together four 1" x 8" boards of proper length (pressure-treated for termites) to form a rectangle. Care must be taken to brace the box firmly at each corner, either with a 2 x 2 nailed on the inside of the corner, or with metal angle braces, or, perhaps better, with both. This bracing is necessary to prevent collapse when the whole neighborhood tightropes around the edges of the box. Next, wheel in white builder's sand to a depth of six inches at the edges and a foot in the center. Finally, turn the kids loose, open a cold one, and sit back to enjoy a well-earned rest.

Causal Analysis

Causal analysis, as the name implies, is a discussion of the causes leading to a given outcome. On an essay test, you might be asked to explain or discuss the reasons for a lost war, a victory in an election, a depression, or the collapse of a bridge. In your life outside school, you might be called on to explain why you have selected some occupation or particular college or why you wish to drop out of school to hike the Appalachian Trail for four or five months.

Causal analysis differs from process analysis in that it does not necessarily involve a chronological sequence. Instead, it seeks the reasons for an outcome and lists them (with necessary discussion) in either ascending or descending order of importance. A certain man once gave this explanation for buying a new car.

> First, you see, my car is two-and-a-half years old, and it's beginning to get some mileage on it. And you know how the car dealers are if you try to trade a high-mileage car; they cut the trade-in allowance way down. Then, too, I've been hearing some strange clanks and rattles from the back of the car and I'm afraid the rear-end might be burning out. Also, I've been thinking that a switch to a nice compact car might save me some money on gas. But if you want to know the real truth, I'm simply tired of the old bus, and that beautiful blue hardtop with the white upholstery and the stereo tape-deck makes my mouth water, and I've just got to have it.

Use of Examples

One of the simplest yet most effective paragraphs states an idea and uses examples to illustrate and explain the idea. It is also useful to insert examples into paragraphs that follow other patterns. The following paragraph explains an idea by using examples.

Youth and beauty are wonderful attributes, and in combination are a wonderful possession. But television commercials and programs extol youth and beauty to such an extreme that those not so young and less than beautiful are made to feel inferior. Cars, beer, clothes, and even lawn mowers are almost always pictured with lithe, beautiful women of tender age or well-muscled young men with luxuriant well-groomed hair. Cosmetics are always portrayed in use by people who have almost no need of them. Beauty, and especially youthful beauty, sells goods, we surmise, and those who do not become young and beautiful after buying the car or ingesting the iron supplement are obviously unfit to share the planet with the favored ones. And the programs themselves emphasize youthful beauty. There are few homely, few truly decrepit people who play regularly in any series. Any family, and any individual, who cannot compare to these perfect people ought to exile themselves from the land of the lovely. We are left to believe that only the beautiful young are acceptable.

DESCRIPTION AND NARRATION

Two important orders of development remain: development by space and development by time, more commonly called description and narration. Each of these patterns involves a direction or a movement. Description requires that you move your writer's eye through a given space, picking out selected details in order to create an effect. Narration demands that you create a progression through time, providing details selected to convey a story and its impact. The success of each pattern depends on the careful selection of details of physical qualities or of action and on the vivid presentation of these details.

Mark Twain wrote a beautiful description of a sunrise on the Mississippi in *Huckleberry Finn:*

> we run nights, and laid up and hid day-times; soon as night was most gone, we stopped navigating and tied up—nearly always in the dead water under a tow-head; and then cut young cotton-woods and willows and hid the raft with them. Then we set out the lines. Next we slid into the river and had a swim, so as to freshen up and cool off; then we set down on the sandy bottom where the water was about knee deep, and watched the daylight come. Not a sound, anywheres—perfectly still—just like the whole world was asleep, only sometimes the bull-frogs a-cluttering, maybe. The first thing to see, looking away over the water, was a kind of dull line—that

was the woods on t'other side—you couldn't make nothing else out; then a pale place in the sky; then more paleness, spreading around; then the river softened up, away off, and warn't black any more, but gray; you could see little dark spots drifting along, ever so far away—trading scows, and such things; and long black streaks—rafts; sometimes you could hear a sweep screaking; or jumbled up voices, it was so still, and sound come so far; and by-and-by you could see a streak on the water which you know by the look of the streak that there's a snag there in a swift current which breaks on it and makes that streak look that way; and you see the mist curl up off the water, and the east reddens up, and the river, and you make out a log cabin in the edge of the woods, away on the bank on t'other side of the river, being a wood-yard, likely and piled by them cheats so you can throw a dog through it anywheres; then the nice breeze springs up, and comes fanning you from over there, so cool and fresh, and sweet to smell, on account of the woods and the flowers; but sometime not that way, because they've left dead fish laying around, gars, and such, and they do get pretty rank; and next you've got the full day, and everything smiling in the sun, and the song-birds just going it!

Two qualities of this description are important to your writing. Note first the direction or movement of the unfolding picture. Beginning with the dim view of the far bank, the narrator observes traces of paleness in the sky. He then notes that the river has softened up "away off"; notice the logical progression from sky to horizon to river. After he gives details of the changing sights and sounds at river level, the mist curling up from the river focuses his attention again on the sky as the "east reddens up." Then he returns to the river and develops the picture as new details become visible in the light of morning. This movement from mid-picture to background to foreground to background to foreground follows a sensory logic, an order of increasing visibility as the sun rises and light increases. It is important to select an order of presentation (or, as here, a logic) and stick with the order whether it be left-to-right, right-to-left, middle-to-left-to-right, or any other easily followed combination.

Second, Twain provides details that appeal to the senses:

Color: Dull line of woods.
Pale sky.
River changing from black to gray.
Dark spots and black streaks.
East reddening.

    Sound: Complete absence of sound.
            Bullfrogs a-cluttering.
            Sweep screaking.
            Jumbled up voices.
            Song birds.
    Smell: Woods.
            Flowers.
            Dead fish.
    Motion: Dark spots drifting.
            Snag in swift current.
            Mist curling up off the water.
    Touch: Cooling off in water.
            Sitting on sandy bottom of river.
            Cool breeze springing up.

Supply your reader with sensory appeal. Keep your description lively and colorful.

Twain also provides us with a heart-stopping piece of narration in *Huck Finn,* the killing of the old drunk, Boggs:

> So somebody started on a run. I walked down street a ways, and stopped. In about five or ten minutes, here comes Boggs again—but not on his horse. He was a-reeling across the street towards me, bareheaded, with a friend on both sides of him aholt of his arms and hurrying him along. He was quiet, and looked uneasy; and he warn't hanging back any, but was doing some of the hurrying himself. Somebody sings out—"Boggs!"
>
> I looked over there to see who said it, and it was that Colonel Sherburn. He was standing perfectly still, in the street, and had a pistol raised in his right hand—not aiming it, but holding it out with the barrel tilted up towards the sky. The same second I see a young girl coming on the run, and two men with her. Boggs and the men turned round, to see who called him, and when they see the pistol the men jumped to one side, and the pistol barrel come down slow and steady to a level—both barrels cocked. Boggs throws up both of his hands, and says, "O Lord, don't shoot!" Bang! goes the first shot, and he staggers back clawing at the air—bang goes the second one, and he tumbles backwards onto the ground, heavy and solid, with his arms spread out. That young girl screamed out, and comes rushing, and down she throws herself on her father, crying, and saying, "Oh, he's killed him, he's killed him!" The crowd closed up around them, and shouldered and jammed one another, with their necks stretched, trying to see, and people on the inside trying to shove them back, and shouting, "Back, back! give him air, give him air!"

Colonel Sherburn he tossed his pistol onto the ground, and turned around on his heels and walked off.

Again, two aspects of the narrative are important. The order is simple, straight chronology. But notice the action words. The girl comes on the run, the men jump, Boggs staggers. Few forms of the verb *to be* intrude to slow the action, and no statements of thought or emotion stop the progression. All of the impact and emotion is conveyed through action, and that use of action is the essence of good narrative.

A FINAL NOTE

Good paragraphs are not necessarily restricted to a single pattern of development. Quite often it is useful to combine patterns to produce a desired effect. The following paragraph on spider webs illustrates such a combination of patterns. The predominant device used here is analysis: The larger unit, spider webs, is broken down into three categories. But the writer uses an additional strategy; he clarifies his analysis by comparison/contrast, pointing out like and unlike details of the three kinds of spider webs.

> Three kinds of webs are constructed by web-spinning spiders. The first type is the tangled-web, a shapeless helter-skelter jumble attached to some support such as the corner of a room. These webs are hung in the path of insects and serve to entangle them as they pass. The second type of web is the sheet-web. This web is a flat sheet of silk strung between blades of grass or tree branches. Above this sheet is strung a sort of net, which serves to knock insects into the sheet. When an insect hits the sheet, the spider darts out and pulls it through the webbing, trapping the insect. Finally, and perhaps the most beautiful of the webs, is the orb. The orb web consists of threads that extend from a center like a wheel's spokes and are connected to limbs or grass blades. All the spokes are connected by repeated circles of sticky silk forming a kind of screen. Insects are caught in this screen and trapped by the spider.

FURTHER CONSIDERATIONS
FOR PARAGRAPH WRITING

In addition to understanding and using the patterns of development already discussed, you need to be able to do three things in order to write successful paragraphs:

1. Write a topic sentence that controls its paragraph.

2. Maintain unity of concept within each paragraph.
3. Produce coherence within each paragraph.

TOPIC SENTENCES

Every paragraph ought to contain one sentence that captures the main idea you are trying to convey to a reader. This sentence may occur anywhere in the paragraph—beginning, middle, or end—but, regardless of its position, the sentence ought to state clearly and succinctly the main idea of the paragraph.

> Roasting marshmallows, an art that flourished in earlier generations, is now almost lost among those under twenty-five. However, *you can produce delectable roasted marshmallows if you follow these instructions.* Select a stick that is slender and smooth and impale two marshmallows on the sharpened end. Hold the marshmallows in the flames of the campfire, moving them back and forth so that they do not catch fire. When they have reached a rich golden brown, remove them from the flame and allow them to cool. Slide them off the stick onto your fingers and enjoy the best campfire dessert in the world.

It is theoretically possible to write a paragraph with no stated topic sentence, with the topic sentence implied and supposedly understood by the reader. Although such paragraphs are possible, in actual practice they seldom seem to succeed. The writer risks losing control of a paragraph that has no topic sentence, and the reader has difficulty following the development of such a paragraph.

Thus, there are two good reasons for using a clearly stated topic sentence. First, most writers need to establish a controlling device to keep them from wandering off the subject established for each paragraph. Second, most readers need as much assistance as possible in decoding written material. A topic sentence that clearly expresses the main idea of the paragraph is a great help to any reader.

Notice how the topic sentence (italicized) in the following paragraph controls it and provides clear direction for the reader.

> Of all the inventions of the last one hundred years, *the automobile assembly line has had the most profound effect on American life.* The assembly line provided a method for building and selling automobiles at a price many could afford, thus changing the auto from a

luxury item owned by the wealthy few to an everyday appliance used by almost every adult in America. Universal ownership and the use of the automobile has opened new occupations, new dimensions of mobility, and new areas of recreation to everyone. In addition, the automobile assembly line provided a model for the mass production of television sets, washing machines, bottled drinks, and even sailboats. All these products would have been far too expensive for purchase by the average person without the introduction of assembly-line methods to lower manufacturing costs. With the advent of Henry Ford's system, every American could hope to possess goods once reserved for a select class, and the hope changed his life forever.

The italicized sentence states the topic and the purpose of the paragraph: The paragraph is going to argue that the assembly line, more than any other invention, changed America's way of life. The writer is controlled by this sentence because everything in the paragraph should serve to support this argument. The reader is assisted by the sentence, for he is led to expect examples supporting the position stated in the sentence.

Formulating a topic sentence is relatively easy. Examine the materials you have collected for the paragraph and establish your main idea. (You can review this process in "Taking Essay Tests.") This main idea will probably emerge as a phrase or a clause, or perhaps as only a word or two. Take this first expression of the idea and develop it into a sentence that contains a complete statement of the idea. Use this sentence to open the first draft of the paragraph. Let it control the ideas and the progression of the paragraph as you work to establish unity and coherence.

UNITY

An essential quality that you need to develop in good paragraphs is unity. A very simple rule says everything necessary to make clear the concept of unity in paragraph writing.

Handle only one idea in a paragraph.

Second and subsequent ideas should be handled in separate paragraphs.

The paragraph originated as a punctuation device to separate ideas on paper and to assist readers in keeping ideas separate as they read. Introducing more than one idea in a paragraph violates this basic reason for the existence of the paragraph.

It would seem to be easy to maintain unity in a paragraph, but sometimes ideas can trick you if you don't pay close attention to your topic sentence. A student wrote this paragraph on strawberries some years ago.

> Strawberries are my favorite dessert. Scooped over ice cream or dipped in powdered sugar, they are so good they bring tears to my eyes. My uncle used to grow strawberries on his farm in New Jersey. Once, I spent the whole summer there and my cousins and I went to the carnival . . . .

Things went pretty far afield from strawberries as the paragraph continued, and you can see how one idea, "grew strawberries on his farm," led to a recollection of a delightful summer on that farm and opened the door to a whole new idea and a change in form from discussion to narration. "Strawberries" and "that summer on the farm" are each a legitimate, interesting, and perfectly workable topic for a paragraph. But they are probably not proper for inclusion in the same paragraph. Unity demands that each topic be treated in a separate paragraph. One paragraph handling one idea equals unity.

COHERENCE

Another important quality that you need to develop in your paragraphs is coherence. The word *cohere* means to stick together, to be united. It is a term used in physics to describe the uniting of two or more similar substances within a body by the action of molecular forces. In paragraph writing, the term *coherence* is used to describe a smooth union between sentences within the paragraph. In other words, the sentences in a coherent paragraph follow one another without abrupt changes. A good paragraph reads smoothly, flowing from start to finish without choppiness to distract the reader from the idea being presented.

The first step in establishing coherence occurs when you select a pattern for developing the paragraph. The selection of a pattern is based on the assignment the paragraph is going to fulfill. You learned in the study of essay-test answers that a question asking for discussion requires one sort of development and a question asking for comparison demands another. Review the section on essay tests and the section on paragraph patterns to keep this idea fresh in your mind.

(Note, however, that it is sometimes necessary to include more than one pattern of development in a paragraph. A narration, for example, may demand a passage of description. Don't hesitate to shift methods where a switch is useful. Do so with care, and with the possibility in mind that a new method of development might suggest the need for a new paragraph.)

The pattern you select will help to establish coherence because it produces a flow and movement in the paragraph and because it serves as a frame for providing details of development. Select the pattern according to the demands of the assignment and follow that pattern through the whole paragraph.

The selection of a development pattern is perhaps the most important step in achieving a coherent paragraph. There are, however, various other writing strategies contributing to the same end.

1. Repetition of nouns and use of reference words.

> My father asked me to dig some postholes. After I finished that, he told me the truck needed washing. It is Father's pride and joy, but I'm the one who has to do such jobs.

These three short sentences show a fairly clear pattern of development that in itself establishes coherence. There is the beginning of a story, suggesting that narration will carry the paragraph further. Events occur one after another, setting a pattern of straight chronology. But note how strongly the repeated nouns and reference words knit the sentences together:

My [father] asked [me] [to dig some postholes].
After [I] finished [that], [he] told [me] the [truck] needed [washing].
[It] is [Father's] pride and joy, but [I]'m the one who has to do [such] jobs.

2. Use of temporal words: conjunctions and adverbs.

A series of short, abrupt sentences, although following a rigid chronological pattern, does not read as though it had coherence:

> I drove down to the corner. I stopped for a red light. A car smashed into the back of mine. I got out rubbing my neck. The driver of the other car sat behind the wheel and wept. I realized that the other driver was an elderly, gray-haired man.

The writer, sensing that something is lacking from the paragraph, might revise it like this:

> I drove down to the corner. *While* I was stopped for a red light, a car smashed into the back of mine. *As* I got out rubbing my neck, the driver of the other car sat behind the wheel and wept. Only *then* did I realize that the other driver was an elderly, gray-haired man.

Two features of the revision have improved on the original draft. First and most obvious, the added words *while, as,* and *then* connect sentences by declaring the chronological sequence. Second, *while* and *as* convert short sentences into dependent clauses, thus replacing four choppy sentences with two longer ones and eliminating the jog-trot rhythm that gave the reader hiccups.

3. Use of transitional words and phrases at or near the beginning of sentences.

The coordinating conjunctions*; adverbs like *however, moreover, therefore, consequently, similarly, thus;* and expressions like *on the other hand, in addition, for example* can produce a subtle transitional effect rather like that of reference words. They force the reader to recollect the preceding material, thus making a tie between the thoughts they introduce and what has already been stated. When you read *But* at the beginning of a sentence, the author is declaring to you in loud tones, "You are to interpret the forthcoming statement as being in opposition or in contrast to what you have just read." *Moreover,* in the same place, suggests that what is coming is in addition to the last remark; *consequently* means "as a result of what you have just learned."

The ploy of cementing the parts of a paragraph together by these words and phrases is used by nearly every writer. It is a perfectly good device, but, unfortunately, it is also a seductively easy one. The unwary writer larding sentences with *howevers* and *therefores* in search of elegance and poise can be lured into a tangle of overwritten prose. The woman who states, "My escort drank too much at the reception. Consequently he threw up," may leave

---

* Disregard the myth that there is something wrong with starting a sentence with *and, but, for, or,* and *nor.* Do realize, however, that these words at the opening of a sentence produce a special effect and call attention to themselves and to what follows them. Don't overuse them, and be sure of your purpose when you do launch a statement with one.

the reader wondering whether the nausea stemmed from the liquor or the date.

A Final Word on Paragraphs: Completeness

Good paragraphs possess these characteristics: a strong topic sentence, a consistent pattern of development possibly supported by other patterns in subordinate roles, unity, and coherence. But, in addition, good paragraphs are complete. They finish the job they begin: telling a story, describing a scene, presenting an idea. Completeness requires that the paragraph satisfy the reader that the idea is fully developed. There should be no questions unanswered, no facts undisclosed, no necessary details omitted.

WRITING ESSAYS

At some point in your college career an instructor is going to smile at your class and say, "Write a paper for me—oh, about two pages long—discussing your position on the state of national politics." Or perhaps the assignment will be more formal: "Discuss the special qualities of concrete as a paving material for streets and highways. Length: two pages."

In the previous sections on writing we have discussed a method for approaching and writing essay-test answers. We have also discussed the nature of paragraph writing, particularly in terms of how paragraphs might be useful in writing answers to tests. Now we shall move to the kind of writing required to create a sustained essay.

A paper or report of approximately two pages is going to contain four to eight paragraphs of supporting material plus an introductory paragraph and a concluding paragraph or sentence. To write such a paper successfully, you need to do some planning. This section on how to prepare and write a two-page paper will build on techniques discussed in the previous sections.

The Assignment

The nature of an assignment for a paper can vary, but you will find that writing assignments usually fall into one of three categories.

1. General: Write a two-page paper on something we've covered in this course.

2. Somewhat specific: Write a two-page paper on some aspect of the novel *Huckleberry Finn*.

3. Very directive: Write a two-page paper explaining why Huck Finn's experiences led him to make his final statement: "Aunt Sally's going to adopt me and sivilize me and I can't stand it. I been there before."

The first example, the general assignment, grants considerable latitude in the selection of a subject for your paper. Often this latitude will prove more of a problem than a blessing, because it is necessary to find something to write about that you *and* the teacher consider interesting and worthwhile. It is of little value to write a fine paper and find that the teacher (the grader) thinks the topic is so insignificant that the whole effort can't be worth more than a *C*. The best approach here is to review the textbook, lecture notes, and previous tests (if any), select from these an important content area, concept, or personality, and use that as a starting point for your work. Be sure to choose an area that interests you, an area in which you have some knowledge and some readily accessible sources of information. Once you have made this initial selection, you have converted the type of assignment from "general" to "somewhat specific." Now we can move to the next step in preparing to write a paper.

As a second step you need to restrict the area you selected or were assigned so that you can develop it fully within the assigned length of the paper. Suppose, for example, the assignment names the novel *Huckleberry Finn* as the subject for a two-page paper. Several areas are open to you:

1. Autobiographical aspects of the novel.
2. Problems of plot and structure.
3. Problems of characterization.
4. Philosophical aspects of the novel.

For the selection or restriction process, choose one of the areas and make a final selection of a topic within that area. The final selection should be fairly small in scope, something manageable within two pages. In the example of *Huckleberry Finn,* the process of restriction might look like this:

1. Philosophical aspects of the novel.
2. The relationship between man and society.

3. Huck Finn's attitude toward the world as he saw it.
4. Why Huck's experiences led him to say that he couldn't stand to be "sivilized."

The final version of the topic (number 4) is probably limited enough for it to be treated adequately within the assigned length. The topic asks a single question about one person, and that question, "Why?" can be answered "because his experiences with civilization were unpleasant or terrifying." That statement and the unpleasant or terrifying experiences can be illustrated efficiently by using three or four examples. The statement of this restricted topic results in a "very directive" assignment and provides the basis for organizing and writing a two-page paper.

The process detailed above is designed to help you derive a topic that is manageable within the scope of a given assignment. There are three stages in this selection process.

1. The selection of a general subject area.
2. The selection of a portion or phase of this general area to form a limited subject area.
3. The final selection of a specific limited topic from within the limited subject area.

Note that the way in which your teacher states the assignment dictates the starting point for your work. A general assignment requires that you do all three steps. A somewhat specific assignment does steps one and two for you by limiting you to a general area. You need do only step three to complete the restriction process for this assignment. A very directive assignment does all three steps and leaves you free to begin work on the organization of the paper itself.

ORGANIZING THE PAPER

Any paper has three basic components: introduction, development, and conclusion, all helping to fulfill the function of the paper, which is to express an idea. Obviously, then, as a first organizational step you must formulate the idea you wish to develop in your paper.

FORMULATING YOUR IDEA

Know where your paper is going!

To formulate your idea, you must be sure to understand the topic you have settled on. Read the final version of the topic again. Decide what is demanded of you and determine the exact nature of the topic. (Review this process from "Taking Essay Tests.")

When you are satisfied that you understand your topic precisely, find out what you know about the topic by collecting materials and by jotting down bits of information about the topic.

Finally, write out the idea you have developed in a sentence that expresses it clearly and concisely. This sentence will guide you as you write the paper, assisting you in staying on the topic (maintaining unity of idea). It will also guide the reader as he or she proceeds into the development of the idea.

WRITING THE INTRODUCTION

Try to provide two services to your reader in the introduction. First, show your interest in the topic and try to make it interesting to your reader. Second, by writing into the introduction a version of the idea statement, guide the reader into the development of this idea.

The introduction ought to help you, too. Refer to the idea sentence, as it appears in the introduction, to guide you in writing the paragraphs of development.

WRITING THE DEVELOPMENT SECTION

Once you have written an opening paragraph that interests and guides the reader, begin to develop the idea of the paper. Development is a generic term for several tactics of explanation and illustration. Providing development may mean

1. Offering examples of the idea.
2. Analyzing and explaining the idea.
3. Giving the history or the background of the idea.
4. Applying the idea to new or innovative areas.
5. Arguing for the truth of the idea.

You may choose to develop the paper following only one of these tactics or you may include more than one as long as such inclusions serve to develop the idea.

You will find it helpful at this point to jot down a list of the materials and illustrations you plan to include in your development. Check this list against your idea statement to be sure that you have not departed from your original intentions for the topic.

Finally, write out a first draft of your development, using the patterns of paragraph development already presented.

WRITING THE CONCLUSION

In writing a conclusion, provide a wrap-up and brief recapitulation of the idea to give the paper a sense of completion. Avoid long summaries and do not introduce new ideas in a conclusion. For a two-page paper, you can often write a successful conclusion in one sentence and add it to the last paragraph of development. If you decide to write a separate concluding paragraph, do not write more than two or three sentences.

WRITING THE FINAL DRAFT: A WORD ON REVISION

After you have written the first draft of your paper, set it aside for a day so that you can gain some objectivity toward it. Then reread your paper. Try to think of yourself not as the author but as a critical reader seeing this material for the first time. On your first reading don't look for small details; read the entire essay to evaluate the organization and the general effect. Then go through the paper again, checking for matters of spelling, mechanics, and grammatical correctness. Use your dictionary. Study the sentences: You may find long sentences that could well be broken up or groups of short, choppy sentences that should be combined and compressed. Rewrite sentences that do not read smoothly. After you have done all of this, make your final clean copy. And since for most of us our handwriting and typing can play tricks on us, you should proofread this final copy before you hand it in to your instructor.

A TYPICAL ASSIGNMENT

How then would you approach the writing of such a paper? As a final demonstration, follow this development of a paper from the statement of the assignment to a complete draft of the paper.

> **ASSIGNMENT:** Write a two-page paper explaining why Huck said that he wanted no more of civilization, that he had been there and couldn't stand it.

Problem 1: Defining the terms of the assignment.
This assignment asks you to explain the reasons for Huck's reaction against the prospect of living a "normal," "civilized" life. Why did he react this way? His experiences in civilization were mostly unpleasant, confining, or frightening.

Problem 2: Establishing what you know about the topic. Having established that his reaction is negative because his experiences were bad, you must provide examples. Some possibilities are these:

1. The confining life at the Widow Douglas' home, and Miss Watson's efforts to teach Huck manners and religion.
2. The brutal shooting of Boggs by Colonel Sherburn, and mob violence of the attempted lynching that was faced down by Sherburn's singlehanded capacity for even greater violence.
3. The Grangerford–Shepherdson feud.
4. Huck's obvious pleasure at living outside civilization with Jim on Jackson's Island and on the raft.

Problem 3: Establishing the statement or thesis of the paper. Huck could not stand to be "sivilized" because his experiences of civilization were either suffocating or frightening. Note that this statement is formulated after you review what you know about the topic.

Problem 4: Writing the introduction. Remember that you must interest your reader and, at the same time, establish your thesis. The introduction might read this way:

> At the close of the novel *Huckleberry Finn*, Huck concludes his story by saying that he intends to "light out for the Territory" because Aunt Sally intends to "sivilize" him and he feels that he can't stand any more efforts to make him an upstanding, moral, and religious citizen. His attitude is understandable, for his experiences in society as it existed along the Mississippi were confining and unpleasant or downright terrifying.

Problem 5: Writing the development. Select materials, illustrations, and examples before writing. Use the list of ideas and illustrations collected under Problem 2. Note that listing one idea may cause you to recollect another. The paragraphs of development might read this way:

> Huck's experiences of "home," or at the two places where he lives at the opening of the novel, were decidedly unpleasant. The home of Widow Douglas and Miss Watson tended to oppress and constrict a boy's natural energy and interests. Regular meals eaten with careful manners and polite small talk worked against Huck's tendency to roam at will through the woods. Lectures on morality and religion tended to confuse him. If one could obtain his desires

through prayer, why were folks poor, or sick, or crippled? If being good made one blessed, why was Miss Watson so sour and seemingly unhappy? Life with Pap may have been more free from the repressions of etiquette, but it also had its frightening side with its drunkenness, violence, and delirium tremens. So Huck decided to leave these situations behind to look for something better.

Something better turns out to be life on the river with Jim, the runaway slave. They meet on Jackson's Island and camp there for a time. Their experiences on the island are mostly pleasant: loafing, camping, fishing, and generally hanging out, all of which suited Huck just fine. The idyll is interrupted by a snakebite (from which Jim recovers) and is ended by the threat of a search party coming out to find Jim. Jim is a slave and, by all the measures of that day, a savage, but in reality he is the only truly civilized person Huck meets in his travels. Jim loves Huck and cares for him, in spite of Huck's tendency to play cruel jokes on him. He shelters Huck from the knowledge of Pap's death and doesn't reject Huck when he discovers the hoax of Huck's dream fabrication when they have been separated in a fog. It is ironic that the only civilized person Huck meets is not considered truly human by those who regard themselves as civilized.

The other people Huck meets in his travels do very little to improve his suspicious view of the world. He and Jim meet some fairly terrible people as soon as they venture out on the river: slave hunters, the gamblers who are trying to kill their partner, and a nonhuman agent of civilization, a steamboat that runs them down and puts Huck back on shore. There he meets the Grangerfords, gentlemen and ladies all, living in a fine house and enjoying prosperity. The Grangerfords are aristocrats and moral churchgoing people who have one fault: They are engaged in a murderous, generations-old feud with the Shepherdsons. One Sunday afternoon Huck witnesses an outbreak of this feud that leaves most of the people from both families dead.

Fleeing from the killing, Huck returns to the river and finds Jim. They continue down the river. Later they meet the King and the Duke, two great con artists who dupe the people in a nearby town and are eventually tarred and feathered for their efforts. During the adventures with the King and the Duke, Huck witnesses the shooting of the harmless drunk Boggs and the attempted lynching of Colonel Sherburn, the man who shot him. Taken on balance, most of Huck's experiences on shore are grim and frightening, good reasons for his lack of enthusiasm for civilization.

Even the last episode of the book does little to increase Huck's desire to live in the civilized world. Huck comes by chance upon the home of Tom Sawyer's Aunt Sally and adopts Tom's identity. When Tom shows up, he is introduced as Cousin Sid. Jim is also on the plantation, being held as a runaway slave. The two boys, with Tom leading, enter an incredible plot to free Jim, although, as Tom already knows but conceals, Jim has already been freed. After a series of cops-and-robber antics, the plot resolves into what looks like a happy ending. It is revealed that Jim is free, Pap is dead, and Huck's personal fortune, presumed lost, is intact. Aunt Sally offers to adopt Huck and raise him properly so that he can become a successful civilized adult. At this point Huck reviews his situation. Life in town and his misadventures on shore with the Grangerfords, the King and Duke, Sherburn, and others suggest only bad experiences to come if he accepts Aunt Sally's offer. His time with Jim, living free and easy on the river, proves wonderfully pleasant when compared to those recollections. Little wonder, then, that he decides to "light out for the Territory."

WRITING RESEARCH PAPERS

An education that will be useful in the late twentieth century and the early years of the twenty-first must include the development of skills needed for learning new materials and new principles after college is far behind. The world is changing so rapidly that the facts and concepts learned today will soon be out-of-date. The graduate going to work in the 1980s will, on the average, move to a new job or learn a completely new way to perform the old job at least three times during his career. Staying abreast of modern developments will require the ability to learn new skills and concepts, to evaluate what is learned, and to apply what is learned.

The place for learning to apply study skills to the acquisition of new skills and concepts is the library; the principal method for organizing and recording what you have learned is the research paper. Performing research and writing research papers are not tasks that will stop at graduation but are, in fact, realistic practice for the kind of work required in many occupations. Engineers spend days and even weeks doing research and writing reports and proposals based on that research. Bankers, investment advisers, doctors, teachers, market analysts, chemists, mechanics—people in all lines of work—pore over books and magazines to learn more about their businesses or professions. Research techniques and report writing are indispensable "real world" skills. The ability to use the library effectively and efficiently and to write in clear, concise language what you uncover is probably the single most important thing you can learn as a student.

BEFORE YOU START

The first step in writing a research paper is the same as the first step in any writing assignment:

Analyze the assignment to determine exactly what is required. (See also "Writing Essays," pages 159–161.) Quite often research assignments are couched in rather general terms:

> Write a ten-page paper on a subject that catches your interest during the term.
> Write a 2,500-word paper on the life and works of James Baldwin.
> Write a brief report on the causes and effects of the War of 1812.

You need to answer several questions before you begin work on these assignments.

> A paper on any subject? What interests me in this course? What do I know that could be developed into a paper? What subjects that interest me are also available in the resources of this library?
> Baldwin's entire life? All his works? Only the best? A sample of the early and later works? Should I include a resumé of each work? Critical opinion?
> If the paper is on the causes and effects of the war, how much shall I summarize the events of the war? Shall I focus on short-term cause and effect, or shall I extend the discussion backward and forward in time?

These are important questions, and they suggest that you must do two things before you begin to work:

1. You must define the assignment so that you know exactly what the subject matter is and what the technical requirements are (length, number of sources, distribution of sources among books and periodicals, and any further directions from the instructor). Be sure that you understand all that is required of you.

2. You must limit the topic so that you can develop it fully within the page and word limitations of the assignment. Don't try to shrink an important topic to fit a limited space. (A definitive history of the Ford Motor Company cannot be written in five pages.) Don't pad a topic of minor importance to meet a specified

requirement in length. (The history and development of the paper clip does not warrant fifty pages of exposition.) Limit the topic so that you can answer the important questions of a careful reader within the limits of the assignment.

BEGINNING THE RESEARCH

The very word *research* suggests that you will need to *search* the available sources of information for material on your topic. But before you rush to the library, take a few moments to jot down what you already know about the general topic area. Some of the notes and readings you have done in the class for which the paper is assigned may help you. Look for some of the following:

1. The names of people who are important to your topic.
2. An outline of the history of the period or some discussion of the background of the topic.
3. The names of authors or the titles of books that are an important part of the scholarship of the topic.
4. The important questions and problems that are a part of the study of the topic.

When you have reviewed and recorded what you know already, take your tools to the library.

A NOTE ON TOOLS: You will need several pens or pencils and a large supply of index cards. Choose a size of card convenient for you, but realize that a 3″ x 5″ card is close to the minimum practical space. You may be tempted to take notes on regular notebook paper. Don't do it. Cards are far more convenient for storing, retrieving, and re-sorting the product of research.

The first stop in the library ought to be the reference shelf where the encyclopedias are stored. (If you are not familiar with the layout of the library, ask for a map or guided tour.) In a comprehensive encyclopedia (*Encyclopedia Americana, Encyclopaedia Britannica, Collier's Encyclopedia*) read the article or articles that pertain to your topic. Remember, you are not undertaking this paper in a vacuum; use what you have learned in the course as a starting point for exploration. You can find articles about, related to, or concerned with your topic by looking in the encyclopedias (always look at more than one if possible) under the key words, important names, and major concepts suggested by your class notes and course readings. Look up the key words and other fundamentals in the index volume of the encyclopedia. You will probably find cross references there that you might otherwise have overlooked. As you read these encyclopedia articles, try to add to your knowledge of the history, people, important concepts, questions, problems, and statistics that surround your topic. Use what you learn here to lead you to additional, more specific sources of information. The bibliographies at the end of the encyclopedia articles will often provide you with several titles for further research.

After reading the articles in these general works, you may find it useful to consult one or more of the specialized encyclopedias and reference works on the reference shelves of the library. The following list, arranged by general subject areas, will help you to recognize a work in the area of your topic.

SPECIALIZED ENCYCLOPEDIAS AND REFERENCE WORKS

HUMANITIES

Art

Encyclopedia of Painting, 3rd rev. ed., 1970
Encyclopedia of World Art, 15 vols., 1968
Larousse Encyclopedia of Byzantine and Medieval Art, 1976
Larousse Encyclopedia of Modern Art, 1965
Larousse Encyclopedia of Prehistoric and Ancient Art, 1976
Larousse Encyclopedia of Renaissance and Baroque Art, 1976

Literature

Cassell's Encyclopedia of World Literature, 3 vols., 1973
The Contemporary Novel: A Checklist of Critical Literature on the British and American Novel since 1945, 1972
Literary History of the United States, 2 vols., 4th ed., 1974
The Oxford Companion to the Theater, 3rd ed., 1967
The Oxford History of English Literature, 12 vols., 1945–1963
Princeton Encyclopedia of Poetry and Poetics, 1975
The Reader's Encyclopedia, 2nd ed., 1965

Music

Encyclopedia of Jazz, 1960
Grove's Dictionary of Music and Musicians, 5th ed., 1954, 1961
International Cyclopedia of Music and Musicians, 10th ed., 1975
Kobbé's Complete Opera Book, 9th ed., 1976
The New Oxford History of Music, 10 vols., 1957–1975

Mythology

Frazer, Sir James G. *The Golden Bough: A Study in Magic and Religion,* 13 vols., 1907–1915; Supplement, 1936

Funk and Wagnalls Standard Dictionary of Folklore, Mythology, and Legend, 1972

Larousse World Mythology, 1965

Mythology of All Races, 13 vols., 1916–1932

New Larousse Encyclopedia of Mythology, 1968

Philosophy and Religion

The Concise Encyclopedia of Western Philosophy and Philosophers, 1960

Copleston, F. C. *A History of Philosophy,* 8 vols., 1947–1966

A Dictionary of Comparative Religion, 1970

Encyclopaedia Judaica, 16 vols., 1972

The Encyclopaedia of Philosophy, 4 vols., 1973

Encyclopaedia of Religion and Ethics, 13 vols., 1962

The New Catholic Encyclopedia, 15 vols., 1967

The New Schaff-Herzog Encyclopedia of Religious Knowledge, 13 vols., 1950

SCIENCE AND TECHNOLOGY

Architecture

Concise History of Western Architecture, 1970

Dictionary of Architecture and Construction, 1975

World Architecture: An Illustrated History, 1963

Biological Sciences

Dictionary of the Biological Sciences, 1967

The Encyclopedia of the Biological Sciences, 2nd ed., 1970

Encyclopedia of Oceanography, 1966

Grzimek's Animal Life Encyclopedia, 13 vols., 1972

General Works

Cowles Encyclopedia of Science, Industry, and Technology, 1969

McGraw-Hill Encyclopedia of Science and Technology, 15 vols., 4th ed., 1977

Van Nostrand's Scientific Encyclopedia, 1976

Mathematics

Dictionary of Modern Engineering, 1974

Engineering Encyclopedia, 3rd ed., 1963

Handbook of Engineering Fundamentals, 3rd ed., 1975

International Dictionary of Applied Mathematics, 1977

Universal Encyclopedia of Mathematics, 1964

Physical Sciences

Encyclopaedic Dictionary of Physics, 9 vols. and supplements, 1965–1975
Encyclopedia of Chemical Technology, 22 vols., 2nd ed., 1963–1972
Encyclopedia of Physics, 2nd ed., 1974
Van Nostrand's International Encyclopedia of Chemical Sciences, 1964

SOCIAL SCIENCES

Business and Economics

Encyclopaedia of Banking and Finance, 7th ed., 1973
Encyclopedia of Business Information Sources, 1976
Encyclopedia of Management, 2nd ed., 1973
The McGraw-Hill Dictionary of Modern Economics, 1973

Education

Encyclopedia of Education, 10 vols., 1971
World Survey of Education, 1955–date
World Yearbook of Education, 1931–date

History

The Cambridge Ancient History, 12 vols. text, 5 vols. plates, 1924–1939
The Cambridge Medieval History, 8 vols., 1922–1967
Encyclopedia of American History, 1976
An Encyclopedia of World History, 5th ed., 1972
McGraw-Hill Encyclopedia of Russia and the Soviet Union, 1961
The New Cambridge Modern History, 14 vols., 1957–1975
New Century Classical Handbook, 1962

Social Sciences and Psychology

Dictionary of Psychology: With Thesaurus, 1977
Dictionary of Social Science, 1959
Encyclopedia of Psychology, 3 vols., 1972
Encyclopedia of the Social Sciences, 15 vols., 1930–1935
International Encyclopedia of the Social Sciences, 17 vols., 1968

LOCATING MATERIALS IN THE LIBRARY

THE CARD CATALOGUE

After you have oriented yourself to the general outline and context of the topic, use the **card catalogue** to locate books that
contain material for the paper. Note carefully the plural "*books*
that contain." No single source will provide everything for a
paper. No source will confine itself exclusively to a treatment of
your topic with your approach. Expect to find information in

several sources, and be ready to combine what you find into one statement that is your own.

The card catalogue lists all the books held in the library. The list is made up of cards, three for each book on the shelves: an author card, a title card, and a subject card. A book may appear on several subject cards, one for each general area the book touches.

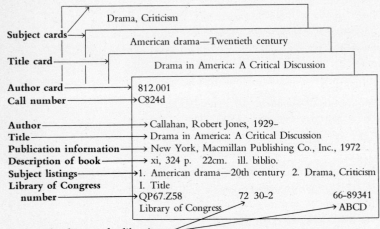

Subject cards	Drama, Criticism
	American drama—Twentieth century
Title card	Drama in America: A Critical Discussion
Author card	812.001
Call number	C824d
Author	Callahan, Robert Jones, 1929–
Title	Drama in America: A Critical Discussion
Publication information	New York, Macmillan Publishing Co., Inc., 1972
Description of book	xi, 324 p. 22cm. ill. biblio.
Subject listings	1. American drama—20th century 2. Drama, Criticism
Library of Congress number	I. Title
	QP67.Z58 72 30-2 66-89341
	Library of Congress → ABCD
Technical references for librarians	

The subject index of the card catalogue contains an additional aid in the search for possible sources of information. At the end of the group of cards filed under a subject heading, there is a card that reads

> *See* (Or sometimes, *See Also*)
> Theater in America
> Literary criticism
> The names of specific plays

These references direct you to other subject headings in the card catalogue, additional references that can open valuable areas of material if you will follow through carefully on each one. Ask the librarian to help you find additional headings for your subject when you have finished working through all that you can find.

The following is a list of filing rules for the card catalogue:

1. Authors are listed alphabetically by last name; books and subject headings are listed by the first word in the title or subject.

A, An, and *The* are not considered in the alphabetical arrangement; thus *The Great Balloon Races* would be listed under *Great,* not under *The.*

2. All initials or titles composed of initials are listed before words that are spelled out; thus *FCC* comes before *Fabulous.*

3. Numerals are filed as though spelled out; thus *10* is filed under *te.*

4. Names that begin *Mc* or *Mac* are filed under *Mac;* thus *McDougal* and *MacDougal* occur in the same place in the file.

5. Alphabetical arrangement does not extend beyond the first word; thus *New York* comes before *Newark,* and *On time* before *One time.*

FINDING ARTICLES IN
MAGAZINES AND PERIODICALS

After you have worked through the card catalogue to locate books on your subject, turn to the *Reader's Guide to Periodical Literature* to locate articles published in magazines and periodicals. (*Periodical* is a name for any publication containing articles and published on a schedule. *Magazine* is generally applied only to popular periodicals for a general readership; it is not used for serious or scholarly works. *Time* and *Newsweek* are magazines; *Publications of the Modern Language Association* is a periodical.)

The *Reader's Guide to Periodical Literature* is published on the 10th and 25th of each month (except July and August, when only one issue appears each month). These semimonthly volumes are cumulated every three months and bound permanently in one volume once each year. Articles in the *Guide* are entered under the name of the author and under as many subject headings as may apply. Titles of articles are not indexed separately, although literary works are entered under title and author.

An *author* listing will contain the following information:

> **HUDNALL, James**
> "In the Company of Great Whales"
> *Audubon* 79:62–73 May '77

The author's name appears first in boldface type on a line by itself. The next entry is the title of the article. The third line gives the name of the periodical (often abbreviated), the number of the volume (79) in which the article appears,* the pages on which the

* All issues in one twelve-month period are given the same volume number.

article is printed (62–73), and the month and year of the periodical issue (May '77).

A *subject* heading contains the same information as the author
entry, but under a new heading and in a slightly different order.

> **WHALES**
> "In the Company of Great Whales"
> James Hudnall. *Audubon* 79:62–73   May '77

(Note that the Hudnall article will be one of many under
"Whales.") Because in the early stages of your research you will
know your topic but probably not the names of authors who have
written on it, you will find the subject headings of the *Guide* to be
the richest source of information. To find subject heading listings
of possibly relevant articles, look under key words associated
directly and indirectly with your topic. The *Guide* uses a helpful
and easily understood system of cross references. The subject
heading you first select may give only a "See" reference to one or
more headings used in the indexing system of the *Guide.* Looking
under the subject heading "Conservation," you may be led to the
article in the preceding example by no more than the simple
instruction:

> **CONSERVATION.** See Whales

At the end of some entries, cross references will give directions to
other headings that may provide additional, useful sources. Some
broad subject headings are divided into subheadings for specific,
convenient reference. Under "Sport," for example, you may find
several subheadings arranged alphabetically in boldface type in the
center of the column:

> **SPORT**
> **Accidents and injuries**
> **Philosophy**
> **Photographs**

Sometimes the index will contain articles by an author and
about that author. In such double listings, the articles by the author
appear first; the articles about the author are listed second under
the italic heading *about,* located in the center of the column. To
save space, the *Guide* uses many abbreviations. All of those used
are listed on a page at the beginning of each volume. Refer to
these lists when you cannot interpret an abbreviation.

OTHER PERIODICAL INDEXES

In addition to consulting the *Reader's Guide,* an index to general periodicals, you may want to look into one or more of the following special indexes:

Agricultural Index
Applied Science & Technology Index
Art Index
Bibliographic Index
Biography Index
Biological & Agricultural Index
Book Review Digest
Business Periodicals Index
Education Index
Engineering Index
Essay & General Literature Index
Index to Legal Periodicals
Library Literature
New York Times Index
Play Index
Short Story Index
Social Sciences & Humanities Index
United States Government Publications: Monthly Index

ADDITIONAL REFERENCE AIDS

The library has other collections of materials for reference that provide sources for a paper. The *Vertical File* is a collection of newspaper clippings, booklets, and pamphlets, many produced by various branches of government. These materials are organized by subject and in a file cabinet. Ask the librarian to explain the contents and the organization of this collection in your library.

In the reference section of the library you will find specialized works cataloguing facts and isolated bits of information.

ALMANACS, YEARBOOKS, AND COMPILATIONS OF FACTS (FOR MISCELLANEOUS FACTS AND STATISTICS)

The Americana Annual, 1923–date
Britannica Book of the Year, 1938–date
Collier's Yearbook, 1939–date
Facts on File, 1940–date
Information Please Almanac, 1947–date

ATLASES AND GAZETTEERS (FOR GEOGRAPHICAL INFORMA-TION)

Encyclopaedia Britannica World Atlas, 1959
National Geographic Atlas of the World, 3rd ed., 1970

DICTIONARIES (FOR RESEARCH INTO THE ORIGINS AND CHANGING MEANINGS OF WORDS)

A New English Dictionary on Historical Principles (also called *The Oxford English Dictionary*), 12 vols. and supplement, 1888–1933
Partridge, Eric. *A Dictionary of Slang and Unconventional English,* 2 vols., 7th ed., 1970

BIOGRAPHICAL DICTIONARIES (FOR FACTUAL MATERIAL ON PEOPLE'S LIVES)

Chamber's Biographical Dictionary, ed. J. O. Thorne, rev. ed., 1969
Current Biography, 1940–date
Dictionary of American Biography, 20 vols. and supplements, 1928–1958
Dictionary of National Biography, 22 vols. and supplements, 1951–1960
Hyamson, Albert M. *A Dictionary of Universal Biography of All Ages and of All Peoples,* 2nd ed., 1951
International Who's Who, 1935–date
Who's Who in America, 1899–date

BOOKS OF QUOTATIONS (FOR LOCATING THE SOURCE OF AN UNATTRIBUTED QUOTATION)

Bartlett, John and E. M. Beck. *Familiar Quotations,* 14th ed., 1968
Bohle, Bruce. *The Home Book of American Quotations,* 1967
Evans, Bergen. *Dictionary of Quotations,* 1968

The library may also have a collection of films, filmstrips, and records that could be used as reference tools. Some schools house this collection in a center connected to the library and catalogue such materials in the card catalogue of the library. Other schools may have a separate division called The Audio-visual Department, The Media Center, or The Instructional Resources Center. Consult with the librarian as to the location and availability of these materials.

DEVELOPING A WORKING BIBLIOGRAPHY

For each source that promises to contain material pertinent to your topic, write out location and publication information on an index card. This card, known as a bibliography card, should contain the following pieces of information:

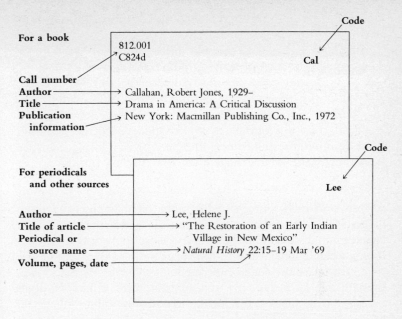

Note the letters in the upper right-hand corner of each card. These letters are an abbreviation of the author's last name and will serve as a code mark for the bibliography card and all the note cards you accumulate as you read the work named on the bibliography card. Some people use numbers or arbitrary letters instead of abbreviations, but the style of code selected is not important. It *is* extremely important that every bibliography card carry some unique mark that can be repeated on each note card from that bibliographic source.

The collection of bibliographic cards listing authors and titles comprises a *working bibliography*. The sources included in the list are starting points in the search for the information and examples of which your paper will ultimately be composed. Six to ten bibliography cards form a reasonable nucleus of sources for beginning a ten-page paper. Read the most general, most recent work first. A general book will introduce you to more aspects of your chosen topic than will a specialized study and will broaden your appreciation of the topic and its literature; a recent work usually summarizes, and sometimes criticizes, previous research, thus giving you an early, preliminary evaluation of your bibliography. The encyclopedia you first consulted probably gives the most general view of all, although it seldom contains the most recent view.

From the encyclopedia and the more general books in your bibliography you should quickly develop a broad, non-specific overview of your topic. As you move to the more specialized, detailed works, try to fit the specific, detailed information they provide into an outline based on the broad overview. Do not, however, treat this outline as a restriction on further reading. Wide reading in search of new ideas and more information is far more important at this stage than a well-constructed outline.

The Note Card

As you read each source listed in your bibliography, and those suggested by the reading of works on the initial list, record each concept you discover and the facts and illustrations associated with it on a separate index card. In the upper right-hand corner of *each* note card, place the code of the bibliography card for the source. Immediately after the code give the note card a number of its own: 1 for the first card, 2 for the second, and so on. When you finish taking notes from that source, count the number of cards from it and enter the total next to the number of the card on each note card: 1 of 9, 2 of 9, 3 of 9, until each card is thus identified. This will allow you to be absolutely certain that you do not misplace a card should the stack be disarranged. Start a new sequence of numbers for each set of note cards under each bibliography card. The code and number will simplify identification when the time comes to acknowledge sources of quotes, facts, or illustrations in footnotes to the paper.

In addition to the bibliography card code and series number, the note card should include the following information:

1. In the upper left-hand corner, the number of the page in the source from which the note card information is taken.

2. On the first line below the source page number, the heading from your tentative outline under which the content of the note is most likely to be used. The heading may begin flush with the left margin or be centered on the card.

3. The content of the note.

CONTENT OF THE NOTE CARD

A note card may contain information from a source in the form of

1. A direct quotation from the source. (Quotation should be reserved for occasions in which (a) the exact wording is essential to understanding—as in graphs, tables, charts, and figures, (b) the original wording is unusually apt, striking, or familiar, (c) an authority of exceptional repute declares his position or conclusion. *Be sure to enclose direct quotations in quotation marks on the note card. Be sure that direct quotations are accurate to the last word.*) See Example 1.

2. A summary of the source statement. (A summary condenses information to its main points and produces a shortened version of the original in which only the essential matter is retained.) See Example 2.

3. A paraphrase of the source statement. (A paraphrase is a rewriting, almost a translation, of a passage to simplify difficult wording or to adapt a distinctive style to one appropriate to the paper that uses the sense of the original. Unlike the summary, the paraphrase does not seek specifically to shorten the original.) See Example 3.

The following examples of the three types of note mentioned above are taken from an anthology of poetry. The bibliography card contains the following information:

A passage is selected from the introduction of the book identified because it contains a brief discussion of the function of poetry and concludes with a clear, concise definition of poetry.

> Poetry probably appeared earlier in human history than any other literary form; indeed, pure lyric outbursts to express joy, fear, outrage, or contentment may have preceded utilitarian communication. Thus the tradition runs without a break from the earliest cultures we know anything about to this present moment, and though our age may be, as we often hear, prosaic or scientific or material, it is also one of the great eras of poetic creation. One source of poetry's durability is its power to adapt to changing circumstances. Homer sang of the wonders Ulysses found on his

long homeward voyage; the poets of the Renaissance celebrated the discovery of the New World; today's poets ponder the meaning of humankind's adventures in space. But poetry is not a news medium; its enduring concern is with the human condition—with adventures in inner space. Hence, whatever new subjects it assimilates or whatever novelties of form it takes on, poetry is unchanged in its essential nature. It not only records and comments on events, but also helps to define our responses to them, for although poetry is thoroughly capable of telling stories or dramatizing ideas, it is especially valuable in expressing emotion. Whatever its diversity, we may still define poetry as *imaginative discourse that gives powerful expression to experience, ideas, and emotion in heightened, patterned language.*

The definition is a good example of the sort of material that ought to be recorded verbatim on a note card for possible use as a direct quotation in the paper.

EXAMPLE 1

P. 2 Poetry: definition of   Alt 1 of 9

". . . imaginative discourse that gives powerful expression to experience, ideas, and emotion in heightened, patterned language."

Example 2 shows how a summary note of that same passage condenses the original without losing the main thoughts. Note that the definition of poetry, still quoted verbatim, is set off with quotation marks.

EXAMPLE 2

P. 2 Function and definition of poetry   Alt 2 of 9

Poetry has endured from earliest times because of its power to adapt to a changing world. Homer treated heroes of the Trojan War; today's poet ponders space flights, but poetry in any setting speaks of human condition. It not only records events, but helps define our responses to them. Its chief value is the expression of emotion. Poetry is thus "imaginative discourse that gives powerful expression to experience, ideas, and emotion in heightened, patterned language."

In Example 3 you see a paraphrase of the same passage. Remember that such a note is useful only in special circumstances. The material quoted from the original is again carefully set off in quotation marks. (If your notes are to include many paraphrases, 5″ × 7″ cards will be much more practical than the 3″ × 5″ variety.)

EXAMPLE 3

P. 2 Function and definition of poetry	Alt 3 of 9

Poetry is probably the oldest form of literature and may have existed as a lyric expression of joy or another emotion before practical communication developed. So the tradition of poetry runs from earliest times to the present. Despite our modern reputation for practicality, science, and material values, our age is a great time of poetic creativity. One reason for poetry's endurance is its ability to change its focus without losing its quality as poetry. Homer described the trials of Odysseus' journey home; Renaissance poets celebrated discovery of the new world; modern poets consider the meaning of space exploration. But poetry is not supposed to be a reporter of the news; it is supposed to focus on the human condition. Thus poetry continues to focus on the same eternal themes, although it takes as its subjects contemporary details. Not only does poetry record events, it helps us understand our emotional responses to them. This is poetry's chief value, that it serves as a means of defining and expressing emotion. Poetry can still be defined as "imaginative discourse that gives powerful expression to experience, ideas, and emotion in heightened, patterned language."

Many libraries provide photocopy machines within walking distance of the stacks. Use the machines to copy important, long, or difficult passages so that you can take the content home and reduce it to note-card form at your leisure. Important quotes or short passages may be taped or stapled to cards to save copying time. If you simply duplicate all material, however, you will defeat the advantages in rearranging information that cards afford and only postpone the process of rethinking and restating that is necessary to working the material into your own paper. When a duplicate is used in lieu of a note, make sure you write in the source on the appropriate bibliography and note cards. Copied pages sometimes carry only part of the bibliographic data and so omit information necessary for complete footnote and bibliographic references.

When you have finished taking notes, and don't stop until you have worked through the available sources and have about twice as many notes as you think you need, sort the cards by idea, putting notes relevant to each idea or each point in a working outline into a separate stack. (At this point you are ready to formulate your idea and can begin to follow the steps outlined in the earlier sections of Part V.)

Read through all the cards and decide exactly what you want to say about your topic. Try to state your objective (sometimes called your *thesis*) in a brief paragraph not much more than three or four sentences long. Some writers blatantly capture their thesis in a declaration that begins, "In this paper I intend to . . . ." Such a statement should not appear in the final paper, although it may be inserted in the working outline, but it will serve as a guide for constructing the final outline and selecting support materials for the content.

A CAUTION ABOUT OUTLINES

The place in this series of steps at which you actually establish the formal outline for the paper will vary from topic to topic. Some topics have an outline built in them from the start; the paper on the life and works of James Baldwin, mentioned at the beginning of this section, will, obviously, contain material on the life and works of Baldwin, and the outline is thus determined almost automatically. Either of the following variations on a basic chronological arrangement will serve.

I. Baldwin's Life
  A. Early
  B. Middle
  C. Later
II. Baldwin's Works
  [Discuss by time or
  discuss by importance]
  A. Early
  B. Middle
  C. Later
    [or]
  A. Major Works
  B. Minor Works

I. Early Life and Works
II. Middle Life and Works
III. Later Life and Works

For another paper, especially one in which you will present a controversy or an issue that has two sides, equally strong, no outline will present itself at the beginning of the research. The paper on the causes and effects of the War of 1812, for example, will have only the most general sort of outline at the beginning of your research: Causes and effects will be discussed, but no order, no list of causes and effects, no additional discussion will suggest itself until after you have completed much of the reading and note-taking for the project. When you have collected materials from your sources, read through the notes to determine what you have learned about the topic. At this time formulate the thesis statement and let the outline develop naturally from that statement. When you have completed both thesis statement and outline, review the entire production and compare it to the notes. You may find it necessary to revise the outline to include additional material or to return to the library to do additional research. Be sure to extend yourself and do this additional work. Only thorough preliminary work will produce a successful paper.

The development of a paper of ten or twelve pages is more complex than the development of a two-page paper because it must cover more territory and control both the writer's skill and the reader's attention for a longer time. It is helpful to think of the longer paper as a series of short ones, to approach the writing of each section in the outline as though it must stand alone. Each section will then have its own thesis and outline; its own introduction, development, and conclusion. Each may be constructed by following the steps for writing short essays and will eventually be integrated with the rest of the paper by an overall introduction and by the careful use of transitional sentences or paragraphs between the sections.

The conclusion of a long paper must accomplish more than the conclusion of a short one. Because more material is introduced in the long paper, the conclusion must summarize and unite the main points of the paper in about one page if it is to leave the thesis of the paper firmly fixed in the mind of the reader. State the points clearly and succinctly, leaving the reader with a capsule version of the whole to remember after the details have been set aside.

DOCUMENTATION

It is absolutely necessary that you make provision for acknowledging your use of materials taken from the works of others. You must acknowledge

1. Quotations from any source, written or oral, published or unpublished.

2. Any version of such quotations, despite minor changes in wording.

3. Any idea or illustration unique to a work or person. (If the idea is not in two other sources, acknowledge the originator.)

Keep track of the material that needs acknowledgment by recording each usage in the rough draft in a note giving source and page for the quote. The identifying tag from the bibliography card of the source and the source page number are usually sufficient. Place them in parentheses (Lee-18) at the end of the quotation.

FOOTNOTES

The actual acknowledgment of adapted or quoted material occurs in a *footnote* written in proper form either at the bottom of the page containing the quote or, in the case of most term papers, on a separate sheet at the end of the paper. The footnote is identified in the body of the writing by a raised number (superscript) at the end of the passage involved. There are several acceptable styles for footnotes, and these styles vary from discipline to discipline and from teacher to teacher. Before completing your research paper, ask the teacher to specify the required style and follow that style down to the last comma and period. If there is no required style, the following models represent acceptable footnotes.

BOOKS BY ONE AUTHOR

[1] Frank E. Halliday, *Chaucer and His World* (New York: Viking, 1969), p. 123.

BOOKS BY TWO OR THREE AUTHORS

[2] Charles R. Baskervill, Virgil B. Heltzel, and Arthur H. Nethercot, *Elizabethan and Stuart Plays* (New York: Holt, 1934), p. 475.

BOOKS BY MORE THAN THREE AUTHORS

[3] Robert E. Spiller et al., *Literary History of the United States* (New York: Macmillan, 1946), p. 263. [*Et al.* is an abbreviation of the Latin *et alii* "and other persons."]

BOOKS IN A SECOND OR SUBSEQUENT EDITION

[4] Robert E. Spiller et al., *Literary History of the United States,* 4th ed. (New York: Macmillan, 1974), p. 57.

A CHAPTER BY AN AUTHOR IN A BOOK ASSEMBLED BY AN EDITOR

[5] Richard W. Bailey and Jay L. Robinson, eds., *Varieties of Present-Day English* (New York: Macmillan, 1973), p. 154. [This citation is to an introduction written by the editors for a chapter by another person.]

[6] William Labov, "Some Features of the English of Black Americans" in *Varieties of Present-Day English,* eds. Richard W. Bailey and Jay L. Robinson (New York: Macmillan, 1973), p. 244. [This citation is to an essay in the specified collection.]

BOOKS IN A SERIES OF VOLUMES, ALL BY THE SAME AUTHOR AND WITH THE SAME TITLE

[7] Carl Sandburg, *Abraham Lincoln: The War Years* (New York: Harcourt, 1939), II, 283. [When a volume is specified, the abbreviation "p." is omitted.]

ANONYMOUS WORKS

List anonymous works alphabetically by title without using "Anonymous" or "Anon."

REFERENCE BOOKS

[8] H. W. Fowler, *A Dictionary of Modern English Usage,* 2nd ed., revised by Sir Ernest Gowers (Oxford: Clarendon Press, 1965), p. 107.

ARTICLES IN ENCYCLOPEDIAS

[9] "The Automobile," *Encyclopaedia Britannica,* 11th ed., I, 204. [If the article is signed, place the author's name in front of the title of the article.]

PAMPHLETS AND GOVERNMENT PUBLICATIONS

[10] *Exterminating Nematodes,* USDA Bulletin No. 638 (Washington, D.C.: Government Printing Office, 1976), p. 12.

SIGNED ARTICLES IN MONTHLY AND QUARTERLY MAGAZINES

[11] James Hudnall, "In the Company of Great Whales," *Audubon,* May 1977, p. 64.

ARTICLES IN WEEKLY MAGAZINES

[12] "Steel Prices Increase," *Newsweek,* 19 Apr. 1975, p. 67.

UNPUBLISHED DISSERTATIONS

[13] Joan R. Michaels, "Robert Frost's Early, Minor Poems," Diss., Univ. of Washington, 1955, p. 176.

UNSIGNED ARTICLES IN NEWSPAPERS

[14] "Fall Kills Three Workers," *New York Times,* 20 Mar. 1975, Sec. C, p. 7. [Signed articles follow the pattern for signed magazine articles.]

THE BIBLE
[15] John 1:21.

WORKS ALREADY CITED IN FOOTNOTES

The first reference to a source is made in a complete footnote, but there is no need to write out the complete citation in the second and following references. Two methods exist for making additional citations of sources previously noted:

1. Simply use the author's last name and the appropriate page number.

[16] Halliday, p. 134.

2. Use abbreviations, never underlined, of Latin words to indicate the relation of the new citation to the first one. This method is cumbersome and has largely given way to the simpler form mentioned above. As it occurs in many older books, however, a brief explanation of its system is necessary.

[17] Ibid., p. 135. [The Latin *ibidem* means "in the same place." This notation can be used only when no note, except another *ibid.,* comes between it and the original reference. The page number is given if reference is to a new page in the cited work; if no page number appears, the reference is to the page of the work as originally cited.]

[18] Halliday, op. cit., p. 48. [*Opere citato* means "in the work cited." The label *op. cit.* indicates that the reference is to a new page of a work already cited but not cited in the immediately preceding footnote. *Op. cit.* is invariably accompanied by a page number.]

[19] Halliday, loc. cit. [This note, like *op. cit.,* refers to a work already cited. It is used when reference is to the page cited in the original footnote and when one or more unrelated references intervene between the original citation and the present instance. *Loco citato* means "in the place cited." *Loc. cit.* is never used with a page number.]

Footnotes may be placed either at the bottom of the page containing the reference annotated or on a single sheet at the end of the body of the paper and in order of their occurrence in the text. If you are typing and setting footnotes at the bottom of the page, you must allow space to type the note without going below the bottom margin of one inch. Count the number of footnotes on a page in the rough draft and mark the corresponding page of the final draft as follows: For one footnote, mark off two inches; for each additional note add one-half inch. Mark a line (to be erased later) at the measured distance from the bottom of the page and stop at that mark as you type the text of the page. When you have typed down to the pencil mark, come down a single space on the typewriter and make a horizontal line. Allow a double space and then type the footnote. To raise the number of the footnote, release the ratchet and roll the platen down one space. Type the number, roll the platen back up, and type the first letter of the footnote without spacing. Single-space the material in each note, but double-space between the notes.

Footnotes at the bottom of a page look like this:

---

[1] Frank E. Halliday, *Chaucer and His World* (New York: Viking, 1969), p. 123.

[2] Charles R. Baskervill, Virgil B. Heltzel, and Arthur H. Nethercot, *Elizabethan and Stuart Plays* (New York: Holt, 1934), p. 475.

(Allow a one-inch margin to bottom of page.)

Endnotes are typed, doublespaced, on a separate sheet headed "Notes" and should be listed consecutively, one after the other, on as many sheets as necessary, numbering all sheets after the first. Indent the first note five spaces and roll the carriage down a half space. Type the number. Roll the carriage back up and, without any punctuation, begin the note.

Be sure to footnote each reference carefully. Be even more careful to footnote every time you use someone else's material. It is dishonest to use the material of another person as though it were your own. The technical name for failure to acknowledge borrowed material is *plagiarism*. Follow the rules of documentation to avoid any suggestion of plagiarism in your use of source material.

BIBLIOGRAPHY

A bibliography is a listing of sources consulted in the writing of a research paper. The list will include all of the sources mentioned in the paper, whether in the body or the footnotes. It will also include other works that were consulted, even though they are neither quoted nor mentioned in the paper. The bibliography is a reflection of the care and interest you have invested in the paper; it should show that you located the important works and important people relevant to your topic. Your instructors will probably know the major works in a given subject area and will expect to see those works listed in your bibliography.

The final form for a bibliography is somewhat like the form for footnotes; enough differences exist, however, to require great care in the preparation of the bibliography page. Place the bibliography on a separate page, or pages, either at the end of the paper itself or following the footnote page if you put the footnotes on a separate page. Bibliographies are presented in alphabetical order by the last name of the author, or the first letter of the first word of an entry (excluding "the," "a," and "an") when no author is listed. An alternative order groups the sources by type (books, periodicals) alphabetically within the groups. Alphabetical listing of all sources is probably the more commonly used arrangement. Bibliographic entries are not indented in the first line, but the second and all subsequent lines are indented five spaces. Bibliographic entries are not numbered. The following models are acceptable forms for bibliographic entries.

BOOKS BY ONE AUTHOR
Halliday, Frank E. *Chaucer and His World*. New York: The Viking Press, Inc., 1969.

BOOKS BY TWO OR MORE AUTHORS
Baskervill, Charles R., Virgil B. Heltzel, and Arthur H. Nethercot. *Elizabethan and Stuart Plays*. New York: Holt, Rinehart and Winston, 1934. [Note that the second and following authors' names do not appear last name first.]

BOOKS IN A SECOND OR SUBSEQUENT EDITION
Spiller, Robert E., Willard Thorp, Thomas H. Johnson, Henry Seidel Canby, Richard M. Ludwig, and William M. Gibson. *Literary History of the United States,* 2 vols., 4th ed. New York: Macmillan Publishing Co., Inc., 1974.

BOOKS WITH CHAPTERS WRITTEN BY VARIOUS AUTHORS AND COLLECTED BY AN EDITOR
Bailey, Richard W. and Jay L. Robinson, eds. *Varieties of Present-Day English*. New York: Macmillan Publishing Co., Inc., 1973.

A CHAPTER BY AN AUTHOR IN A BOOK ASSEMBLED BY AN EDITOR
Labov, William. "Some Features of the English of Black Americans" in *Varieties of Present-Day English,* eds. Richard W. Bailey and Jay L. Robinson. New York: Macmillan Publishing Co., Inc., 1973.

BOOKS IN A SERIES OF VOLUMES BY THE SAME AUTHOR AND WITH THE SAME TITLE
Sandburg, Carl. *Abraham Lincoln: The War Years,* Vol. II. New York: Harcourt Brace Jovanovich, Inc., 1939.

REFERENCE BOOKS
Fowler, H. W. *A Dictionary of Modern English Usage,* 2nd ed., revised by Sir Ernest Gowers. Oxford: Clarendon Press, 1965.

ARTICLES IN ENCYCLOPEDIAS
"The Automobile." *Encyclopaedia Britannica,* 11th ed. Chicago, 1935. Vol. I, 204.

PAMPHLETS AND GOVERNMENT PUBLICATIONS
Exterminating Nematodes, USDA Bulletin No. 638. Washington, D.C.: Government Printing Office, 1976.

SIGNED ARTICLES IN MONTHLY AND QUARTERLY MAGAZINES
Hudnall, James. "In the Company of Great Whales." *Audubon,* May 1977, pp. 62–73.

ARTICLES IN WEEKLY MAGAZINES
"Steel Prices Increase." *Newsweek,* 19 Apr. 1975, p. 67.

UNPUBLISHED DISSERTATIONS
Michaels, Joan R. "Robert Frost's Early, Minor Poems." Diss., Univ. of Washington, 1955.

UNSIGNED ARTICLES IN NEWSPAPERS
"Fall Kills Three Workers." *New York Times,* 20 Mar. 1975, Sec. C, p. 7.

THE BIBLE
John 1:21.

The Final Draft

The final draft of the paper ought to include the following parts:

1. A title page containing the title of the paper, the course for which the paper is being submitted, the date, and your name.

2. A table of contents or outline.

3. The paper itself with introduction, body, and conclusion neatly typed or handwritten between proper margins and in the required double spacing.

4. Footnotes in order of occurrence, placed either at the bottom of the page of text to which they relate or on a separate sheet or sheets after the last page of the paper proper.

5. A bibliography on a sheet separate from any footnotes and listed in alphabetical order. (The style of the footnotes and bibliography must be consistent with the style sheet selected for the paper.)

The final draft is a reflection of your pride of workmanship and your abilities. Proofread the paper carefully, eliminating mistakes in spelling, grammar, and mechanics. (If you find it difficult to read only for errors in spelling and punctuation, try reading the paper backwards, from end to beginning. Individual words and marks of punctuation will stand out vividly under that torture.) Turn the paper in on time, carefully stapled or bound in a folder.

ONE LAST WORD

Before you commit your paper to the mercies of an instructor, make sure you have a copy of the complete, final draft for your records as a protection against loss by fire, theft, civil disturbance, human frailty, or acts of God.

Appendix A
Reminders About Style

INTRODUCTION

Style is the quality of writing that produces effect, much as character is the quality of a person that creates an impression. Like character, style is determined not by one or two distinctive elements or traits but by the way all the elements blend. A writer's spelling alone no more determines the writer's style than a man's absentmindedness by itself establishes his character. But each such detail contributes to the realization of a whole, and when style or character must be measured, its measure is set by analysis of detail.

Character is measured by impression—loosely speaking, in degrees of amiability or of esteem. Style is measured by effect, by its success in transmitting information under the proper conditions for the reader to react, to learn, to enjoy, or to decide. It is not judged by correctness, as is usage; indeed, for the sake of style the writer may consciously break the conventions of usage to arrange words, phrases, or sentences to suit the purpose of the moment. Innovation, however, is risky even for the master of the craft, and the right to violate rules is a privilege of understanding them. Most writers generate their styles by manipulating standard English to achieve variety and effect within familiar limits. Those limits are broad enough to permit a good deal of discretion.

Because style is a matter of perception, originality, taste, *and experience,* few of its principles can be called rules. The comments that follow are not rules but suggestions for controlling the details that constitute style. They are arranged in three categories: *"Use of the Right Word," "Sentence Style,"* and *"Common Sense."*

USE OF THE RIGHT WORD

DICTION

Diction is the selection and arrangement of words. Good diction consists of the exact word set in the best possible order of words for occasion and audience.

Take the case of Harry, who has an old car to get off his hands. An announcement in the classified advertisement listing of his local newspaper offers a simple, inexpensive way of letting people know his car is for sale. It also imposes a limit on the number of words he can use to describe his property, unless he cares to pay more for the ad than he can hope to get from a buyer. After a quarter of an hour's experiment and revision, Harry comes up with the following concise, accurate statement:

> For Sale: '71 Chevy. Some body damage. Needs front-end work and two tires. Runs.

Before calling the paper to place the ad, Harry shows what he has written to his wife, Matilda, who shakes her head and says that he has let candor run away with him. His diction tells the truth but in words that suggest the worst. "Damage" sounds beyond repair, "front-end *work*" and the need for two tires present the buyer with considerable immediate expense, while "runs" implies no more than barely functioning. With Matilda's emendations the advertisement eventually appears in the paper thus:

> For Sale: '71 Chevy. Mechanically perfect [*best feature first*]. Two tires nearly new [*let the buyer make his own guess about the other two*]. Some body blemishes [*intentionally vague and less emphatic than "damage"*]. Needs front-end adjustment [*maybe all that's required is a few turns of a wrench*].

The issue is not, alas, honesty, but which statement will sell the car.

DENOTATION AND CONNOTATION

The difference between an apt word and a vaguely suitable one is a matter of *precise* meaning. English is rich in words of similar sense but distinct in power of suggestion and emotional appeal. A person who is widely known may be variously described as famous, renowned, celebrated, noted, notorious, distinguished, eminent, or illustrious. The adjectives share a general sense of *conspic-*

uously well known, and this general sense is their *denotation,* the fundamental meaning they hold in common. Someone who is *notorious,* however, is noted for evil; the *illustrious* man or woman is respected as an example of the best human qualities. Years of use and misuse have built a deposit on the original meaning of *notorious* (notable) until the word cannot now be assigned without implications of infamy and skulduggery. Such deposits on a word's root sense form its *connotation,* its unique meaning.

Insensitivity to a word's connotation can lead to blunders. The statement "Critics often point to the *sensual* imagery in Keats's poem 'Hyperion'" makes it clear that Keats's imagery appeals to touch, taste, sight, sound, or smell; but *sensual* has a specific connotation of lascivious, erotic feeling. Keats was not strong on the erotic; his imagery is innocently *sensuous,* a simple appeal to the senses.

The *cohort* was a Roman military unit comprising 300–600 men and roughly equivalent in function to a company in a modern army. A *cohort* when used to refer to a single associate or colleague is thus illogical, as is its plural applied to two or three individuals.

THE CONCRETE, THE GENERAL, AND THE ABSTRACT

A concrete word stands for a particular object, sight, sound, odor, taste, person, place, or action; a general word stands for a class of related objects, sights, sounds, odors, tastes, persons, places, or actions. An abstract word names an idea, something that has meaning and definition in the mind rather than in the tangible world. Of the three classes of word, the concrete is the most specific. Two people reading the words *cereal bowl* will envisage roughly the same shape and substance. Let the same two people see the general word *china,* however, and one will think of a plate and the other of a figurine. If the word is an abstraction like *liberty,* the notions it elicits are likely to be even more diverse—and more dangerous, for each holder of a notion is sure his is the true one. If the concrete is readily understandable, the abstract is just as readily misunderstandable. Careful writers usually observe two precautions in recognition of these three degrees of specificity:

1. They stick to the concrete whenever possible.
2. They restrict each unavoidable abstract or general term to one indisputable meaning by full explanation and definition.

Analogy. One effective way of defining the abstract is to render it in concrete terms by *analogy*. In an analogy the unfamiliar or vague concept is made explicit through reference to something familiar and usually concrete.

> An organization [abstraction] is a hybrid form of machine [concrete analogy]—one part tool or system, the other part human.
>
> —CHARLES A. REICH "The Limits of Duty"

> The animal mind is like a telephone exchange; it receives stimuli from outside through the sense organs and sends out appropriate responses through the nerves that govern muscles, glands, and other parts of the body.   —SUSANNE K. LANGER "The Prince of Creation"

The two examples demonstrate two forms of analogy: the *metaphor* and the *simile*.

Metaphor. The first analogy is a metaphor. The author makes his comparison by declaring that an organization actually *is* a form of machine.

Simile. In the second quotation, the author uses a simile. She does not say that the animal mind is a telephone exchange but that it is *like* one. A simile is a straightforward, announced comparison; two things not ordinarily thought to be similar are shown to be like each other in certain aspects. A metaphor is an overstated comparison; it claims for the sake of effect that one thing is something completely different.

Both metaphor and simile freshen and illuminate definition, but metaphor, because it is overstated by nature, requires the more careful treatment. Karl Marx's assertion "Religion . . . is the opium of the people" is a metaphor so sweeping and pithy that it has become a clever witticism independent of logical or suitable application. Metaphor should not overwhelm reason. Analogy, of course, can be applied successfully in concrete, factual discussions as well as in abstract ones.

> Portions of the [earth's] crust are under constant tension, *like a bent bow*. At frequent intervals, when the strain becomes intolerable, the rock gives way at some weak point, often far beneath the surface.
>
> As the crust makes this sudden shift, it releases pent-up energy in enormously powerful waves that make the whole earth vibrate *like a giant bell*.   —MAYNARD M. MILLER "Our Restless Earth"

WORD VARIETY

If repetition of an important word prevents misunderstanding or adds emphasis, do not be afraid to repeat the word.

> *Junk* is a generic term for all habit-forming preparations and derivatives of opium, including the synthetics; any form of *junk* can cause addiction. Nor does it make much difference whether it is injected, sniffed, or taken orally. The result is always the same— addiction. The addict depends on his *junk* just as a diver depends on his airline. When his *junk* is cut off he suffers agonizing withdrawal symptoms. —WILLIAM S. BURROUGHS "Kicking Drugs"

The writer does not achieve effective style by saying the same thing twice in different words. An unnatural clawing after synonyms to hide a failure to develop a topic naturally produces not a style but a mannerism. Nouns essential to the topic discussed, as *junk* is essential to the passage above, are best repeated or referred to by appropriate pronouns. Adjectives and adverbs, on the other hand, are qualifiers and of secondary importance. Their recurrence in proximity attracts notice and may be interpreted as a sign that the writer's vocabulary is poorly stocked. A verb, although indispensable to the development of its subject, may also benefit by the use of an alternative when its appearance in two or more close but different situations will draw disproportionate attention to it.

> How do you *recruit* strong verbs? Mainly by *impressing* into service [recruiting] verbs that *express* action, that *show* [express] an instant and subliminal picture of men and ideas in action.
> —CHARLES W. FERGUSON "Mind Your Verbs"*

If they occurred twice in the example, *recruit* and *express* would, paradoxically, lose vitality as they became more prominent.

PROPRIETY

The propriety of words does not mean their decency or decorum but their fitness or suitability to their subject. A stubbed toe is not a catastrophe; a fire in the wastepaper basket, and confined to the basket, is not a holocaust. If you miss your bus, do not say you are

---

* Even professional writers stumble. *Impress,* used in the sense of the example, means *force into service.* By adding "into service" the author commits a tautology (see "Common Sense").

devastated by the mishap—unless you mean to be funny. Extravagant phrasing, especially the misapplication of overwrought adjectives, destroys credibility in writing. "I am suffused with gratification at the receipt of your latest epistolary efforts" is generally less suitable than "Thank you for your last letter"—and will leave the recipient wondering what you could say if he saved your life. By all means experiment with new words, new analogies, new images. But scrutinize the results. If they sound unnatural, go on too long, or if they cannot be read aloud with a straight face when they should be, they are probably better dropped for something less striking. The search for an alternative that ends in an obscure derivative from the Greek invites scorn, especially when unfamiliarity with the word leads to misuse. Groping for an elegant variation on *short,* one writer ended a letter with the words "I must close now; my time is becoming laconic." *Laconic* means "brief" or "minimal" but is applicable only to speech in the sense of *concise, terse,* or *short-spoken.* What the word *short* lacks in originality it would have gained in propriety under the circumstances.

CLICHÉ

"Cliché is a dead metaphor" is the cliché used to define cliché. In other words, a cliché is a once-novel turn of phrase that has been used too often. How much sparkle is left in catch phrases like "Go bananas," "Out of his gourd," "No way," "Tell it like it is," "The whole thing," "You better believe it"? And, as clichés go, these are fairly fresh. A piece of writing full of them, or of such automatic word combinations as "solemn occasion," "bountiful harvest," "time and trouble," "reigns supreme," suggests that its writer found no inspiration other than prefabricated sentiment. Words that have already been chewed are unappetizing. No image at all is better than a jaded one.

EUPHEMISM

A gentle term or phrase used in lieu of a harsh or unpleasant one is a *euphemism.* Euphemisms have their place; there may be some point in telling relatives that Aunt Sophia has "passed on" and in referring to her corpse as "her remains." As no one is sure of the technical name for that essential piece of plumbing in the bathroom, it's convenient to call it "the toilet" and let it go. Euphemism employed for considerations other than simple politeness, however, is suspect. "What are they trying to hide?" the reader asks. "Is that 'discrepancy' in the accounts an error or a fraud?" A euphemism used deliberately to veil the truth is dishonest. A euphemism used unnecessarily to add elegance is pompous. Potatoes are dug with a spade, not with an agricultural implement.

JARGON, OFFICIALESE, GOBBLEDYGOOK

Jargon. *Jargon* has several meanings that range from nonsense to hybrid forms of language, such as pidgin English. It is often used as a mildly derogatory name for any style or vocabulary unique to a particular group of people, especially to members of a distinct profession. There is nothing wrong with jargon, in this sense, as long as its use is confined to the audience equipped to understand it. An economist addressing students nearing the end of their first course in economics can comment on air pollution thus:

> From the point of view of the economic analyst, urban air pollution is a dramatic case of the operation of external diseconomies. Pollution almost invariably represents an external cost that the individual or private business firm places upon society without charge to himself. When such externalities exist, a divergence between private and social interest will arise, and some form of collective intervention will be required if the problem is to be solved. —RICHARD T. GILL *Economics*

His point could be made without drawing on words like "diseconomies" for expenses without benefits and "collective intervention" for government regulation, but because the author knows his readers are familiar with a basic economics vocabulary he uses it as the shortest and most exact means of exposition. A writer, however, should not use the jargon of his clique or allude obliquely to experience restricted to members of the clique unless he is writing solely for the clique. Jargon cast among persons ignorant of its special uses will breed misunderstanding, frustration, hostility, and murk.

Officialese. *Officialese* is a form of false jargon adopted by people who are afraid of being easily understood.

> It is only when the student sees good writing against the backdrop
> of his own social and value development that an environment
> conducive to internalization of course goals is possible.

This sentence means that students in a writing course will buckle
down to studying the subject when they are convinced the effort
will benefit them. The writer apparently recognized the concept
for a truism, a commonplace assumption, and so tried to dignify it
with officialese. Spores of officialese speckle many business and
government communications like mildew. They should be kept
out of plain, honest writing.

Gobbledygook. *Gobbledygook* is officialese carried to the extreme
of obscurity, often with the aid of illogical structure.

> At the same time, deep historical, social, and political inhibitions to
> immediate and effective regional mutual security arrangements
> in some areas must be recognized.

The firmest ground in this sentence is the flabby verb "must be
recognized." Unfortunately, it can be reached only by passing
over a bog of almost meaningless abstractions. Thus does illogical
structure add to the gap between reader and sense. After a good
deal of thought, it is just possible to guess at a relatively useful
paraphrase of the statement.

> In some areas, historical, social, and political circumstances may
> hinder the establishment of mutual security arrangements [and
> we can only hope that *they* are defined somewhere else].

Thorough gobbledygook is less an accident than an art. The art is
not worth the trouble to acquire it.

AUDIENCE

Good writing does not occur in a vacuum. Even very personal
journal writing is set down for a reader. Write, therefore, as
though your words were being read. Summon up a phantom
reader to sit before you as you write. Will this ghost be insulted if
the words are too simple? Will it sneer at an overblown phrase?
Will it understand (*or be willing to learn*) that unusual, big word, or
should you select a more common one? Will it challenge what
seems a safe general assumption in the first paragraph? Will it
appreciate that analogy of the concerto and the split-T formation?
Will it find this sentiment trite, that phrase a cliché? Will it catch
the allusion to the sorority rush? Will it follow the logic of the

fourth paragraph? Will it enjoy that anecdote? Does it know who you are? Does it care? Can you assume it will be interested in the same points you are? How can it be brought to an interest in them if it has none? How much of the technical language of the subject can it be expected to know? Will your writing strike it as artificial or posed? If you can satisfy your ghost in these respects, you will probably keep a general, unspecified audience contented.

Experienced writers carry their audience analysis further, often to the point of writing in one style for the serious, well-educated reader who knows a good deal about the subject in hand and in quite another for the uninformed person who has, at best, only a passing interest in the writer's topic. Only an experienced writer, however, can make effective use of these distinctions, for they can be applied only when the writer commands a variety of styles well enough to write with ease in each of them. An accurate appreciation of any specific audience, moreover, requires a breadth of knowledge and human understanding few of us possess. No cause is as lost as that of the paper written in a forced style based on the wrong conclusions about an audience. For the average person, five minutes spent testing the writing itself for clarity and logic are worth an hour's guesswork about the intellectual pedigree of the potential reader.

TONE

Tone is the effect of diction. It is the indicator of the writer's attitude toward subject and audience. Tone informs the audience that the writer regards the subject seriously or flippantly, critically or enthusiastically. From it the reader understands that the writer addresses him to instruct, amuse, convince, entertain, or persuade and by it gathers whether the writer's relation to him is one of equal speaking to equal, of inferior respectfully submitting a proposal to a superior, or of an expert dispensing information to the uninformed. The words and phrases of the writer's diction establish either a close, informal association with the reader or a distant, formal one.

TONE AND OPINION

What the writer thinks of a subject inevitably affects the tone of his writing, but if he adopts a scornful tone without stating and thoroughly justifying a scornful opinion, the reader will be confused, if not repelled. An opinion, where one is called for, must be supported and argued if it is to be accepted. A tone cannot be tested by logic and is therefore suspect as an emotional product without rational foundation.

> Numerous self-proclaimed experts have argued that a two-hundred mile offshore fishing limit will stimulate the United States economy.

Whether the argument goes on to prove that a new fishing limit will, or will not, stimulate the economy, the writer is still at fault to asperse the experts as "self-proclaimed," unless he introduces specific evidence, relevant to the discussion, that they have no right to the title of "experts."

CONSISTENCY OF TONE

Although it is possible, and often beneficial, to lighten a serious discussion with a touch of humor, the overall tone of an essay should be consistent from beginning to end. If you open with a formal, arms-length attitude to the reader, don't suddenly descend to casual familiarity.

> The committee has delegated me to convey the results of their review of personnel performance over the past three months, and I'm just tickled to death to be able to slap you on the back for all of them and tell you that you're doing one hell of a job, Marcia. There's just one thing, tho; they're kind of negative on those two-hour coffee breaks you've been taking after lunch.

A flippant introduction, on the other hand, demeans a serious proposition and spoils its chances of success.

> It must sound pretty chintzy, I bet, but I'd like you to pay my expenses for a world tour that will materially advance our nation's cultural image abroad.

PERSON

When the writer makes statements in the first person—*I* believe, *I* have found, *I* realize—and addresses the reader in the second—*you* will agree, as *you* know, *you* have seen—the tone is informal, almost conversational. If he refers jointly to the reader and himself as *we,* the tone becomes conspiratorially intimate.

> Then as *I* studied the problem further, *I* didn't think the Seven Deadly Sins were holding up much better. For it seemed to *me* there is hardly one *we* could do without . . . . I.e., if *I* hadn't

envied *my* neighbor his watertight roof, *my* own would still leak, and the children would catch cold. And *we* need Avarice, with taxes the mess they are, for *you* must want more in order to get more, and *you'd* better get more unless *you* want Big Daddy to take ultimate care of *you*—see Pride. And without Lust *we* wouldn't be here discussing it. And so on.

—PEG BRACKEN "It's a Funny Thing About Me, But Not Very"

The informality of the example results from more than the free use of first and second person pronouns (*didn't think* and *you'd better* are more conversational than *did not think* and *you had better*), but the pronouns keep the issue personal, that is, something between the writer, *I,* and the reader, *you.* No meaning is lost without those pronouns.

> Subsequent further study of the problem indicated that the Seven Deadly Sins weren't holding up much better, for hardly one appeared to be dispensable . . . .

The treatment is, however, more formal and noticeably less direct. In reminiscence and anecdote, *I* must do a lot of the talking.

> *I* used to remember *my* brother Henry walking into a fire outdoors when he was a week old. It was remarkable in *me* to remember a thing like that, and it was still more remarkable that *I* should cling to the delusion, for thirty years, that *I* did remember it—for, of course, it never happened; he would not have been able to walk at that age.   —MARK TWAIN *Mark Twain's Autobiography*

But reiteration of *I* in argument or persuasion produces an egotistical effect that detracts from the force of reason.

> When *I* say Madison Avenue has done more than all the illiterates born or yet to be born to corrupt the English language, *I* mean that advertising has assaulted *my* eyes and ears with more verbal misuse urged with more persistence than *I* ever met from man, woman, or child. The time has come, *I* think, to muzzle those who claimed a cigarette tasted *like* a cigarette should. Why should *I* or any other person who cares for his mother tongue suffer torture from slovenly commercial exhortation? Why indeed; but what can be done about it? *My* solution is simple. *I* propose that all advertising copywriters be required to pass a standard high school equivalency examination in verbal achievement and that their future salary increases be deferred for prescribed punitive periods on the commission of each grammatical fault.

One may agree with the speaker, but one cannot like his arrogance.

If overuse of *I* draws unfavorable attention to the writer, incessant references to *you* may force a familiarity the reader is unwilling to permit or imply an inferiority he resents. In the following example the effect of writer domination is intentional as part of the humor. It is achieved by driving each point home with a tap on the reader's chest.

> *Your* job as hostess is not complete when *your* guests have been properly fed. *You* must see to it that they are also entertained.
> *Your* family and friends will expect *you* to be able to relate amusing stories which *you* have heard at the butchers, at a meeting of Hadassah, or which *your* husband has told at previous gatherings of these same people. Familiarize *yourself* with the following formula for successful storytelling and in no time at all *you* will have a widespread reputation as a *raconteuse*.
>
> —DAN GREENBURG "How to Be a Jewish Mother"

The *I/you* relationship is essential when the writer wishes to move a particular person to take some action or make some decision. An applicant for a job or a salesman with a pitch must rely on the first and second person to deliver the message. In the specialized cases of applying and selling, the reader's reactions are so important that as much emphasis should be placed on *you* as circumstances permit.

> Dear Ms. _____:
> The personnel office of your company has recommended that I direct my inquiry about employment opportunities to you. Your division, I understand, hires proofreaders on a freelance basis as work is available for them, and I should be very grateful if you would consider my suitability as a reader for you on those terms. You will find a copy of my resume enclosed.
>
> Dear Mr. and Mrs. _____:
> Congratulations on the arrival of your new daughter. With the pleasure an addition to the family brings, comes added responsibility, as I am sure you are aware. Now that you have another person to care for, perhaps you are considering taking out a new life-insurance policy or adding to the one you have. You will certainly want to enroll the newcomer in a medical plan. As an independent agent, I can show you a wide variety of health and life insurance programs, one of which is certain to suit your particular needs.

May I call on you to learn your requirements and to explain the policies I can provide?

In most narrative and expository prose, however, the relationship between writer and a specific reader is less obviously direct. A sparse scattering of the personal pronouns *I* and *you* serves as well as a saturation to hint at a personal tone in such writing, and interjection of no person at all is perfectly acceptable. The statement of facts and their analysis without reliance on *you* or *I* does not sound stuffy. What, after all, could be more natural when the subject is not *you* or *I?*

Parody is the most aggressive form of impersonation, designed not only to deflate hollow pretense but also to destroy illusion in all its forms; to undermine pathos by harping on the trivial, all-too-human aspects of the victim. Stage props collapsing, wigs falling off, public speakers forgetting their lines, dramatic gestures remaining suspended in the air—the parodist's points of attack are all situated on the line of intersection between two planes: the Exalted and the Trivial.   —ARTHUR KOESTLER *The Act of Creation*

One danger of impersonal address is the temptation to fall back on *it is* and *there is* (*are*) constructions. There are few occasions when it is impossible to substitute a definitive noun or other part of speech for these vague references. (Why not say instead: A definitive noun or other part of speech can usually replace these vague references?)

Two styles indicating person should probably be avoided altogether. The first is the elaborately distant allusion to the writer in the third person. A degree of objectivity is preserved in saying "In his research for this article the author discovered several disagreements between the commentaries of two critics . . . ." But the advantage, such as it is, is wiped out by the strained pose and the implication that the writer is trying to shirk responsibility for his own words. The second style is known as the "editorial we." Instead of using the simple *I,* the writer adopts the loftily plural *we* as if he embodied all human virtues and knowledge. "We have given the proposal our consideration, and we find it unacceptable." If the words really apply to a case accurately summed up in "I have looked the proposal over and don't like it," the choice of the plural pronoun constitutes inflated posturing.

As is true of other aspects of tone, use of personal pronouns to establish relation between writer and reader requires logical consistency. Once the writer has determined the number of parties to be involved, explicitly or implicitly, in the passage he should stick to his choice.

> I was walking down one of the flaming avenues of autumn maples in the older section of town, when I came across Vernon, the junk dealer, and his son trying to heave an enormous grand piano up onto their crazy swaybacked pickup. Two conflicting emotions at work in the old man struck you at once, for you could see clearly his elation at acquiring an obviously valuable and unexpected piece of property and his frustration at being unable to haul it away. I watched the efforts of the pair for a few minutes before I worked up enough nerve to offer to help. Vernon's horror at any gesture putting him in the position of owing something was proverbial in Marriettasburg.

The paragraph begins as a narrative in the first person and ends with a general remark that is still credibly within the narrator's experience. In the second sentence, however, the writer inserts a jarring second person point of view. The effect is a disturbing, shadowy fourth presence in a story involving, so far, only the people in the narrator's ken. Who is this *you* on the spot and capable of drawing conclusions? The question is a nagging, distracting one that ought never to have been raised.

WEAK MODIFIERS

A writer must often qualify a statement to acknowledge exceptions. (Remove *often* from that sentence, for example, and the assertion is partly wrong.) But if modifiers have important functions, they should not be wasted in situations that do not need them. A *pretty* safe guess is a safe guess made by a guesser hedging his bet. An *extremely* satisfactory agreement is much rarer than a simply satisfactory one. Unnecessary qualifiers brand a writer as either uncertain or indiscriminately emphatic. If omission of intensifiers like the following leaves the important meaning intact, omit them: *very, really, extremely, significantly, considerably, measurably, frequently, truly, wonderfully, awfully, greatly, highly, genuinely, sincerely, deeply, gravely, severely, acutely, widely, seriously, exceptionally, grossly.* The same principle applies to the belittling modifiers: *pretty, rather, somewhat, practically, probably, virtually, almost, moder-*

ately, relatively, essentially, basically, little, nearly, sometimes, few, slightly, rarely, partly. Remember, the object is not to shun these words and their likes altogether, but to reserve them for uses that count.

CAUTIONS

A good dictionary is the surest aid to using words accurately. Consult one regularly. Dictionaries, however, may lag behind the actual changes in our language, and they may not answer a question about very current usage. When writing, be conservative toward the adoption of nondictionary words. Observe at least three cautions.

BEWARE OF VOGUE WORDS

The realm of slang is an obvious breeding ground for vogue words; indeed, slang survives by replacing its colorful terms as their vividness fades. But slang is an issue beyond the comprehension of these suggestions for practical written style. The writer need know the slang applications of "dudes" for men, "fuzz" for police, and "bread" for money only if he intends to reproduce speech in a dialogue among characters. On the other hand, the writer must be aware that standard language, as opposed to slang, has its vogue words too, apparently respectable words useful in ordinary exposition that rise to a height of fashion. And once they are fashionable they are sure to be perverted to meanings for which they were never intended. The recent rise of *insightful* is an example. Although *perceptive* has been available and serviceable for many years, someone thought that *insightful* suggested an extra degree of intellectual penetration, as in some cases it does. From that moment *perceptive* was rated inadequate, whatever the occasion, and we now rarely hear of a perceptive remark, but the air is heavy with insightful ones.

There is no crime in the word's ascendancy, only suspicion that its popularity grows from indifference rather than deliberate choice. The writer should avoid suspicion. No one can challenge the ancient and honorable applications of *perceptive;* some can, and do, question the new ones of *insightful.* In any case, a vogue word is on its way to becoming trite.

When a word rears suddenly from the herd of common usage, the writer proposing to adopt it should ask:

1. Do I really know what the word means?

2. Does it improve on the common word or words I might use in its stead?

An odd and modish word calls attention to itself, and the effect is not always positive.

BEWARE OF CREATING NEW WORDS

Our language constantly absorbs new words promulgated by writers and speakers. The right to add to the vocabulary belongs to everyone, but a new word's place in diction depends on its being the only word appropriate to the immediate circumstances. Its claim is weak if a familiar term will serve just as well.

The noun *summary,* for example, has long had a verb counterpart, *summarize. Synopsis,* distinguished by only the finest of shades from summary, has not yet acquired a fully sanctioned verb: *synopsize.* One cannot tell whether the writer who uses *synopsize* is ignorant of *summarize* or knows it too well. Any doubt will diminish the force of the argument involving the questionable term.

Conversion of a noun to a verb by the suffix *-ize,* as exemplified in *synopsize,* produces a new word at the cost of less invention than any other process, with the possible exception of forming adverbs by the addition of *-wise,* as in *moneywise, powerwise, timewise,* and so forth. An application of either formula *may* earn the writer a share of derision, and its use in the creation of a neologism, a new word, when no such innovation is necessary will draw abuse. A damp towel is *moist;* to make a towel damp, one *moistens* it; the noun of *moisten* is *moisture.* Why, then, do advertised cosmetics invariably *moisturize* rather than *moisten?* The language is not enriched when a verbal poverty forces some unfortunate to coin with -ize or -wise a word that merely duplicates an established one. (See "A Glossary of Usage.")

When the temptation is strong to invent a new word or to use a new one you have recently picked up, check the dictionary. If your selection is not given, search thoroughly for an authorized replacement. If no alternative suits the particular need, proceed cautiously with the novelty, but demonstrate your powers of discrimination by defining the new word where it first appears. The vocabulary of modern English has been accumulating for nearly four centuries, remember. A great many situations have found suitable terms in that time.

BEWARE OF PUTTING OLD WORDS TO NEW USES

The chance of confusion is always present when a word with an accepted function is diverted to a new application. The contemporary use of *hopefully* to mean *it is to be hoped* or *I/we/you hope* is a weary controversy now. But what is meant by

> Hopefully, Carmen teed off for the seventh hole?

Was she hopeful, in the old sense, of making par at last on this seventh hole; or does the reporter hope, in the sense of "it is to be hoped," that she teed off for the seventh and not the fifth or ninth hole, because he was in the clubhouse at the time and didn't see the drive?

Purists dislike the transfer of a word from one part of speech to another:

> Jean recoiled from the *contact* with Bruce's clammy palm and declined his offer to *contact* her that evening. [Noun to verb.]
> He has *fun* in Memphis, but he doesn't think Memphis is a *fun* city. [Noun to adjective.]

Numerous words, of course, already function unchanged as nouns and verbs (view, suspect, caress, tumble) or nouns and adjectives (many, choice, light, red), and the objections to *contact,* the verb, are pedantic and perhaps illogical.* What the writer must keep in mind is that any unusual use of a word singles the word out. If the unexpected twist emphasizes a point or sets a properly striking tone for the content, very well; but if the variant contributes nothing that a more conventional choice gives, it will stand out as an eccentricity, a distraction, or a revelation of a threadbare vocabulary. Worse, it may not accurately communicate the writer's meaning. The writer, moreover, can never be certain that his reader will not be a purist. If the purist has no grounds for complaint, the adulterationist will seldom quarrel. Consult the dictionary when questions of word function arise.

SENTENCE STYLE

NOUNS AND VERBS

Nouns are cannonballs—heavy, impressive, and immobile. A sen-

---

* The chief objection is to the use of *contact* to mean "to establish communication with"; one object that *contacts* (touches) another will arouse much less ire.

tence loaded with them is ineffective unless it is also charged with verbs forceful enough to move the contents. The following sentence is perverted from the original to eliminate, as far as possible, the verbs that give it strength.

> The mathematically straight and barometrically level road westward from a town by the Mouths of the Rhone is one of the world's measured miles for record-setting motorists.

One essential but insipid linking verb, *is,* serves twenty-six other words. Sense is there, but it is incongruously suspended like the fat man in the cartoon who can hang from the cliff by a twig. The original reads:

> Westward from a town by the Mouths of the Rhone *runs* a road so mathematically straight, so barometrically level, that it *ranks* among the world's measured miles, and motorists *use* it for records.
> —RUDYARD KIPLING "The Bull That Thought"

Three unexceptional, active, indicative verbs enliven a static, descriptive sentence with metaphors of movement, rhythm of imagery, and short, comprehensible clauses. The greater the proportion of action verbs a sentence contains, the greater the probability that the sentence will read easily, express its point forcibly, strike deep into the memory, and join successfully with the thoughts preceding and following it.

Nothing makes the importance of a verb so obvious as a delay that frustrates expectation of the verb or a misplaced emphasis that conceals the verb's significance.

> With respect to money, three of its functions which were clearly stated by the classical economists relatively early in the last century stood out as salient.
> —TALCOTT PARSONS "Social Structure and the Symbolic Media of Interchange"

In this example not only is the false primary verb "stood out" tied to the end like a tug pushing a string of barges, but the verb of real meaning, "stated," is buried in a relative clause. Try the revision:

> Relatively early in the last century, classical economists clearly stated three salient functions of money.

Let the verbs lead, and the rest of the words will follow.

Natural Expression and Sentence Variation

The art of varying sentences from long to short and from loose to periodic form is not acquired through mechanical concentration. Reading a passage aloud will usually reveal monotony of tone and unsatisfactory repetition of structure. Without thinking consciously of the terminology of variation, the writer should follow instinct in setting words down and revise as necessary later.

LOOSE AND PERIODIC SENTENCES

A *loose* sentence states the point or action at the beginning and amplifies it with succeeding details and modifiers.

> The mob broke into open riot, throwing cobblestones and bottles in place of the insults that had satisfied it before.

In contrast to the loose sentence, a *periodic* one, beginning with subordinate detail, saves its point for the end.

> Throwing cobblestones and bottles in place of the insults that had satisfied it before, the mob broke into open riot.

An uninterrupted sequence of either loose or periodic sentences lulls the reader's interest. Every reader needs an occasional jab in the ribs to keep his attention from flagging.

LENGTH

If you find your sentences all trotting out to the same moderate length, throw in a short one to vary the pace. Don't write all short sentences. On the other hand, don't strive for extra long sentences. A series of short ones may be dull, but a series of long ones will be duller.

RHETORICAL QUESTION AND RHETORICAL IMPERATIVE

What makes a reader sit up and take notice more than a question? Anticipate your exposition occasionally by posing a *rhetorical question,* that is, one that either requires no answer or receives an answer in the discussion that immediately follows it. Similarly, order your reader to do something at times: "Look at the previous example," "Read the label on your next can of soup," "Compare the alternatives," "Take any five cab drivers." These are *rhetorical imperatives.* Your reader will not respond by dropping your essay to round up five cab drivers—unless he or she is pathologically literal. The standard reaction is to imagine five cab drivers from memory and read on to see what the writer intends to do with them, now that they have been mentally summoned to the room.

Both the rhetorical question and the rhetorical imperative are strident variations in tone. A paper littered with them to the exclusion of logic, reason, and development will read like a propaganda broadside, one of those melodramatic handouts designed to get people jumping to conclusions without knowing why. Be selective in applying these devices to any discourse.

VARIETY IN THE BEGINNINGS OF SENTENCES

Unless a sequence of related points needs special emphasis, repetition of the same word or words at the beginnings of several successive sentences produces monotony.

> She was an interesting young woman who challenged the values of contemporary society. She was tall and heavy, with mousy brown hair reaching to her waist and a face ravaged with the strip mining of adolescent acne. She was not interested in money, although she could have had as much as she wanted from her wealthy father, who doted on her. She was well educated as far as her education went, but that was no farther than the sophomore year of college. She was passionately fond of music and convinced that the salvation of mankind, or at least a part of it, could be achieved through her guitar. She was playing once a week as stand-in for the regular at a third-rate nite spot when I first met her.

A clever writer might adopt such a deadpan series of "she was's" to lead up to a startling conclusion, but for good, journeyman style the formulaic chant is too wearisome to be used without risk of losing the audience.

There Is AND It Is

See suggestions under "Tone: Person." A paper saturated with sentences beginning "There is . . ." and "It is . . ." relies too much on the vague and the abstract. Whenever possible reword such phrasings to get a real subject in the driver's seat.

NOTE: This suggestion does not mean that the question "How's the weather out there?" must invariably be answered, "Rain is falling." It is perfectly adequate to say "It is raining" in such circumstances.

EMPHASIS

The structure of a sentence should leave the reader in no doubt as to what is the main point and what is dependent or supportive detail.

> We drove to the park, and we got out of the car, and our dog Sherlock slipped his leash, and he ran away, and he frightened some small children.

The example consists of a string of *coordinate* clauses, clauses of equal structural weight. The effect is of a child's recitation in which every element receives the same stress, and, like the adult listening to the child, the reader is left to distinguish the jewel of information from its setting. The remedy for this sentence is *subordination* (see "Subordination" in Part II), the placement of secondary information in a secondary structural form.

> When we got out of the car after driving to the park, *our dog Sherlock slipped his leash and ran away* [the main or dominant clause], frightening some small children.

The revision not only denies independence to all parts of the sentence except Sherlock's, it also settles the issue of importance between the dog's running away and his frightening the children. The revision could have read:

> *Our dog Sherlock frightened some small children,* having slipped his leash and run away as we were getting out of the car after the drive to the park.

The original leaves the question wide open, but if Sherlock's break for freedom is more important to the situation than his frightening the small children, then the second revision (which is overloaded in any case) produces *inverted subordination;* it gives prominence to the wrong fact.

> *They were sitting in the living room reading* when a bolt of lightning struck the oak tree that stood only twenty feet from the window.

The example might be appropriate under certain conditions, but a lightning bolt at close quarters usually commands more respect.

> As they were sitting in the living room reading, *a bolt of lightning struck the oak tree that stood only twenty feet from the window.*

The reporter who inserted the following news story in the local weekly was probably a member of the town's volunteer emergency squad.

> The Principal was informed that the local fire department's presence on the school property last Saturday resulted from a severed "fire sensor" wire, which was triggered by the collapse of part of the auditorium ceiling. Before leaving the premises, firemen and school officials made a thorough inspection of the building. There was no observable damage to any structure other than the auditorium.

Those shiny red trucks certainly caught the writer's eye, but, surely, the damage to the school building concerns us more than the arrival of the fire fighters. The first sentence would prepare the reader better for what follows if it read:

> The Principal was informed that part of the school auditorium ceiling collapsed last Saturday, severing a "fire sensor" wire that summoned the local fire department.

If the writer fails to hand over the stick so that it can be grasped in only one way, he cannot blame the reader who takes hold of it by the wrong end.

ACTIVE VOICE AND PASSIVE VOICE

In Part III the different emphases of passive voice and active voice are explained. Use the passive voice (the subject receives the action of the verb) if the action is more important than the performer of the action.

> The window had been broken. [The breaking of the window, regardless of who broke it, is important.]
> Harry broke the window. [Harry, the culprit, is more important than the window.]

The passive voice, applied with respect for its particular emphasis, supplies variety of pace in writing, the speed with which one image or thought proceeds to another. Sometimes a temporary slackening of the action increases a general tension beneficially.

> In television violence does not hurt too much, nor are its consequences very bloody or messy. *Physical pain and details of injury or death are shown to be a consequence of violence in only one out of every four TV exposures. In other words, there is little connection evinced between the*

use of violence and the suffering such acts would inflict in real life. This is perhaps the worst sin of all.

—RICHARD L. TOBIN "When Violence Begets Violence"

The passive voice of the two italicized sentences tempers what violence does as cold water tempers hot steel, leaving "the worst sin of all" sounding, if possible, even worse.

WORDS THAT BELONG TOGETHER

Words that relate to each other should be kept together in a sentence; phrases should appear in proper sequence.

> I only smoked one cigarette. [Do you mean "All I did was smoke one cigarette," or "I smoked no more than one cigarette"?]

It is less ambiguous to say:

> I smoked only one cigarette.

> He stepped cautiously like a man on a plank walking over an abyss. [The plank is probably not walking.]
> He stepped cautiously like a man walking on a plank over an abyss.

SPLIT INFINITIVES

Despite the many proofs offered to show that infinitives can be split with impunity, the world is still full of people who relish hailing each occurrence of a split one as a peccadillo. The writer is foolish to give any reader an excuse to quibble with the language rather than the argument, and so the prudent expositor keeps infinitives intact—unless rupture clearly avoids an artificial mouthing. The split infinitive has some justification in this sentence:

> You must see him at work to really appreciate his zeal.

In the example the word "really" is so vague—it can mean *thoroughly, truly, fully, genuinely*—that it may actually benefit from being sandwiched between "to" and "appreciate." Any of the more specific words, however, has more effect if placed to modify the complete infinitive.

> You must see him at work to appreciate his zeal thoroughly [fully, genuinely, truly]. [Note that "you must see him at work truly to appreciate . . ." allows "truly" to modify "work" and thus create an ambiguity.]

UNNECESSARY WORDS

Practice economy of expression. Why say

> We must increase our budget in order to cover new costs

when

> We must increase our budget to cover . . .

serves the same purpose? Instead of "taking the matter under consideration," try simply "considering the matter." Where possible, replace a two-word expression with a single word: for "leave out" *omit,* for "take off" *remove,* for "send away" *dismiss,* for "wake up" *awake,* for "in back of" *behind,* for "have got" *have.*

On the whole the advice to cut superfluous words is good, but remember that the interests of variety must be met as well. Sometimes the more leisurely phrase is the more natural one and will mitigate unwanted abruptness. Every recommendation for style must be judged against the particular situation at hand. Perfect adherence to every suggestion made here will result in a paper that is perfectly unexceptional—and dry and wooden and posed and forced and anonymous. Never be afraid to take a chance with your eyes open.

COMMON SENSE

TAUTOLOGY

Some automatic combinations of words form clichés: "due process," "idle rich," "vital statistics"; other words seem to get thrown together out of some indistinct feeling that one alone is not enough. These combinations may be clichés, but they may be worse; they may be *tautologies,* also known as pleonasms or redundancies. Two different words or phrases joined together constitute a tautology when one of them serves only to repeat, in whole or in part, the sense of the other. Writers commit tautologies when they fail to gauge the meaning of each word independently, and so repeat when they think they are intensifying. How often have you seen these combinations: "consensus of opinion," "excessive verbiage," "new innovations," "component parts," "bisected in half," "return back"? A *consensus* is a general opinion, and the word *opinion* is tautological when tied to it; *verbiage* is an *excess* of words; an *innovation* is something *new;* the *parts* of a watch are its *components;* something *bisected* is divided into two equal segments, or *halves;* the *re-* of *return* supplies the sense of *back.* In each pair, one word comprises the total meaning; the additional term adds nothing but a false oratorical rounding out. Tautologies lessen verbal efficiency; they obscure meaning; they signify ignorance. If the precise definition of a word eludes you, refer to the dictionary. (Don't, however, refer *back again* to the dictionary.) An accurate vocabulary is the surest defense against the tautological blunder.

CONTRADICTION

Do not accidentally negate a word by coupling it with a modifier of incompatible or opposite meaning. The adjective *unique* means one and only, single, sole, or having no equal. One feature cannot, therefore, be *more unique* than another. An argument can *center on* an issue, but it cannot *center around* one. As *proceed* means go ahead, one cannot *proceed back* to the start. Sometimes it is not the denotation of a word that fouls the association, but the connotation. Clothes made from *genuine synthetic* fabrics do exist; they sound irregular only because we equate *synthetic* with *phony* through connotation.

Intentional contradictions, in contrast to accidents, glow briefly with a certain originality.

> He's ninety-three and seems to be suffering from terminal longevity.
> Her vicious morality would be unbearable if it were uncontrolled.
> Francis undertakes every task in a spirit of dynamic lassitude.

A reader will put up with one such ploy in an essay, but he probably won't stomach two. The official name for such intentional contradiction is *oxymoron.*

CIRCUMLOCUTION

Circumlocutions (*Circum*—"around"; *loqui*—"to speak") may be made up of clichés, tautologies, euphemisms, or just a mass of empty words. They are complicated equivalents for simple, direct statements. Without circumlocution, officialese and gobbledygook would be lost. "The reason why is on account of" is a circumlocution for "the reason is that" (or even for a simple "because"). A "terminological inexactitude" is circumlocutory for a lie. When a student "internalizes the behavioral objectives of an experience delimited by an oral and interpersonal instructional medium," he is the victim of a circumlocution meaning that he gets what he should from a lecture. Circumlocutions are invaluable to the propagandist who wants to blind reason with words and to the writer with a certain number of words to write and nothing to say. The insidious attraction of circumlocution is its power, at its bombastic best, to sound genuinely inspired.

> The plaintiff is a widow; yes, gentlemen, a widow. The late Mr. Bardell, after enjoying, for many years, the esteem and confidence of his sovereign, as one of the guardians of his royal revenues, glided almost imperceptibly from the world, to seek elsewhere for that repose and peace which a custom-house can never afford.
>
> —CHARLES DICKENS *The Pickwick Papers*

But the product of circumlocution, intentional or otherwise, is an obstacle between the reader and the point. A conscientious writer eliminates circumlocutions from his work.

CONSISTENCY OF VERB TENSE

Narration that begins in the past should stay in the past.

> I *walked* down the street and *see* this old fellow rooting in the trash cans.

As *walked* is past tense, *see* should be in the past as well, that is, *saw*. On the same principle, the present should remain the present and the future the future. An infinitive, however, does not adjust its form to reflect the tense of the verb dominating it.

> It would have been better to cash a check yesterday. ["Would have been" suffices to set the time for all events. "To have cashed," when the cashing and the being better are simultaneous, merely repeats what is already established.]

The infinitive *does* have a distinct tense when its time and the time of the main verb differ.

> I *should like to have cashed* a check yesterday. [My feelings are present, but they depend on what I did not do in the past.]
> Tomorrow I *shall be* glad *to have cashed* a check today. [Rewording without the infinitive shows the distinction in time: "Tomorrow I shall be glad that I cashed a check today."]

Unnecessary use of the *perfect infinitive,* to have _____, is about all the writer need guard against. Proper acknowledgment of differences in time between infinitive and main verb comes fairly naturally. If the action represented by the infinitive takes place in the time designated by the main verb, the *present infinitive,* to _____, is correct, whatever the tense of the main verb.

When a verb or a clause in a sentence expresses a state that is contrary to known fact, one that is uncertain, probable, possible, or desirable, the verbs of related clauses reflect that state consistently.

> *Were he to go* about his work with less noise, you *would realize* that he is not very diligent.
> *If she had been* there, I *should* (or *would*) *have been* pleased.

The writer should be careful, however, not to weaken a statement by mistaking the indicative mood in a *clause of contingency,* a clause that declares a simple choice of action yet to be made, for the subjunctive mood of a *clause of condition,* a clause that implies a hypothetical state in which the choice of action is assumed to have been made.

CLAUSE OF
CONTINGENCY: *If you go* down that street [choice of action], you *will reach* the square.

CLAUSE OF
CONDITION: *If you went*
Were you to go
Should you go
down that street [imagine, for the sake of argument, yourself in the act of going down that street], you *would reach* the square.

CLAUSE OF
CONTINGENCY: *If you can give* me your answer by tomorrow, I *shall* [not should] *be* grateful. [In this sentence "I should" would mean "I ought to," which is no doubt true, but the reader would rather know that you very definitely *will* be grateful.]

A related injurious tendency is to qualify indicative verbs with the auxiliaries *may* and *can* to dodge responsibility for a result. When a genuine doubt exists, *may* and *can* are important:

> If we drive all night, we may arrive by lunch time.

Indiscriminate application of *may* or *can,* however, suggests a lack of conviction.

If the writer omits unnecessary *may's* and *can's,* the writing *will* [not *may* or *can*] be improved.

MIXED CONSTRUCTIONS

Two distinct words, images, or statements rammed together in defiance of their individual meanings create a *mixed construction.* The most common cause of mixed construction is the writer's failure to respect the units of composition in haste to get the whole work finished.

MIXED METAPHOR

A figure of speech in which one object, abstract concept, or state of being is declared directly or indirectly to be another object, concept, or state for purposes of effect or definition is a metaphor. A *mixed metaphor* occurs when the writer forgets, or never realizes, the properties of the object, concept, or state involved.

> The present government is blithely sailing the ship of state down the road to destruction. [Ships do not sail on roads.]
> His enthusiasm was quenched by the fiery reaction that met his proposal. [Water, not fire, quenches.]
> She caught a chill sitting in the draft of an open mind. [Not all mixed metaphors are without merit.]

OMISSION OF NECESSARY WORD

A word, or words, left out can cause a ludicrous mixed construction.

> He is a veteran of World War II and father of one. [Without the obligatory word "child," the sentence suggests he fathered an unnamed global conflict.]
> People remember failures but forget successes are unjust. [People *who* remember . . . .]
> The driver said he could cope better with a bus load of monkeys fresh from the jungle than a party of conventioneers. [. . . than *with* a party of conventioneers.]
> King Lear felt the pain of a thankless child more keenly than a serpent's tooth. [. . . more keenly than *that* of a serpent's tooth.]
> Briar Aspirin contains more of the pain relievers doctors recommend most than any other aspirin. [This common commercial claim needs an extensive refit to caulk all the loopholes for ambiguity: Compared to other aspirins, Briar Aspirin contains more of the pain reliever that doctors most often recommend.]

NON SEQUITUR

We use the Latin phrase *non sequitur* (literally: "it does not follow") to describe a statement that is not truly supported by the facts intended to suggest it. Style suffers from *non sequitur* when the meaning of part of a sentence is not logically related to the meaning of another part.

> She must be corrupt; she's a politician. [She is corrupt because she is a politician *only* if it is proved that *all* politicians are corrupt by definition.]

Occurrence of *non sequitur* is not confined to a single sentence. Often two or more sentences set one up.

> Mr. Randolph has presented cogent arguments against capital punishment. He is a famous linguist, and his views command respect. [Not in the least so! On the subject of capital punishment a linguist, however eminent, commands no more respect than you or I.]

ZEUGMA

A word forced to do double duty in a sentence creates a mixed construction known as *zeugma*. In a faulty zeugma the word does not serve its two masters equally well.

> The roads are bad, the journey long. [*Are* fits roads, but the journey requires *is*.]

Deliberate zeugma, where all the elements agree, can be used to surprise or amuse the reader.

> As far as justification for the theft was concerned, the case, but not the coast, was clear.

PERSONIFICATION

Personification, which also goes by the names of *anthropomorphism* and *pathetic fallacy,* is a mixed metaphor in which human capacities for thought, emotion, or action are ascribed to an inanimate object or abstraction. It is permissible to speak in poetry and dramatic prose of the "cruel and violent sea," the "raging tempest," and the "pitiless desert sun"—permissible, that is, if one turns a deaf ear to the clichés involved. Some extremes of personification are excused for their lofty nonsense.

> If it is introduced to a gustatory circle by a sufficiently urbane apéritif, this normally naive and diffident little wine is capable of an astonishing effrontery.

For the purposes of plain expository prose, however, personification should be curbed. Purists object to frequent use of conceits such as "The writing should demonstrate sensitivity to the merits of personification while it avoids the dangers of personification's excess." Because "writer," a real person, is an easy and natural substitute for the inanimate subject "writing," the purist's objection is justified. The revision, which is better for all purposes, is "The writer should demonstrate sensitivity to the merits of personification while avoiding the dangers of personification in excess." (The argument against personification extends to the application of the possessive formed by adding *'s* to non-persons, as in personification*'s*.)

And, as we have mentioned them, let us not forget the *merits* of personification. Concepts that are best expressed through personification do arise in expository prose.

> A good argument appeals to the listener's judgment without challenging it.

Although the arguer and not the argument actually makes the appeal, to brand the figure as therefore illogical and inexcusable is to tax ingenuity beyond practicality. How is one to express the same thought differently? "The speaker will construct an argument that is good when he or she addresses points in the form of an appeal devoid of challenge to the listener's judgment." The revision is a monumental circumlocution.

As is true of so many decisions of style, the permissible extravagance of personification is up to the writer's common sense. If the figure of speech is used sparingly so that it does not become a mannerism, and if its effect is natural in contrast to a prosy alternative, then let it alone. Some purists pine if they are not given offense.

One of the first reminders about style is that the conventions of usage may be broken in the interests of style. Perhaps it is fitting to end on a convention that is probably broken, for good reasons, as often as it is observed. The essence of good style is the ability to interpret, adapt, and even reject the prescriptions of standard usage. The more experienced a writer is, the greater the liberties he or she may take. If you examine the work of professional writers, however, you will find the abuses of convention remarkably few and, where they do occur, excused by uncommon situation and purpose.

APPENDIX B

A Glossary of Grammatical Terms

NOTE: References headed *see* are to other entries in this glossary. Of the additional cross references, those to page numbers call attention to more detailed definitions, explanations, and examples; those using letters plus numbers refer to handbook rules to which the unit being defined has direct application.

Absolute phrase. A subordinate unit consisting of a noun or pronoun plus a verbal, most often a present participle. The participle is sometimes understood, not actually expressed: "The mob reached the courthouse, *their leader* [*being*] *a swarthy man in a red sweater.*" These phrases are called "absolute" because they modify the whole sentence; unlike subordinate clauses, they have no subordinating connective tying the phrases to particular words in the sentence. (Pages 128–29; P 8.)

Accusative case. See *Case.*

Active voice. See *Voice.*

Adjective. A word that modifies a noun or pronoun. (See *Modifier.*) True adjectives name a quality (size, shape, color, and so on) of the noun being modified, for example, *big, shaggy* dogs. Other words used as adjectives have the functions of pointing out or identifying the noun or naming an action associated with the noun: *those two* big, shaggy, *snarling* dogs. (Pages 78, 96; P 2, U 41–U 44.)

Adjective clause. A subordinate clause, introduced by a relative pronoun, relative adjective, or relative adverb and modifying a noun or pronoun. (See *Clause.*) (Pages 122–24; P 6, P 15–4, Sn 1, Sn 6, Sn 7, Sn 10, U 17, U 24, U 38, U 40.)

Adverb. A word that modifies anything except a noun or pronoun. (See *Modifier.*) Most adverbs modify verbs, adjectives, or other adverbs; but adverbs may also modify prepositions, conjunctions, and whole sentences. (Pages 78–79, 97; P 16, Sn 11, Sn 13, Sn 14, Sn 16, U 41–U 43.)

Adverbial clause. A subordinate clause, usually introduced by a subordinating conjunction, modifying a verb, an adjective, or another adverb. (See *Clause.*) Some adverbial clauses are used parenthetically to modify the sentence as a whole. (Pages 124–26; P 4–1, Sn 1, Sn 7, Sn 8, Sn 23, U 10.)

Affix. A unit of one or more letters added at the beginning or the end of another word or stem to produce a related or derived word. *Prefix* is the affix added at the beginning and *suffix* is the affix added at the end. The prefix *un* and the suffix *ly* affixed to *usual* produce the word *unusually.* (Pages 94–95, 96; M 7–2.)

Agreement. The principle that dictates the form of a word to correspond to that of another word with which it has a grammatical relationship. The three main situations in which agreement must be observed are these:

1. A verb agrees with its subject in person and number.

2. A pronoun agrees with its antecedent in person, number, and gender.

3. A demonstrative adjective agrees in number with the noun it modifies.

(See *Person, Number, Gender.*) (Pages 63–64, 68, 99; U 12–U 19, U 25–U 29.)

Antecedent. The word or words (sometimes a statement) to which a pronoun refers. (Pages 67–68; U 17, U 20–U 29.)

Appositive. A noun unit inserted after another noun unit to rename or supplement the first noun. Appositives may be restrictive and written without a comma (The poet *Donne*) or nonrestrictive and set off by commas (My favorite poet, *Donne*). (See *Restrictive.*) Infinitive phrases, gerund phrases, and noun clauses may also be used as appositives. (Pages 120–21; P 7, P 15–5, P 31, U 37.)

Article. A subclass of adjectives consisting of the *definite article* (*the*) and the *indefinite articles* (*a, an*).

Auxiliary verb. A "helping" verb used with the main verb to show some verbal aspect such as time, voice, or mood. The most common auxiliary verbs are *be, have,* and *do.* Others, called *modal auxiliaries,* are *shall, will, should, would, can, could, may, might, must, ought.* (Pages 105–106, 114–17; Sn 4–1, Sn 4–2.)

Case. In highly inflected languages like Latin or German, case refers to the alterations in the form of nouns, pronouns, and adjectives dictated by the grammatical function of the word within the sentence. In such a language, for example, when an article-adjective-noun unit is used as a direct object, the three words differ in form from that of the same words when the unit is used as a subject. Although we traditionally say that Modern English has three cases, the *nominative,* the *genitive* (or *possessive*), and the *objective* (or *accusative*), adjectives have lost all distinctive case endings; nouns have only two forms, the *common* case and the possessive; and the personal pronouns (except *you* and *it*) and the *who* pronouns retain the three distinctive forms. (Pages 73–74; U 30–U 40.)

Clause. A combination of words containing a subject and a verb. An *independent clause* may stand by itself as a sentence. A *dependent* or *subordinate clause,* which functions within the sentence as a noun, an adjective, or an adverb, cannot stand by itself as an independent utterance. (Pages 117–26; P 4–1, P 6, P 15–1, P 15–4, P 16–P 19, P 25, Sn 1, Sn 3, Sn 4–3, Sn 6–Sn 9, Sn 23, U 10, U 17, U 40.)

Collective noun. A noun the singular form of which refers to a group or collection of individual things. (U 15, U 27.)

Comma fault (also called **comma splice**). The use of a comma—or no mark of punctuation—between independent clauses that normally would be written with a semicolon or as two separate sentences. (Pages 118–19; P 16.)

Common case. See *Case.*

Common noun. The name that is common to all members of a class (for example, *woman, city*), as opposed to a *proper noun,* the name of a particular member of a class (*Elizabeth, Akron*). (Page 94; C 2–C 9.)

Comparison, comparative degree. See *Degree.*

Complement. A noun (or other noun unit such as a pronoun, noun clause, gerund phrase, infinitive phrase) or an adjective that must be added to a subject and verb in certain sentence patterns before the sentence gives complete meaning. The four complements ("completers") that determine the patterning of basic sentences are the following:

    1. *Direct object.* Following a transitive verb, the direct object names the person or thing that receives the action of the verb. (Pages 107–112, 114; U 33, U 34, U 38–U 40.)

    2. *Subjective complement.* Following a linking verb, the sub-

jective complement is a noun unit renaming the subject or an adjective describing the subject. (Pages 109–110, 114; U 36.)

    3. *Indirect object.* Used with a direct object, the indirect object names the person to whom or for whom or the thing to which or for which the action is performed. (Pages 110–11, 114.)

    4. *Objective complement.* Used with a direct object, the objective complement is a noun renaming the direct object or an adjective describing the direct object. (Pages 111–12.)

Complex sentence. A sentence made up of one independent clause and at least one dependent clause. (Pages 119–26.)

Compound sentence. A sentence made up of two or more independent clauses. (Page 118; P 1, P 16, P 17, P 26, Sn 7, Sn 9.)

Compound-complex sentence. A sentence made up of at least two independent clauses and at least one dependent clause. (Page 126.)

Conjugation. An orderly listing of the forms of a verb to show the variations of tense, person, number, voice, and mood. (A partial conjugation of the verbs *earn, grow,* and *be* is given on pages 99–101.)

Conjunction. A class of words used to join words, phrases, and clauses. Conjunctions are conventionally divided into the following:

    1. *Coordinating* (*and, but, or,* and so on). (Pages 98–99, 117–19; P 1, P 17, Sn 6, Sn 7.)

    2. *Correlative* (*either . . . or, not only . . . but also,* and so on). (Page 98; Sn 12.)

    3. *Conjunctive adverb* (*however, moreover, therefore,* and so on). (P 16.)

    4. *Subordinating* (*because, although, that, since,* and so on). (Pages 121, 125–26; Sn 4–3.)

Conjunctive adverb. See *Conjunction.*

Coordinating conjunction. See *Conjunction.*

Correlative conjunction. See *Conjunction.*

Declarative sentence. A sentence that makes a statement.

Definite article. See *Article.*

Degree. The property of adjectives and adverbs to change form to heighten or make more inclusive the descriptive quality. Comparisons use three degrees, the *positive* (*small, delightful, fast, rapidly*), the *comparative* (*smaller, more delightful, faster, more rap-*

idly), and the *superlative* (*smallest, most delightful, fastest, most rapidly*). (Pages 96–97; Sn 15–Sn 19, U 43, U 44.)

Demonstrative adjective, demonstrative pronoun. *This, that, these, those* when used to point out or designate. (U 24.)

Dependent clause. See *Clause.*

Direct address. The use in a sentence of a person's name, title, or designating common noun to show to whom the utterance is directed. (P 10.)

Direct object. See *Complement.*

Direct quotation, direct question. A sentence or part of a sentence that uses the exact words of the person being quoted. An *indirect quotation* or *indirect question* gives the substance but not the exact words.

> *Direct:* Bert told me, "I have already paid the fine."
> "Have you paid your fine?" Bert asked.
> *Indirect:* Bert told me that he had already paid the fine.
> Bert asked me if I had paid my fine.

(P 11, P 34, P 35, P 37, P 44.)

Elliptical construction. A sentence or part of a sentence in which a word or words necessary for grammatical completeness but not necessary for meaning have been omitted. (Sn 4, Sn 23, U 35.)

Exclamation. An abrupt or emphatic utterance, also called an interjection. (P 46, P 47.)

Fragment. See *Sentence fragment.*

Future tense. See *Tense.*

Future perfect tense. See *Tense.*

Gender. In grammar, gender refers to any alteration in a word on the basis of its reference to something masculine (male), something feminine (female), or something neuter (neither masculine nor feminine). In English, gender is shown by certain pronoun forms (*she, him, it, hers, its* and so on), by a few suffixes (*actor, actress*), and in some cases by separate words (*king, queen*). (U 25, U 29.)

Genitive case. See *Case.*

Gerund, gerund phrase. One of the three verbals. (See *Verbal.*) The identifying feature of the gerund is the *ing* ending, on either the simple form (*seeing*) or an auxiliary (*having seen, being seen*). Gerunds, with their modifiers and/or complements, constitute *gerund phrases*. Gerunds function as nouns within the sentence. (Pages 54, 127–28; Sn 21.)

Imperative mood. See *Mood.*

Imperative sentence. A sentence that gives a command, order, or request. A characteristic of the imperative sentence is that the subject *you* is normally not expressed. (Page 101.)

Indefinite article. See *Article.*

Indefinite pronoun. A pronoun that refers to an unspecified group or member of a group, such as *all, several, some, each, either, one, somebody.* (Page 95; P 21, U 13, U 26, U 31.)

Independent clause. See *Clause.*

Indicative mood. See *Mood.*

Indirect object. See *Complement.*

Indirect quotation, indirect question. See *Direct quotation.*

Infinitive, infinitive phrase. One of the three verbals. (See *Verbal.*) In most of its modern uses the infinitive has the "to" marker and, with the auxiliaries *have* and *be* to show tense and voice, exists in six forms. Infinitives with their modifiers and/or complements constitute *infinitive phrases* and are used within the sentence as nouns, adjectives, or adverbs. (Pages 54, 129–30; Sn 14, Sn 22, U 7.)

Intensifier. A subclass of adverbs (for example, *too, very, quite*) used to heighten or strengthen the descriptive quality.

Intensive pronoun. A pronoun ending in *self* when used as an appositive to add emphasis, as in "The governor *himself* interceded in the case." (See *Reflexive pronoun.*)

Interjection. See *Exclamation.*

Interrogative. A pronoun (*who, which, what,* and so on), adjective (*which, whose,* and so on), or adverb (*when, how,* and so on) that is used in an independent clause or a dependent clause to mark a direct or indirect question. (Pages 95, 115–16, 121–22; U 38, U 39, U 40.)

Interrogative sentence. A sentence that asks a direct question and is punctuated with a question mark. (P 44.)

Intransitive verb. A verb that does not require a direct object because no reaction is transferred to a receiver of the action. (Pages 106–107.)

Irregular verb. See *Regular verb.*

Linking verb. A subclass of intransitive verb that requires the addition of a subjective complement to rename or describe the subject. (Pages 109–110.)

Modal auxiliary. See *Auxiliary verb.*

Modifier. Any word, phrase, or dependent clause that is used with another sentence unit in order to describe, to limit, or to make more exact the meaning of the sentence unit.

Mood (also called **mode**). A property of verbs that shows how the speaker regards the verbal idea, whether as a statement of fact, a command, or a supposition or wish. The three moods in English are the *indicative,* to make a statement of fact or to ask a question, the *imperative,* to give a command or request, and the *subjunctive,* to show that the utterance should be construed as a wish, a supposition, or a condition contrary to fact. The subjunctive mood is sometimes shown by an inflectional change in the form of the verb (*be* or *were* instead of *am, is,* or *was*) but more often by the use of a modal auxiliary such as *should, must, might,* and so on. (Pages 99–101; U 10.)

Nominative case. See *Case.*

Nonrestrictive. See *Restrictive.*

Noun. Conventionally defined as being words that name a person, a place, or a thing, nouns can be identified by their function in the sentence (subject, object, and so on), by their having a possessive case and plural number (*boy, boy's, boys*), and sometimes by their distinctive suffixes (act*or*, happi*ness*, exist*ence*, and so on). (Pages 94–95.)

Noun clause. A subordinate clause that functions in one of these noun positions: subject, direct object, subjective complement, object of preposition, or appositive. (Pages 119–22.)

Number. The property of nouns, pronouns, verbs, and demonstrative adjectives by which the form of the word shows whether the reference is to one thing or to more than one thing.

> *Singular number: This girl is* writing *her theme.*
> *Plural number: These girls are* writing *their themes.*

(Pages 63–64, 99–101; U 12–U 19, U 25–U 27.)

Object of preposition. The noun or noun unit introduced by a preposition that shows the relationship of the object to the rest of the sentence. In a sentence such as "He walked down the aisle from his bench to the stage with his father," *aisle, bench, stage,* and *father* are the objects of the prepositions *down, from, to,* and *with.* (Page 98; U 33-2, U 38.)

Objective case. See *Case.*

Objective complement. See *Complement.*

Parenthetical element. A word or phrase inserted, as an aside or incidental observation, into a sentence that is grammatically complete without it. (P 9.)

Participle, participial phrase. There are two forms of the participle, the *present participle* and the *past participle.* As principal parts of the verb, they are used with various auxiliaries. (See *Progressive verb, Tense, Passive voice.*) As verbals, the participles—as single words or expanded into *participial phrases* by the addition of modifiers and/or complements—are used as adjectival modifiers: *Speaking softly and offering him some candy,* the nurse comforted the *frightened, weeping* little boy. (Pages 54, 128–29; Sn 20, U 1, U 7.)

Passive voice. See *Voice.*

Past participle. See *Participle.*

Past tense. See *Tense.*

Past perfect tense. See *Tense.*

Person. The property of certain words, chiefly the personal pronouns, that distinguishes the person(s) speaking (*first person—I, my, mine, me, we, our, ours, us*), the person(s) spoken to (*second person—you, your, yours*), and the person(s) or thing(s) spoken about (*third person—he, his, him, she, her, hers, it, its, they, their, theirs, them*). The irregular verb *be* has distinctive forms for the present tense singular and the past tense singular (I *am,* you *are,* he *is,* I *was,* you *were,* he *was*). For all other verbs the only distinguishing marker for person is the *s* ending for the third person present tense singular. (This marker is not found on the auxiliary verbs.) Nouns are always third person singular or third person plural. (Pages 99–101; U 17, U 25, U 28.)

Personal pronoun. A word that substitutes for persons or things named in the context, either the speaker(s), the person(s) spoken to, or the person(s) or thing(s) spoken about. (See the listing of personal pronouns in the preceding entry.) (Page 95; U 20–U 23, U 25–U 29, U 30–U 37.)

Phrase. A group of words not containing a subject and a verb and used to modify a part of the sentence or the sentence as a whole. (See *Absolute phrase, Gerund, Participle, Infinitive, Preposition.*)

Positive degree. See *Degree.*

Possessive case. See *Case.*

Predicate. A term sometimes used to designate that part of the clause or sentence containing the verb with its modifiers and/or complements, in other words, everything in the sentence except the subject and its modifiers.

Prefix. See *Affix*.

Preposition, prepositional phrase. A preposition is a connecting word that ties a noun unit, called its object, to some part of the sentence. (See *Object of preposition*.) Prepositions are sometimes modified by adverbs (*almost* onto the rocks, *even* before breakfast). A preposition with its object and modifiers constitutes a *prepositional phrase*. (Pages 97–98, 126; U 45–U 47.)

Present participle. See *Participle*.

Present tense. See *Tense*.

Present perfect tense. See *Tense*.

Principal parts. The principal parts of a verb are the base form or infinitive (*talk, speak*), the past tense (*talked, spoke*), and the past participle (*talked, spoken*). Some grammarians, wanting to include as principal parts all of the possible distinctive forms, add to these three the present participle (*talking, speaking*) and the third person singular present tense (*talks, speaks*). (Pages 102–104; U 1–U 5.)

Progressive verb. A verb formed with the auxiliary verb *be* and the present participle to show that the time involved is not fixed at one moment but is continuing. Progressive forms are used in all six tenses (*is helping, was helping, had been helping,* and so on) and in the present and past tenses of the passive voice (*is being helped, was being helped*). (Page 105.)

Pronoun. A word that substitutes for a noun or a noun equivalent. (For a listing of the various kinds of pronouns, with examples, see page 95 and other listings in this glossary.)

Proper noun. See *Common noun*.

Reflexive pronoun. Any pronoun ending in *self* when used as a complement or object of a preposition and having reference to the same thing as the subject. *Intensive pronouns* and reflexive pronouns are identical in form but differ in use:

> *Intensive:* You *yourself* must make the decision.
> *Reflexive:* Be careful; you might hurt *yourself*.

Regular verb. Regular verbs, also called weak verbs, are those with the *ed* ending for both the past tense and the past participle (*talk, talked, talked*). *Irregular verbs,* also called strong verbs, show internal changes and/or other endings in the past tense and past participle (*eat, ate, eaten; run, ran, run; steal, stole, stolen*). With a few irregular verbs all three forms are identical (*hit, hit, hit; set, set, set*). (Pages 57, 102–104; U 2.)

Relative pronoun, relative adjective, relative adverb. A word that subordinates an adjective clause by relating to the noun or pronoun that the clause modifies and substituting for it in the adjective clause. (Pages 122–24; U 17, U 24, U 38.)

Restrictive. Any modifier (adjective clause, participial phrase, appositive) of a noun or pronoun that is not set off by commas because the modifier is vital to the identification of the noun or pronoun. Its purpose is to distinguish that noun or pronoun from all other members of its class. A modifier that does not serve to identify the word it modifies is called *nonrestrictive*. (P 6, P 7, P 15–4, P 15–5.)

Sentence. A self-contained grammatical unit, usually containing a subject and a verb, that conveys to the listener or reader a meaningful assertion, question, command, or exclamation.

Sentence fragment. A word or group of words that, because it lacks a subject, a verb, or both, or because it is controlled by a subordinator, is not a complete and independent sentence. (Pages 42–43; Sn 1–Sn 3.)

Simple sentence. A sentence made up of one independent clause.

Squinting modifier. A modifier, usually an adverb, so placed in the sentence that it could relate to either of two words. (Sn 13.)

Subject. The noun unit that functions with an active verb to name the doer of the action or the thing being described, or with a passive verb to name the thing acted upon. (Pages 106–114; U 12–U 19, U 32, U 35, U 37, U 39, U 40.)

Subjective complement. See *Complement.* Subjective complements are sometimes called predicate nominatives; sometimes they are classified under the three terms predicate nouns, predicate pronouns, and predicate adjectives.

Subjunctive mood. See *Mood.*

Subordinate clause. See *Clause.*

Subordinating conjunction. See *Conjunction.*

Subordinator. Any word that marks the unit it introduces as being a clause that cannot stand by itself as a sentence. Subordinators may be conjunctions (*that, if, because,* and so on), pronouns (*who, which, whatever,* and so on), adjectives (*whose, which,* and so on), or adverbs (*when, how,* and so on). (Pages 99, 119–26; Sn 4–3, Sn 7–Sn 9.)

Suffix. See *Affix.*

Superlative degree. See *Degree.*

Tense. The property of verbs that shows the time of the action, being, or state of being. (See pages 99–101 for the forms and uses of the six tenses; U 1, U 6, U 7.)

Transitive verb. A verb that requires the addition of a direct object to name the receiver of the action expressed by the verb. (Pages 106–113.)

Verb. A word that expresses an action, an occurrence, or a state of being and that can combine with a subject to produce a statement, question, or command. (Pages 95–96, 99–106; Sn 4–1, Sn 4–2, U 1–U 19.)

Verbal. A form derived from a verb but used in the sentence as a noun, an adjective, or an adverb. The three verbals are the *gerund,* the *participle,* of which there are two forms, the *present participle* and the *past participle,* and the *infinitive.* (See *Gerund, Participle, Infinitive.*) A verbal with its modifiers and/or complements is called a verbal phrase. The verbals are sometimes called nonfinite verb forms. (Pages 127–30; Sn 14, Sn 20–Sn 22.)

Voice. The property of verbs that shows whether the subject is the doer of the action or the receiver of the action. The two voices are the *active* (Mr. Berg *trapped* the coyote) and the *passive* (The coyote *was trapped* by Mr. Berg). (Pages 99–100, 113–14; U 8, U 9.)

INDEX

All references are to page numbers. *Italicized* numbers refer to rules, examples, and explanatory material in the handbook section of the text.

could of, 86
couple, 86
criteria, 86
criticize, as instruction work in essay test, 138

Dangling modifiers
  defined, 54
  elliptical clauses, 56
  gerund phrases, 55
  infinitive phrases, 55
  participial phrases, 54–55
  test for, 54
Dashes
  before summarizing statement, 13
  misused, 13
  to set off appositive, 13
  to set off parenthetical insertion, 12–13
  to show abrupt shift, 12
data, 86
Dates
  commas with, 7, 8
  figures for, 21
Deadwood, 138
Declarative sentence, 225
define, as instruction word in essay test, 136
Definite article, 225
Definition, as method of paragraph
    development, 144–46
Degree. See Comparative degree; Positive
    degree; Superlative degree
Degree, adverbs of, 97
Degrees and titles, commas with, 6
Delayed object, delayed subject
  infinitive as, 129
  noun clause as, 120
delineate, as instruction word in essay test, 136
Demonstrative adjectives, 226
Demonstrative pronouns
  defined, 226
  vague reference of, 70–71
Denotation, 192–93
Dependent clauses. See Adjective clauses;
    Adverbial clauses; Noun clauses
Description
  as method of paragraph development, 150–
    52
  sensory appeal in, 151–52
desert, dessert, 29
Diction, 192
Dictionaries, 176
different from, different than, 86
dining, dinning, 29
Direct address
  commas with, 6
  defined, 226
Direct object
  case of pronoun, 75–78
  defined, 107–108, 226
  following passive verb, 114
  gerund phrase as, 127–28
  in basic sentence patterns, 107–13
  infinitive phrase as, 129–30
  noun clause as, 120
  whom(ever), 77–78
Direct question
  defined, 226

Direct question [cont.]
  question mark with, 16–17
Direct quotation
  colon introducing, 11
  defined, 226
  in research paper, 179–81
  quotation marks with, 13–15
discuss, as instruction word in essay test, 137
disinterested, uninterested, 86–87
do
  auxiliary in negatives, 116–17
  auxiliary in questions, 115–16
Double comparison, 53
due to, caused by, 87

e, spelling of words ending in, 26–27
effect. See affect
Elliptical clauses
  dangling, 56
  defined, 56, 226
Elliptical periods, 23
emigrate, immigrate, 87
Emphasis within sentence, 211–12
Encyclopedias
  general, 168–69
  special, 169–71
enthuse, 87
er/more, est/most, 52, 81
Essay tests
  deadwood, 138
  instruction words in, 135–38
  point values in, 133
  preparation for, 132–33
  topic sentence, 139, 141
  writing the answer, 141–42
Essays
  conclusion, 163
  final draft, 163
  introduction, 162, 164
  methods of development, 162
  organization of, 161
  revision, 163
  thesis sentence, 162, 164
  types of assignment, 159–60
et al., 184
etc. See and etc.
Euphemism, 196–97
evaluate, as instruction word in essay test, 138
everyplace. See anyplace
Examples, use of in paragraph development,
    149–50
except. See accept
Exclamation marks
  to show strong feeling, 17
  unacceptable use, to show humor, 17
  with quotation marks, 15
Exclamations
  defined, 226
  punctuation with, 17
explain, as instruction word in essay test, 137

f, fe, plural of words ending in, 31
farther, further, 87
fewer, less, 87
figure, 88
Figures. See Numbers